CODE NAME
MADELEINE

Noor Inayat Khan

CODE NAME
MADELEINE

A SUFI SPY IN NAZI-OCCUPIED PARIS

ARTHUR J. MAGIDA

W. W. NORTON & COMPANY
Independent Publishers Since 1923

For information about permission to reproduce selections from this book, write to
Permissions, W. W. Norton & Company, Inc., 500 Fifth Avenue, New York, NY 10110

For information about special discounts for bulk purchases, please contact
W. W. Norton Special Sales at specialsales@wwnorton.com or 800-233-4830

Manufacturing by Lake Book Manufacturing
Book design by Chris Welch
Production manager: Lauren Abbate

Library of Congress Cataloging-in-Publication Data

Names: Magida, Arthur J., author.
Title: Code name Madeleine : a Sufi spy in Nazi-occupied Paris / Arthur J. Magida.
Description: First edition. | New York, N.Y. : W. W. Norton & Company, [2020] |
Includes bibliographical references and index.
Identifiers: LCCN 2019053511 |
ISBN 9780393635188 (hardcover) | ISBN 9780393635195 (epub)
Subjects: LCSH: Khan, Noor Inayat, 1914–1944. | World War, 1939–1945—
Secret service—Great Britain—Biography. | Women spies—
Great Britain—Biography. | Radio operators—France—Biography. |
World War, 1939–1945—Underground movements—France. |
World War, 1939–1945—Prisoners and prisons, German.
Classification: LCC D802.F8 K4856 2020 | DDC 940.54/8641092—dc23
LC record available at https://lccn.loc.gov/2019053511

W. W. Norton & Company, Inc., 500 Fifth Avenue, New York, N.Y. 10110
www.wwnorton.com

W. W. Norton & Company Ltd., 15 Carlisle Street, London W1D 3BS

1 2 3 4 5 6 7 8 9 0

You are my witnesses.

—ISAIAH, 43:10

CONTENTS

PART THREE: THE POWER AND THE GLORY

PART FOUR: IN THE WORLD OF NO WORLD

CODE NAME
MADELEINE

THE MOON GODDESS

There was a full moon that night. There had to be. That was the only way to fly. The pilot of the lightweight plane that was taking Noor to France used no lights, not even a flashlight to help him scan the crumpled-up map that rested on his knee. Stripped to meet weight and space restrictions, Frank Rymills's Lysander also carried no guns, no armor, no radios, no navigator—a challenge for flights that demanded pinpoint navigation: when seen from the air, Rymills's target was virtually a needlepoint in a dark, hostile countryside. But everything the Lysander lacked gave Rymills a major advantage over the Germans: if his radio was on and the Nazis were listening, they knew he was up there, but they didn't know where. It was a big sky, and being unable to determine his location was a big benefit.

Of all the ways Britain pierced occupied France, the air was the greatest surprise to the Germans. The Nazis knew from the beginning of the war that they would have a hard time securing France's long coastline, especially in Brittany with its hundreds of bays and inlets. The same with the Pyrenees, where downed airmen and desperate Jews were soon going one way as incoming spies went the other. But the Germans had barely pondered that their empire could be penetrated from the air (except for high-flying bombers) until they began hearing about mysterious aircraft flying into territory that had no obvious strategic value. The planes didn't drop bombs and they weren't conducting reconnaissance. They were dropping agents and crates with weapons and wireless transmitters. The Germans weren't ready for this kind of war.

They also weren't ready to detect these planes, tiny as they were. By 1943, Britain had better radar than the Nazis. For that, the Germans could thank Hitler. The Fuehrer believed that defense wasted time, money, men, weapons. Only one thing mattered to Hitler when countries smashed up against each other: advance, advance some more, and with each advance, crush your enemy's army and shatter his confidence and his courage until what's left is a glaring and shameful defeat.

Hitler's creed served him well, at first. But he hadn't reckoned on England's refusal to buckle under the bombing of its cities and the torpedoing of its fleets and the rationing of its food. Hitler couldn't understand why England didn't wave a white flag and call it quits. And he surely hadn't counted on these gnat-like Lysanders: ten feet shorter than Germany's legendary fighter, the Messerschmitt Bf 109, Lysanders crawled along at 212 miles an hour, about thirty-five percent slower than Messerschmitts. Lysanders took about an hour and a half to bounce from their secret bases in England to fields in France, literally *fields* where cows grazed and crops grew: places no one would normally call an airfield. Ideal for their missions, Lysanders could land in less than the length of a football field, and they were equipped with extra fuel tanks that upped their range to 1,150 miles. The British had discovered that high-flying German planes could spot Lysanders silhouetted against the ground. Applying camouflage colors to the upper part of every Lysander's fuselage and the top surface of its wings made the planes nearly invisible. Also, ladders were bolted near the rear door to let passengers out in a flash, cutting the planes' turnaround time. When Lysanders landed in the dark somewhere in Europe, every extra second on the ground could cost the pilot and his passengers their lives.

Give Lysander pilots a full moon and they were ready to go. For them, said a British general, "The moon was as much of a goddess as she ever was in a near eastern religion." The moon determined when someone would go into France or come out of it. No one flew when there was solid cloud cover on a moonless night. This made navigation difficult because ground features were barely discernible. A clear night with a full moon was better. Best was a full moon with cloud cover around 2,000 to 3,000 feet: then the planes were difficult to detect and their pilots had optimal visibility. In France, members of the Resistance tagged comrades by the phase of the moon when they had flown a Lysander: someone was coming on "the next moon," or they had already arrived on "the last moon," be it the "March moon," or the "June moon," or the "September moon." Unlike the rest of humanity, theirs was not a heliocentric universe. It was lunar-centric.

By the time Frank Rymills was making this flight in mid-June 1943, Lysanders had already flown into France 101 agents who belonged to a top-secret British operation—the Strategic Operations Executive. The planes' routes were proven; the pilots were some of England's best; and the English Channel—barely twenty-one miles across at its narrowest point—was proving more penetrable than the Nazis let on. Sometimes Rymills had three passengers: one on the floor, two on a seat. Tonight, he had two. He knew little about them beyond their code names. Lysander pilots never knew the real names of their passengers. That was too dangerous. He quickly sized up Cecily Lefort, and he didn't like her. A courier for an SOE cell in south-eastern France, Lefort "looked like a vicar's wife" and her French "wasn't all that hot." His other passenger, Noor Inayat Khan, was more intriguing. Her light-brown skin, good looks, and vague, not quite placeable accent puzzled Rymills as much as his inability to figure out why someone so easy to spot was being sent to France. The general thinking in the SOE was that the less interesting an agent, the easier it was for her to blend in. The best agents were so bland that they rarely got a second look. Noor was just the opposite. She warranted attention, and invariably she got it. One SOE agent who had trained with Noor called her "a splendid, vague, dreamy creature, far too conspicuous. Twice seen. Never forgotten."

Rymills couldn't question his passengers about anything. That was against the rules. So he fell into his usual routine of being a good host. Some of his gestures bent RAF protocol, like asking his passengers to pass around the flasks he had stowed in front of their seats—one had black coffee, the other coffee laced with rum. Other gestures were fine, like reminding his passengers that once they were over France they would see the graceful, swooping loops of the Loire. From the air, the river was a brilliant illusion, appearing firm and supple, almost idle, a calm counterbalance to what awaited Noor once they landed. Viewing the Loire would be Noor's last chance for repose on the flight, probably her last until she returned to England.

As they crossed into France, Rymills jumped into his role as a tour guide.

"Now, madame," he said into the intercom that connected him with Noor, "we are approaching your beautiful country. . . ." Rymills spoke to Noor like this because he had heard rumors that she had French roots. Despite the ban on Lysander pilots knowing anything about their passengers, something usually leaked out about them.

"Isn't it lovely in the moonlight?" he asked Noor.

"I think it is heavenly," Noor shouted into her intercom, a noisy four feet behind Rymills. "What," she inquired, "is that town over there?" pointing to the sort of view she had heard about from poets and dreamers, but had never expected to enjoy herself.

For the next thirty minutes, Rymills shouted over the roar of his engine about the landmarks below—châteaus, some of the finest in France; and bridges that dated back to the Romans; and towns that were treasures of history and architecture. If Rymills had been flying higher—halfway across the Channel, he had dropped from around eight thousand feet so he would be below the Nazis' radar horizon—the gleam of Paris would have been visible. But Paris was dark, and Rymills was flying low, and Noor was happy just to be returning home.

Eavesdropping on the radio was often the only way the Germans knew Lysanders were up there. That didn't help them locate the planes, but a pilot's carelessness would let the Germans know what they were saying. Which was why Jimmy McCairns, who was flying his Lysander near Rymills—pilots often flew missions in tandem like this—was miffed that Rymills was letting half of Europe listen to his breezy conversation with Noor about the French countryside. Soon McCairns's annoyance turned to bemusement. He realized that the chitchat between Rymills and Noor was making the Germans even more frustrated that they hadn't been able to end, once and for all, these damnable, never-ending flights by such ordinarily inconsequential planes.

Earlier that evening, Vera Atkins, one of the SOE's top officers, had picked up Noor in an open-air cabriolet. Noor and the other agents were flying that night to France. It was a "perfect June day," Atkins would later recall, with "the smell of the dog roses." Still, "taking the agents to the aerodromes . . . was very tiring."

In a cottage next to a secret airfield in Tangmere, a small village in eastern England, Atkins referred to each passenger only by their code name. Making sure each agent remembered the password they would need when they met their contacts in France, Atkins gave each of them a French identity card, a ration book, and a small pistol. There might be trouble when they landed. The Webley M1907—four inches long and ten ounces in weight—looked like a water gun. Experts knew better. Calling it "a little hunk of dynamite," they proudly described the trajectory of its bullets: when they "struck flesh . . . there was a tendency for the bullet to go giddy and turn sidewise. . . . Humanitarians condemned the tippy bullets. Those who knew war were not surprised or even shocked." To an American aficionado of pistols, Webleys connoted "quality and reliability from 'way back, just as our Colt and Smith & Wesson names do. About this gun there was some of the forthrightness that helped make the British Empire great."

Atkins then went through the agents' pockets and examined every inch of their clothing, searching for any sign that they had come from England—labels, scraps of paper, cigarette packs, matchbooks, movie stubs, underground tickets, monogrammed handkerchiefs. Even teeth were inspected to make sure the SOE's dentist had replaced English-style fillings with gold in the French manner. Agents had already gotten French-style haircuts from French barbers who were living in England, and they were wearing clothes that were either genuinely French or had been scrupulously copied from French styles by the SOE's expert tailors. Sometimes name tags were sewn into the clothes from tailors whose shops were in the neighborhoods where the agents would be operating in France. Finally, Atkins pulled out a few items that would lend small, convincing details to the agents' outfits—a pack of French cigarettes, a recent French newspaper, a photo of a "relative" for a handbag or wallet. If an agent needed a last-minute dash of authenticity, Atkins sewed on French clothing labels or French-style buttons.

In a few minutes, Atkins produced several "citizens" of the now-defunct French republic, a country that existed barely in name and hardly in spirit. Pierre Raynaud, an officer in de Gaulle's Free French Army, was watching Atkins. Waiting in that same cottage at Tangmere for his own flight to France, Raynaud was impressed with Atkins's eye for detail. Nothing escaped her. Then he glanced at Noor. She was studying a *prewar* French railway timetable. Raynaud concluded she was out of her depth.

Atkins asked if anyone wanted to meet with her privately. She did this with all of her outgoing agents. The custom contradicted Atkins's reputation for being gruff and haughty. Noor requested a few minutes with her. Going upstairs, they closed the door to a bedroom. Noor was in such a good mood that she complimented Atkins on a brooch she had pinned to her lapel: "You are so clever. You always make sure you wear something pretty." Removing the pin—a silver bird—Atkins pressed it into Noor's hands. The gift was actually part of a long-standing tradition in the SOE—departing agents were frequently given a warm memory of England before leaving for the continent, usually something made of gold. For women, this might be a powder compact; for men, cufflinks or a fountain pen. None of these could bear any compromising marks that might link them to Britain. These small gifts had two purposes: in a pinch, they could be sold to a pawnbroker, and they reminded agents how much they were cherished back home.

Around 10 p.m., a Ford station wagon drove the agents in Noor's group to the tarmac. After a squadron leader introduced the passengers to Rymills, Atkins gave each agent a farewell embrace, whispering to some of them "*Merde alors.*" Loosely translated as "You're in deep shit now," this was Atkins's standard sendoff to departing agents. It was also what the SOE's code wizard wryly called the agency's "ultimate benediction." To Noor, until recently the semi-cloistered daughter of a mystic, this may have sounded crude and vulgar. But Atkins's crudity may have been exactly what Noor needed. Simultaneously harsh and benign, it hammered home to Noor the danger she had gotten herself into.

One by one, the agents climbed the ladder into the Lysander. Noor was too slight—only five feet, three inches tall—to raise either foot onto the ladder. An airman gave her a boost. Settling into the cramped passenger section behind the cockpit, Noor took several deep breaths. Tonight marked two "firsts." One for her, one for the SOE. This was the first airplane ride in her life, and she was the first female radio operator the SOE was sending to France. For the colonel who headed the SOE's French division, radio operators were the linchpin of the SOE. They let the French know there was a world beyond the occupation, that they had friends and allies, and that freedom wasn't dead. Radio operators, said Maurice Buckmaster, helped "nerve the French to far greater degrees of endurance than if they felt themselves all alone. The greatest service we can render these patriots is the link with freedom . . . through our radio operators, a link which brings them gifts from heaven in the form of arms and explosives (and perhaps cigarettes and chocolate)."

At the age of twenty-nine, Noor was about to bring gifts to patriots she had never met.

Past midnight, Rymills approached a landing field northeast of the town of Angers in the Loire Valley. Frequently used by the SOE, the field was officially known as B20/A. Its code name that may have summed up the experience of others who had been flown into it: "Indigestion." A few months before, the Nazis had executed sixty Resistance fighters in Angers's town square. Tonight, everything was still. Rymills knew where to land when he saw his "reception committee" flashing a prearranged Morse-code letter with a flashlight. If Rymills had seen the wrong letter, he would have returned immediately to England. The field was laid out with a miniature flight path: three flashlights arranged in an inverted L-shape: the crossbar was at the upwind end; at the downwind end, the head of the reception committee and his outgoing passengers were waiting. Rymills landed just past the downwind light, taxied in a right-hand turn around the other two, then circled back to the first. Turning upwind again, he halted.

As Rymills's passengers scrambled out of his plane, Noor clutched her pistol. She wasn't afraid to use it. Shooting, she'd written in an essay she had never shown anyone during her SOE training, was like meditating. Both demanded fierce, intense concentration; both narrowed your attention to "the pure essence" of your task—"focusing one's mind in a certain direction" until there was no distinction between outer and inner, other and self.

Noor's notion of firearms was consistent with her upbringing. Raised in a spiritual cocoon near Paris, her father, Hazrat Inayat Khan, an internationally renowned mystic, had raised her to be "chivalrous," an archaic term to the rest of us though to Sufis one pregnant with meaning and purpose. Early on in this miserable war, Noor had concluded that if she didn't fight—and fight in *her* way—then she would betray her heritage and betray her father. He had taught her to love others, to serve them, to never shirk from the dangers and difficulty of improving the world. Not fighting the Nazis would have been heresy, and Noor was not a heretic. Her plane had taken off from England on a Wednesday, a day, according to her father, "for taking an initiative. . . . All that is done on this day must bear fruit." She landed on a Thursday, "a day of inspiration, of revelation." If Noor had to use the Webley M1907 she was holding, it could have been a revelation. Of sorts.

After three minutes on the ground—the longer Rymills stayed there, the greater the chance the Germans would find him—he was back in the air, his engine at full blast. He'd had a good flight. He always did. Yet for the entire trip back to England, he couldn't get Noor out of his mind. Flying north, Rymills kept his eyes on the sky and on his instruments, occasionally scanning the horizon for England's coast, while Noor remained behind him in France. Rymills was confident that "Madeleine" (Noor's code name) could handle whatever came her way. He'd sensed that she was capable of absenting herself from the immediacy of the moment, then returning to it refreshed and invigorated. She seemed to have done that even while flying in a noisy, rickety Lysander. If she could do it in a Lysander, Rymills figured, she could do it while nosing around France for the SOE.

B y the time Rymills reached the Channel, Noor was on her way to a safe house near Paris, perhaps remembering that her father had wondered in one of his lectures "if it is bad for children to play with tin soldiers." His answer was surprising: even toys can prepare us for the harshness of life, for vicissitudes that some mystics pretend don't exist or that they say can be transcended by burrowing into our own personal nirvana. But Noor's father was a practical mystic. He didn't seek students who yearned for an elusive transcendentalism that could buffer them from the rigors of the world. Rather, he taught the value of meeting the quotidian challenges of life with the wholeness of one's spirit and the truth of one's soul. "We should first try to become human," Inayat wrote. "To become an angel is not very difficult; to be material is very easy; but to live in the world, in all the difficulties and struggles of the world, and to be human at the same time, is very difficult.

If we become that, then we become the miniature of God on earth." For Inayat, spirituality didn't reside in another realm. It was here. It was now. And it was real.

Surveying the ups and downs of life, Inayat rarely provided simple answers, especially when it came to being a citizen of a nation. He knew that the price of defending a country's safety, dignity, and honor could be war and it could be death: unsettling confessions for a man of peace and a man of God. As much as Inayat Khan disliked war, he also disliked citizens dodging their responsibility for their country's stability and preservation, and for its very existence. Now, more than a decade after Inayat's death, tin soldiers had turned into live ones, and his beloved daughter Noor, who had been raised in peace and for peace, was among them. Frank Rymills and his compact Lysander had seen to that.

For Lysander pilots, "The moon was as much of a goddess as she ever was in a near eastern religion."

PART ONE
THE RISING

The soul has no birth, no death,
no beginning, no end.

—HAZRAT INAYAT KHAN

CHAPTER 1

THE AIR OF HEAVEN

The Khans were royalty, a lineage they traced to Tipu Sultan, Inayat Khan's great-great-grandfather. In the eighteenth century, Tipu had stubbornly resisted Britain turning India into a colony of its vast empire, fighting against England more than any sovereign in the Asian sub-continent. Having Tipu in the Khans' family tree was like a Vietnamese having Ho Chi Minh as an ancestor or an American having Patrick Henry. In fact, Tipu and the Americans were fighting the British at the same time— the Americans for their independence, Tipu for his freedom. Though their wars were halfway around the globe from one another, they recognized allies where they could find them: Tipu sent money to the Americans along with a letter to the Continental Congress proclaiming, "For every blow that is struck in the cause of American liberty throughout the world, . . . and so long as a single insolent savage tyrant remains, the struggle shall continue." Touched, Benjamin Franklin sent Tipu a copy of the Declaration of Independence. The Americans won their war. Tipu lost his. In four long military campaigns, he earned the respect of the British, but never their defeat.

Inayat Khan was born in 1882 into a family of Muslims, Brahmins, brilliant musicians, revered holy men, and brave warriors. ("Inayat" means "kind," "generous." "Khan" translates as "lofty," "chief," or "ruler.") At an early age, he was fascinated by the dervishes who traveled through his town, and he was riveted by the stories his father told him that always had an elevating and instructive moral. But at the age of fourteen he was annoyed that he still had no proof that God heard his prayers. His grandfather's advice—"The signs of God are seen in the world, and the world is seen in thyself"—inspired him to seek God everywhere, and in everyone, and in himself. A pilgrim in search of a way, a truth, a path, he studied with Hindu gurus, Zoroastrian saints, Buddhist monks, and Sufi masters, learning yoga, meditation, and breath control, the poetry of Rumi, the wisdom of the Koran and the Bhagavad Gita, and how to sink into reveries from holy music for hours on end. He learned about community, about solitude, and about power. Watching a herd of elephants in Nepal bring a tiger to bay by surrounding it in the woods, Inayat concluded that "unity can stand against any power, however great"; and meditating with holy men convinced him of the power of a quiet, still mind. Soon, myths grew about Inayat: he was superhuman, superwise, holy, sacred, luminous. In truth, he was a seeker like any other man.

Inayat married a cousin when he was twenty. She died a few days after the wedding. Grieving, he set off on a pilgrimage, performing for maharajahs and prime ministers in distant provinces. He married again, then mourned again when his second wife died a year later. Again he searched for solace, eventually performing in Hyderabad for a prince who, soothed by Inayat's music, invited him to join his court. For four years, Inayat studied there with a Sufi master. In 1908, his dying teacher told him to go "into the world, harmonize the East and the West with the harmony of thy music," and "thereby spread the wisdom of Sufism, for thou art gifted by Allah, the most merciful and compassionate."

Two years later, Inayat, two of his brothers, and a cousin—all musicians— left for New York. Inayat found Western music more disciplined, systematic, and dignified than music in India. There, musicians—offering empty "amusement" for the idle rich—knew little about the theory of music, and were often afraid their students might outshine them. Though Inayat left India "to admire the works of God by appreciating music in the different parts of the civilized world," he always planned to return: "I wish to . . . pick up foreign music and give [it] to my friends."

America wasn't what Inayat expected. Soon after arriving, he was touring the country with Ruth St. Denis, a "modern" dancer influenced by the pioneering choreography of Isadora Duncan and the melodramas of Sarah

Bernhardt. St. Denis was sure her dancing was a respectful bridge between the West and the best of Japan, India, Egypt—lands she had visited only in her imagination. She dubbed Inayat's ensemble the Royal Musicians of Hindustan—the centerpiece for her new seven-act dance that appropriated Hindu gods, priests, and temples, none of which, by the time she was done, had anything to do with her dancing. Perhaps more upsetting to the Royal Musicians was how St. Denis whirled around in costumes that were pleasingly erotic to her audiences and scandalous to her Indian accompanists, who were new to the West.

The tour made dozens of stops along the way to California. In Salt Lake City, the musicians refused to perform, preferring, according to a local newspaper, to observe a religious holiday "in true Oriental fashion." St. Denis fumed that in the future her contracts with musicians would include clauses about religious holidays. Before they got to the West Coast, Inayat (and the other Royal Musicians) left St. Denis when she insisted he certify that she was performing authentic dances from India. He left just in time. She was about to debut a new dance she called "The Sufi." One critic who sat through it sniffed that St. Denis "alternatively blinked at the painted sky, proudly examined her bare toes and tied herself into a knot as the curtain descended. . . . The audience giggled."

On their own now, the Royal Musicians gave concerts and Inayat gave lectures on Sufism, trying to find the best way to reach Westerners. A mystical offshoot of Islam, Sufism, like all mysticisms, aspired toward a personal relationship with God, one that was beyond words and legalisms and the empty outwardness of rituals. Sufism's force extended from the hidden meaning of Islamic scripture, especially from this verse from the Koran about creating the first human: "I have fashioned him and breathed into him of My spirit." That spark of divinity, Sufis said, is in each of us, and Sufism could help us know it, and expand it.

The few Americans who knew anything about Sufism found it alluring, tantalizing. Ralph Waldo Emerson wrote a poem about the thirteenth-century Sufi, Sa'di; Thoreau's pursuit of nature at a pond twenty miles west of Boston could have earned him a merit badge from a Sufi summer camp; and Whitman sang of the "last lesson" from a "graybeard Sufi":

Allah is all, all, all—is immanent in every life and object . . .
It is the central urge in every atom . . .
To return to its divine source and origin, however distant . . .

Sufism fascinated these men though they had never met a Sufi. There were no Sufis in the United States, where almost anything connected with Islam was theologically unwelcome—the Prophet Muhammad had preached that Islam was the final revelation that had begun with Abraham. To Jews, revelation ended with the last of the prophets in the Old Testament. To Christians, it ended with Jesus. In the Judeo-Christian tradition, Muhammad was an impostor. Inayat also faced difficulty in the United States because Islam was maligned as a danger to American society—many slaves who had come from Africa were Muslims. Anything that comforted slaves disturbed their masters.

Inayat was not the first Sufi in the West. The year after Inayat left India, a Swede, Ivan Aguéli, had founded a secret Sufi group in Paris after studying Sufism in Cairo. But Inayat was the first Sufi in the United States, and he had to find a way to teach Sufism to Americans. He also had to find a new Sufism. The old one, the one he had known, was too esoteric, too Islamic for most Westerners. Teaching Sufism in India had been "like sailing in the sea, smooth and level." Teaching it in the West was like "traveling in a hilly land." To level the hills, Inayat constructed a "Sufism" that would have been unrecognizable in India. He didn't rely exclusively, and overtly, on the Koran, like a traditional Sufi. Instead, Inayat melded Christian, Jewish, Buddhist, Hindu, and Muslim scriptures into an original gospel, emphasizing the universality of all faiths and of all humanity. Like any true mysticism, Inayat's Sufism demolished barriers and distinctions; unlike more orthodox Sufism, there was scant mention of Islam or of its five "pillars": faith, praying five times a day, donating to the poor and the needy, fasting during Ramadan, and making a pilgrimage to Mecca at least once in your life. Eventually, Inayat's Sufism had such modest Islamic content that he rarely mentioned it.

This was a Sufism in which everyone was welcome—Jew, Christian, Buddhist, Hindu, Muslim. As Inayat asserted, "divine wisdom is not limited to a certain people." And if there was a compulsion to call what he was crafting a religion, then it was a "religion of love, harmony and beauty."

Noor's father, Hazrat Inayat Khan.

Truth was the foundation of this trinity. Truth, Inayat said, "was all the religion there is. It is truth which will save us."

Several American scholars have waded into why Inayat distanced Sufism from the mysticism he had known back home. As a British colonial subject, said one, Inayat "felt inferior" in the West. Uncertain whether Sufism could hold up to Western scrutiny, Inayat didn't want Westerners to know it had originated in the East, and surely not that it stemmed from Islam. That would have damaged his project from the start. Another academic added that if Inayat had taught the Sufism he'd known in India, "everyone would have deserted him." Many ordinary spiritual seekers in the West, usually open and accepting, had little tolerance for anything that smacked of Islam.

Yet, the debate continues—was Inayat a reformer of Sufism, determined to prove its elasticity by adapting new ideas for a new world? If so, say some observers, then he was an absolutely authentic Sufi. Sufism rejected formalities and canon and edicts. And since Sufism emphasized individual-ism, why shouldn't Inayat exercise his? Still, that notion is anathema to an Iranian Muslim who teaches Islamic Studies at George Washington University in Washington, DC. "Sufism without Islam is a total absurdity," scoffed professor Seyyed Hossein Nasr. "That's like not calling water wet. Inayat was not a reformer. He was a deformer."

In the end, it may not matter if Inayat was a reformer, an apostate, or a nontraditionalist. At their core, his teachings reflect the central tenet of Sufism—*mahabba*, a love in which the trinity of lover, loved, and love itself arises from a compassionate and merciful God. Like any Sufi, Inayat never deviated from this.

On the West Coast of the United States, Inayat was attracting attention, sometimes as a spiritual teacher, sometimes for entirely different reasons. The *Los Angeles Times* called him a "polished gentleman" with the "grace of a man born to a high caste." (The headline was less respectful: "Sinuous Gent from the Orient.") Women swooned when they saw his photo: rugged and dashing, he defied the usual image of gurus and holy men—dyspeptic, chaste, and prudish. In San Francisco, he attracted his first student in the West—a thin, bespectacled Jewish woman who yearned to bask in Inayat's "great and illuminated intelligence." He taught her yoga, breathing techniques, meditation, and the virtues of modesty ("conceal your practice and its results and its effects upon you from others") before returning to New York for more lectures and concerts. Most were at the New York Sanskrit College—a warren of threadbare rooms at 250 West 87th Street, an apartment building a quarter-block west of Broadway. The "college" was little more than a yoga studio, a second room with some rickety chairs sitting on top of a faded Persian carpet, and a revolving "faculty" of gurus, sages, and masters of the arcane and the esoteric.

The founder of the "college" was Pierre Bernard, who was neither a "Pierre" nor a "Bernard." Originally Perry Baker from Leon, Iowa, a town with a mere 1,400 residents, he preferred "Pierre Bernard" for its European air. Having escaped Iowa in his late teens, Baker traveled around the country, dispensing Eastern wisdom that he'd picked up from a self-taught yogi. Eventually, he settled in Manhattan, teaching his version of mysticism and the occult to the curious, the rich (wives of Broadway producers, sons of Wall Street financiers), and the famous (Lillian Russell, the illustrious actress). Women were Bernard's weakness. First he shared an apartment near Central Park West—what newspapers would soon call a "love nest"—with a young woman from the Bronx who suffered from a weak heart. He promised he had the cure for her. She was soon disappointed: he had other things in mind. Then there was Gertrude Leo, whom he brought to New York after one of his yoga hustles in Seattle. When the police learned about this, they claimed he had crossed state lines with an unmarried woman for "immoral purposes." Stuck in prison for three months—Bernard couldn't raise the $15,000 bail—he was released when both women dropped their charges against him, deciding they cared more about preserving their reputations than trashing his. Soon, Bernard was running the Sanskrit College with essentially the same moneyed clientele as before.

Bernard liked flaunting his credentials. By his own count, he belonged to more than sixty "learned societies and academies" on three continents. One of these "societies"—the American Medical Association—went to considerable lengths to state that Bernard had never graduated from a medical college, never been licensed to practice medicine anywhere in the United States, and never belonged to the AMA itself. Responding to a query about Bernard, the association stated that its investigators "seemed to get the impression that . . . [Bernard's] cult or circle was devoted to sex worship." Despite the scandals that followed him for decades, by the 1930s Bernard was so wealthy that he purchased an estate in Rockland County, about twenty miles north of New York City, and he was so adroit at mingling the aspirations of spiritual seekers with the balderdash of a sideshow that he owned several elephants. Baby, Budh, Juno, and Old Man entertained local kids, swam in the pool Bernard built for them, and rode oversized tricycles in Bernard's annual fetes.

Inayat arrived in New York a few months after Bernard's disgrace from the "love nest" where he had kept nubile young women. Inayat never learned about the scandals. He probably never wanted to. He was there to teach, not worry about headlines like the police breaking "in on weird Hindu rites" or about "The Great Oom," the tabloids' moniker for Bernard. In any case, Inayat had to be careful. His stay coincided with a resurgence of hysteria about Eastern religions. According to the *Washington Post*, women, brain-washed by gurus and swamis, were "deserting home and husband and children to 'follow the light'" and flee to India. A journalist who attended Inayat's classes noted that after he proclaimed, "We are love ourselves, and we must love," "fair bosoms rise and fall" and "an attraction" and "obsession" sprang up between "American women and a dark-skinned master."

One of those women was Ora Baker, Pierre Bernard's twenty-year-old sister and legal ward. Willowy and petite, with long blonde hair secured by a barrette just above the nape of her neck, Ora fell in love with Inayat. Tall and handsome, he was a relief from the scrawny holy men who usually passed through her brother's "college." Summoning her courage, Ora told Bernard she wanted to marry the new "professor." Bernard was furious. Inayat had no job, no future. He couldn't provide for a family. He could barely provide for himself. Many brothers would have had similar concerns. What really bothered Bernard was Inayat's color: he didn't want a dark-skinned man in his family. "Your blood will never mix with his," he told his sister. (Despite all his talk of love, Bernard forbade his students to ever discuss "in the presence of niggers and chinks and snakes" what he taught. His wisdom was too precious for these lower life forms just as Ora was too lofty for a brown-skinned man from India.)

Soon, Inayat had to leave the United States for concerts and lectures that had already been booked in England. Bernard ordered Ora to stay in the United States, and to never see Inayat or write to him. Bernard also began keeping a gun in a drawer. Had Inayat shown up, he was prepared to kill him. Virtually a prisoner in her brother's house, Ora called herself "the saddest girl in the world." While going through Bernard's desk one day, she came upon the address of Inayat's family in India. Writing to him there, she asked that her letters be forwarded to Inayat in England. In the next few months, Ora wrote almost sixty letters to Inayat, all of them full of longing and yearning, lamenting in one, "Oh, my soul, my soul, how can I ever live through this separation?" and in another, "Who could be so heartless as to keep us apart. . . . My eyes are blind with tears," and in still another, "Where is my love, where is he now / Just to see his face again . . . / I would die a thousand deaths."

In February 1913, Ora secretly bought a ticket for a steamer to Europe.

Wearing a plain black dress and tucking her long blonde hair under a hat, she barely left her cabin for the entire trip. Even her meals were brought there. Inayat met her in Antwerp, a safer port than London in case Bernard had detectives looking for Ora there. On March 20, Ora and Inayat were married in a civil ceremony in London; a few weeks later, they had a Muslim ceremony. Ora never returned to the United States.

Though Inayat and his brothers gave concerts and lectures all over Paris and London, they were barely making a living. To make more of a splash, they teamed up in Paris with Mata Hari—the Dutch dancer Margaretha Geertruida Zelle, whom the French would execute as a German spy after World War I. The brothers were happy to soon leave Mata, embarrassed by her partially nude performances and her phony versions of classical Indian

Noor's mother, Ora.

dancing. Years later, they were still making fun of her. "First," the brothers recalled, "she swayed to the right, then to the left, and then she stood still for a bit. And all the bald gentlemen with white beards on little gold chairs would murmur, '*Ah, c'est charmant.*'"

More satisfying was Inayat's friendship with the composer Claude Debussy. Debussy, who had long been interested in nonwestern music, would incorporate into several of his symphonies the Indian melodies that he had learned from Inayat.

Then an offer came to perform in Moscow. Inayat was accustomed to being asked to perform for royalty in India. He assumed the invitation had come from the czar himself. Inayat was wrong. The offer came from Frederick Bruce Thomas, an African American whose parents had been slaves in Mississippi. After the Civil War, Thomas's parents, Lewis and Hannah, bought a farm—one of only six owned by blacks in Coahama County. They were threatened by the Ku Klux Klan, shunned by their neighbors, and swindled by a rich white landowner to sign their two hundred acres over to him to ease their debts. After they moved to Memphis, Lewis was murdered, his wife struggled to get by, and Frederick—exhausted from sorrow, misery, and humiliation—headed north. Eighteen years old, he worked as a delivery "boy" in St. Louis and Chicago, a valet in New York, and a waiter, butler, and headwaiter in London, Paris, Monte Carlo, Milan, Rome, Vienna, and Budapest. Looking for a place where he could put down roots, Frederick found it in Russia. In 1912, he bought a club in Moscow, Maxim, with rich fabrics on its walls, glittering chandeliers hanging from its ceilings, and, soon, "first-class variety theater" that he imported from Europe. "Mature" entertainment began around 11 p.m. as men reclined on low settees in Maxim's Salon Café Harem, sipping champagne at fourteen rubles a bottle (several hundred dollars in today's money) while the Royal Musicians of Hindustan played their vinas and tablas, and Princess Chukha Mukha, the dancer they'd brought with them from Paris, slithered her way through showbiz hoofing and phony Indian gestures.

When some theosophists heard that holy men from India were performing at Maxim, they convinced the Royal Musicians to quit. Maxim was no place for them. The Royal Musicians were meant for a higher purpose than playing background music in a smoky nightclub. To thank the theosophists, Inayat invited them to join him and Ora to celebrate the recent birth of their first child.

The theosophists bought a dozen white lilies for Ora at Noev F.F. and Sons, a noted florist at 14 Petrovka Street. In the Khans' hotel room, they talked politely with Inayat and his brothers, wondering where the mother and her new baby were. Finally, everyone fell silent as a curtain separating the sitting room from the bedroom parted and Ora entered, cradling Noor in her arms. As Ora settled into an armchair, Inayat announced to everyone that Noor, barely two months old, was already a mystic. The theosophists were impressed. They believed it was rare, though not impossible, for a baby to be a mystic. To Inayat, this didn't make Noor unique: for him, *every* baby was a mystic. Babies knew that their most important task was to preserve the "air of heaven" they had brought to earth—a small vestige of the pristine paradise they had left behind.

Noor-un-nissa—"Light Among Nations"—had been born on the first day of 1914. She was a princess through her father's ancestors: through Tipu Sultan who had fought the British in India in the eighteenth century, then through her great-grandfather Maula Bakhsh—"the Beethoven of India"—whom the Maharajah of Mysore had awarded in the 1860s for his musical excellence. The jewel for his turban, the scepter, the gold chain, and the golden umbrella the maharajah gave Maula were all emblems of royalty. This was royalty by selection, not by lineage or birth. Without these accoutrements, and the subsequent elevation in Maula's rank, he could not have married Tipu's daughter: in India, as in most countries, only royalty married royalty. With that, Noor would have royal roots through a military hero (Tipu Sultan) and a musical savant (Maula Bakhsh) who married the daughter of that hero.

At birth, Noor weighed 7¾ pounds and her skin was a light tan. Precisely where in Moscow she was born is hard to pinpoint: birth certificates were rarely issued in prerevolutionary Russia. One story is that she was born in the home of Sergei Tolstoy, the eldest son of the Russian novelist Leo Tolstoy. Though Sergei and Inayat were good friends, it is improbable Noor was born in Tolstoy's apartment. A birth in the home of a new friend would have been a considerable imposition.

Birth information of the Khan children in their
mother's handwriting. For Noor: 10:15 p.m.,
Moscow, December 15, 1913, in the Russian
calendar; January 1, 1914, in the Roman calendar.

Noor and her father, Moscow, 1914.

Another account is that Noor was born in the Monastery of St. Peter, a two-hundred-year-old complex about a quarter mile from where the Khans were living in Moscow. Yet the monks' cells were never used as delivery rooms, and the monastery didn't have an infirmary. In any case, only sixteen monks were living in the monastery in 1914—a fraction of what was needed to properly attend to the six churches that were inside the monastery's high walls. A monastery that could barely sustain itself had little time in which to help strangers deliver their first child.

A third possibility is that Noor was born in a hospital a block north of the monastery. The hospital was part of Catherine the Great's plan to improve Moscow. After a plague killed one-fifth of Moscow's population in the late eighteenth century, Catherine set out to modernize the city and make it healthier. Factories and slaughterhouses were moved from the city center; cemeteries were placed outside the city limits, downwind from inhabited neighborhoods; water supplies were cleaned up; and new hospitals were built. The most impressive was the Catherine Hospital, with eighteen acres of gardens and wards, and a towering entrance whose twelve Ionic columns may have convinced peasants fortunate enough to receive medical care there that they had already died and gone to heaven. By 1914, when Noor was born, the hospital had expanded considerably, but the quality of its care had declined just as much. Equipment was old, beds were rusty, and in the summer patients often lay on beds with no sheets. Luckily, Noor and her mother were not there during the summer. The hospital provided warm blankets in the winter, and mother and daughter would have been reasonably comfortable.

Free of Maxim, thanks to the theosophists' intervention, Inayat's life in Moscow was decidedly different. He had long discussions about Sufism and music with the composer Alexander Scriabin, even giving him some melodies from India, one of which, the Afghan Sword Dance, Scriabin incorporated into a symphony. Inayat's dinner with the opera singer Chaliapin lasted so long that he didn't return home until the next day. And he and Sergei Tolstoy began collaborating on a musical based on an ancient Hindu story. But after four years in the West, Inayat missed India. He hoped to return there on a British passport that stated he was a "Protected Person" and a "Native of the Indian State of Baroda." But his way was blocked. For almost a century, Great Britain and Russia had been jockeying for power in central Asia—wooing allies and splitting countries into fiefdoms run by surrogates and puppets. Britain called this The Great Game—a global chess match bloodied by thousands of casualties, mostly in Afghanistan, Bukhara, and Turkey, where Britain lost every war it fought. Traveling directly from Moscow to India would have taken the Khans through countries that were either fiercely anti-British or reeling from recent massacres by the czar. No one's safety was guaranteed. India would have to wait. In early summer, the Khans left Moscow for a conference of musicians in Paris. Inayat was ambivalent about leaving. He had learned to admire the Russian people—their idealism, their hospitality, their friendship. They were, he said, a "warm people in a cold land."

Traveling with a baby is difficult. Traveling with a baby in a foreign country is harder, especially in Russia in 1914. Inayat and Ora's journey with Noor turned out to be a blessing, if family lore is true. An angry crowd stopped the Khans' carriage near the border: their elegance and apparent wealth infuriated the local peasants. Worried that they would never get out of Russia, Inayat threw open the carriage door. Emerging in his full height, Inayat towered over the peasants. With his black cape flapping around him in the wind, he held Noor high above him. Seeing the infant, the crowd pulled back, and the Khans slipped away in the night, never to return to the country where Inayat felt most at home outside of India.

If nothing else, Noor left Russia with a nickname her Tatar nurse had given her—"Babuli," Father's daughter. Noor's family would call her this for the rest of her life.

CHAPTER 2

NEVER BE A
"NAUGHTY GIRLY"

After a brief stay in Paris, the Khans moved to London, wanting to put some distance between themselves and the war in Europe that everyone believed was imminent. They settled in Notting Hill. Until recently, Notting Hill had been known as the district of "potteries and piggeries." It was still not much more than a slum. The family's timing was impeccable—hostilities broke out a few weeks after they left France. Soon, Inayat was giving concerts throughout England to benefit the war effort. He sent what money he could back to London for Ora and Noor. As it turned out, Ora's brother had been right about what would happen if she married Inayat: she would be poor and she would be hungry. On some days, Ora had no more than a loaf of bread to share with the rest of her family. A meal of rice and dal was a rare feast.

Almost every week, Zeppelins were dropping bombs on London. Traveling up to 85 miles an hour and carrying as much as two tons of explosives, some Zepps were as long as 650 feet—longer than three blocks in London. By the end of the war, Zepps would kill 557 people and injure another 1,358, and H. G. Wells would say the airships had ended the fiction that England was an "inaccessible island," protected by the Atlantic on one side and the channel on the other. When Noor was three, Inayat wrote to her from the road. Pray, he asked, "that the Zeppelins may not drop [a] bomb on him." A terrifying request, but Inayat rarely coddled anyone, not even his children.

In the summer of 1918, Noor began kindergarten. Teachers admired her "musical little voice," her conduct ("very good"), and how well she "listens

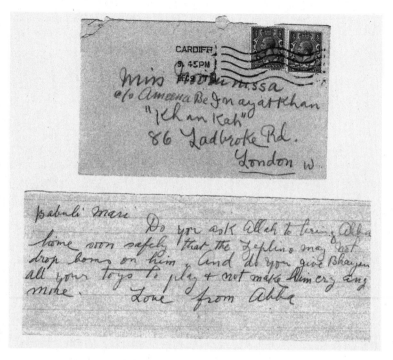

Inayat's letter to Noor: No bombs, please.

and enjoys stories and can tell one herself." Her major faults were her chattiness ("too talkative") and her difficulty concentrating ("needs steadying and strengthening"). In the middle of the school year, Ora gave birth to the sister Noor always wanted. With Claire's birth, Ora and Inayat had four children. (Two boys, Vilayat and Hidayat, had been born in 1916 and 1917.) For the rest of their lives, the oldest two, Noor and Vilayat, would be preternaturally close, largely because of their intense interest in Sufism and the family's mystical legacy.

When the war was over, the Khans (along with Inayat's brothers) returned to France, eventually moving into a large house near Paris which a wealthy Dutch disciple, Mevrouw Engling, bought for them. Inayat named it "Fazal Manzil"—the House of Blessings.

Fazal Manzil ended the wandering of the Khan family. Without Mrs. Engling's generosity, the family might have continued to reside in near-poverty, uncertain about where they would live, how long they would be there, and how they would pay for it. Contributing to their precarious situation was Ora's brother's refusal to help them in any way from the United States. Living now in a mansion north of New York, Pierre Bernard's yogic proselytizing had earned him fame and some wealth—enough to help Ora, if he wished. But smarting from her marriage to Inayat, Bernard had disowned her soon after she left the country.

Fazal Manzil was in Suresnes, a largely blue-collar town directly west of Paris along the Seine. Its nineteen thousand residents were mostly farmers, vintners, merchants, and factory workers who made cars, ambulances, and taxis. Suresnes was no industrial backwater: in the 1920s, the Darracq auto factory located here produced ten percent of France's cars every year. Some residents of the city worked in plants that blended expensive scents for France's finest perfumers—Coty, Volnay, and Worth. At the same time, Suresnes was so informal that you could walk into one of its wineries, buy a bottle of Chardonnay, and enjoy it with your meal in a restaurant a few blocks away, no questions asked and no fee charged. If you attempted to do this across the river in Paris, you'd either be billed for decorking—or asked to leave.

Near the Seine was a maze of shops and cafés and a cluster of cottages that emulated the Tudor style that was fashionable in England. All these were near a new bridge that had recently shut down the small ferries that had carried passengers to Paris for over a century. The bridge provided a new way to enter Suresnes: on the Paris side, first you passed through Bois de Boulogne, two and a half times the size of New York's Central Park. Then the river opened up before you at almost the same time that you saw Mont Valérien, the formidably steeped hill that loomed over Surenses. The entry was as majestic as it was convenient.

Thomas Jefferson had been familiar with Mont Valérien. While ambassador to France in the 1780s, Jefferson often left Paris—"Away to my hermitage," he told friends as he turned his horse toward a monastery that sat on the crest of Mont Valérien. Jefferson was often drawn toward Mont Valérien's solitude. In the monastery's silence, he could read and walk and think. No amateur oenophile, he also enjoyed the monastery's wine, harvested from vineyards that had flourished on Valérien's slopes for nine hundred years.

Noor (far left) and her siblings enjoyed playing dress-up in Indian clothes.

Fazal Manzil was two-thirds up the steep slope of Mont Valérien. Square and stolid, its thick stone walls made it seem larger than its 3,500 square feet. A stone balustrade along the edge of the flat roof lent balance to the overall design; the eight-foot-high stone wall surrounding the house ensured privacy; and the upper floors provided a stunning view of Paris—in the 1920s, the home of Gertrude Stein, Ernest Hemingway, Scott Fitzgerald, Picasso, and Dalí: expatriates and experimentalists trying to make sense of a world shattered by the Great War. In Paris, they hoped, you could start over and forget about everything that was rotten in life. For the French, there was little starting over, not after 1.4 million of their countrymen had been killed in the war that didn't end all wars. Fazal Manzil had little to do with the lost, grieving city of Paris. In fact, it had little to do with Suresnes.

As Noor grew older, she played games and climbed trees in a large field across the street from Fazal Manzil, often picking apricots that her mother used for jam or playing dress-up—with a white sari and a long scarf that reached her waist, and her neatly braided hair draped over one shoulder, pretending, however briefly, that she was in the India that she had heard about from her father.

On the first floor of the house was a room where Inayat met privately with students and a dining room whose long table was rarely underused: a lot of people lived (or visited) here. A wide staircase led to the upper floors. Though Engling had given the house as a present to the Khans, Inayat invited her to move in. In India, this was how you treated a respected relative. He also hoped she would provide company for Ora, who was increasingly isolated from her husband, who was often traveling to teach Sufism. Ora was also isolated from Inayat's brothers, who lived on the third floor.

Half of the second floor of Fazal Manzil was devoted to Engling's bedroom, so large it was almost a salon. The other half was divided into a large bedroom for Ora and Inayat and two smaller bedrooms for their children, the boys in one room, the girls in the other. Engling provided allowances to Inayat's family, paid for the upkeep of the house, and ruled Fazal Manzil with a starchiness at odds with Ora's American informality.

As if that wasn't enough for Ora, Inayat's brothers were freezing her out of life at Fazal Manzil. They hadn't liked her since she set her sights on Inayat in New York. Their dislike hardened in Moscow when one of Inayat's brothers, Musharaff, fell in love with the daughter of the Tatar nurse who cared

Noor's family's home opposite Paris. A "house of blessings," sometimes.

for Noor. Ora opposed the marriage. Married to Inayat for barely a year, she was the only non-Indian in his entourage. She didn't want another relative who wasn't a Westerner. Ora vetoed the marriage, and Inayat sided with her.

Until then, Inayat's brothers had been willing to tolerate Ora. Now she had ruined Musharraf's chances for happiness, and the brothers had little doubt Inayat had made a terrible mistake by marrying her. She could never be one of them. As far as the brothers were concerned, Ora cared about one person: herself.

In this unsettled house, Noor always wrote a birthday poem to Ora. When her brothers and sister were young, she signed the poems with their names and hers. When Ora was taken to a friend's house in Paris to recover from an illness, Noor sent her a drawing she had made of herself and her siblings. And when Ora needed a boost, Noor wrote her another poem:

> *Even if the whole world,*
> *Would serve us and help us e'er,*
> *Still it would not equal*
> *Your tender motherly care.*

The level of Noor's devotion to her mother was what was expected if Inayat Khan was your father. He provided a detailed roster of dos and don'ts for his children: Never interrupt a conversation. Never contradict your elders. Never desire something if that would deprive others of that same thing. Never frown or be blunt or angry. Never interrupt others' enjoyment by asking to join them. And never, in the presence of others, ask your parents for something they could not give you. Doing that only made someone who overheard your request feel they were obliged to give it to you. Inayat also dispensed a few "always": Always deprive yourself of something instead of asking someone to do a favor for you that would satisfy your desires. Always tell the truth. And always be more devoted to your mother than even to your own prayers.

Constantly, Noor's "first and most sacred duty" was to Ora. God, Inayat said, did not hear prayers from children who ignored their mother or didn't give her the attention she deserved. "Heaven," Inayat taught, "lies at thy mother's feet." Noor should never forget to express her gratitude for Ora's "selfless love and devotion and constant sacrifice." Noor was obliged to do this even if that meant not joining in games or amusements that gave Ora "the least displeasure." In Inayat's catechism of proper behavior, not much was left to chance: everything Noor did was another element in her devotion to her mother, the one human being she should never forget, the one from whom all blessings flowed.

During most of the year, Noor waited for Inayat to return from his latest trip. Usually it was a long wait. In 1923, Inayat was in the United States for five months. He spent most of that time—six weeks—in San Francisco. The next year was less demanding—about fifteen days in Holland, and most of October and November in Sweden, Germany, Norway, and Denmark. The pace picked up after that, with extensive stays in Switzerland, Italy, and Germany during the first third of 1925, followed by a six-month tour, December 1925 through May 1926, of Denmark, Norway, and the United States—lecturing, teaching, meeting scientists (Luther Burbank) and moguls (Henry Ford), embracing America as if it were the New Jerusalem, "nursed," he said, "with the milk of . . . ideal brotherhood from its infancy" and noting that other countries watched the United States "with anxious eyes . . . , eager to take up whatever progressive movements America may start." In this most spiritually awakened of all nations—"America sets the example for the world"—even its women "respond more quickly to spiritual principles than others I know."

Every June through August, Inayat stayed home, devoting himself to the Sufi "summer school" that was held at Fazal Manzil. With the endless stream of visitors, he was less of a father and husband than he was *everyone's* father—to his children and to the Sufis who overran the house and the field across the street where they held meetings and classes. On most days, Noor managed to be with her father during his private audiences with devotees, serving tea silently and unobtrusively.

Every morning when he was home, Inayat gave each of his children a theme for their day—virtues like patience, tolerance, forgiveness, kindness, humility. That evening, to prove they had done their "homework," the children told Inayat what they had done to advance the topic they had been assigned. If any of the children had misbehaved, *they* had to decide on their own punishment—a way to instill responsibility about their own conduct. If Inayat suspected a child had been up to trouble, but lacked proof, he asked if they had been naughty, hoping their conscience would loosen their tongues. When Inayat asked Noor about her behavior one day, she answered, "I wanted to be bad, but my goodness prevented me."

The children were both proud and ambivalent about being insulated from the rest of the world. "We were brought up in such a way," Vilayat later said, "that we could not be like other children. The whole atmosphere was rarefied. . . . It was as though we looked at life through stained glass windows." When Inayat was home, he began his mornings with breath exercises, a small breakfast, vocal exercises while accompanying himself on the piano, and two hours of private meetings with students. He lectured in the afternoons, gave initiations, and dictated teachings and sayings for books. His evenings were devoted to lectures or private meetings with advanced students. At the end of the day, his family sat around him cross-legged on the floor of the Oriental Room in Fazal Manzil, meditating and reciting prayers and the names of God.

This was not how most children were raised in Suresnes. Inayat knew

Always dutiful, Noor never strayed.

that, and he wanted them to feel connected to the rest of the world. Out there, he told his children, was a world where people suffered, fought, starved, and killed. To help them appreciate their duty toward others, Inayat relied on their ancestor, Tipu Sultan, the eighteenth-century ruler who had fought several wars to keep the English out of India. "You are royal," Inayat reminded his children. "Nothing in the world can take that away. Do not be afraid to hold up your heads in any court in the world." Between their royal heritage and their Sufi legacy, the children were obligated to be compassionate, to lift up others spiritually, to help anyone who was in pain or doubt. Inayat didn't give his children much leeway about this. "Keep burning the fire I have lit . . . ," he encouraged. "The fuel needed is your every thought, your faith, your prayers, and your sacrifices." Noor never forgot about her faith or her prayers. She also never forgot about sacrifice. This would be the prevailing motif in her life, the fulcrum that supported everything else, and without which her life was vacant and purposeless.

Wherever he went, Inayat wrote to his family. But he wrote more to Noor than to the others, sometimes on letterhead from hotels where he stayed (the Waldorf Astoria in New York, the Copley Square in Boston), sometimes on postcards with photos of the local sights (canals in Venice, the Spanish Steps in Rome, the Japanese tea garden in Golden Gate Park in San Francisco). In almost every piece of correspondence, Inayat reminded Noor to help Ora "every night and every morning when you go to bed and when you get up" and to never be "a naughty girly." Once from New York, he suggested that Noor and her siblings could benefit from knowing about a five-year-old's table manners he had observed during a dinner where he had been a guest. She "sat with dignity" and said "good evening" when she entered the dining room, and she said "thank you" when food was placed on her plate, and she said "excuse me" when she left the room. "I wish," he told Noor, "our little ones would know this." (Inayat was fairly strict during meals at Fazal Manzil. If a child spoke without an adult first speaking to him, Inayat immediately asked, "What are the rules of the table?" The garrulous child would then be silent until he or she was invited to enter the conversation.)

From the road, Inayat encouraged Noor to develop her interest in writing poems. Most of the poems she sent him were about fairies—Noor had a vivid, personal relationship with these small creatures. She knew what to do if you met one:

> . . . *behave in courteous fashion, show respect—*
> *lest their great powers find some defect . . .*
> *. . . should a radiance in your sight appear,*
> *Be sure that some Good Fairy must be near.*

And if they appeared out of nowhere:

> *Fairies of an enchanting sphere,*
> *Whisper your secret in my ear.*

And if they came at night:

> *Take me gently by the arm,*
> *When I'm in dreamland . . .*
> *Take me to your land of charm.*

Inayat took Noor's fascination with fairies seriously. He believed that whatever we imagine exists in the physical plane or in our minds. This was especially true for children, whose imaginations were wild and fertile. What a child believes, "it believes seriously," he said. Therefore, it is "a real belief. If that belief is destroyed, it is a great pity and a great loss." At the same time, the imagination could be dangerous. If, for example, a child decides Santa is a myth, he won't trust anyone who tells him Santa is real. On the other hand, Inayat said, telling the child that Santa isn't real could destroy a child's faith in his own imagination. Inayat preferred a middle path—saying Santa lives in a world that is distinct and parallel to ours, not quite with us and not quite apart. Eventually, Inayat was certain, all children learn the truth about Santa for themselves.

· · ·

Inayat was away more than ever, crisscrossing the United States and Europe for months on end to further Sufism. He was also away to find relief from Fazal Manzil, where there were too many disputes and not enough peace. His brothers were impatient with Ora, whom they found distant and stubborn and determined to raise her children as Westerners as well as Sufis. And some of Inayat's students, especially those who were financing his Sufi organization, wanted Inayat to be more than a teacher. They wanted a messiah, and that wasn't his way.

No matter where he was and sometimes every day, Inayat continued to write to his family and, especially to Noor. But letters and promises to take her out in his new "motor car" when he returned home did not satisfy her. "Peace," Noor wrote in a notebook, "is harmony. . . . Peace is beauty. . . . Disharmony is illness. Disharmony is the curse of life. Harmony leads to perfection. Harmony unites love and beauty. Harmony attracts all human beings." Noor wanted harmony. She wanted her father.

Under one roof in Suresnes, then, were three cultures (Dutch, Indian, and American); two elders (Inayat and Mrs. Engling); several purists (Inayat's brothers) who were not happy with Western modernity and who intensely disliked their sister-in-law; one frustrated mother (Ora) who was adrift from the country of her birth, disowned by her brother, and increasingly reliant on her husband (who was rarely around) and on her four children (who were just getting their bearings in life). While the arrangement may have been the only way Inayat was assured that his "little ones are sheltered from heat and cold under a roof," the shelter came with a price.

Noor found some relief from the tensions at Fazal Manzil by visiting her best friend, Raymonde Prenat, who lived around the corner on rue de l'Hippodrome. The two girls were six weeks apart in age, in the same classes at school, and always made birthday cakes for each other, bringing them to the other's home with candles and good cheer. Noor also brought a homemade card with an original poem, like the one she wrote on Raymonde's twelfth birthday which celebrated their "dear past" and anticipated their "joyous future." Noor's poems never failed her.

At school, a seven-minute walk from her home, Noor's grades were good and, being shy and reserved, she was neither disliked nor exceptionally popular though she was apparently respected: one year, she received the Good Comrade prize. Noor stood out in other ways, like her faith, and her family, and her accent—a blend of British, French, Indian, and American inflections. Noor was an anomaly in a Suresnes that was almost entirely made up of French-born Catholics, farmers, factory workers, and vintners. This wasn't a town of mystics and spiritual seekers (except when Inayat's students descended on the town for his summer school: most stayed at a large building around the corner from Fazal Manzil that had been purchased as their dormitory). Yet, one Christmas, Noor was as French as her friends. At midnight on Christmas Eve in 1925, Noor and her brothers and sister tiptoed down the stairs in Fazal Manzil to the Oriental Room, the most special room in the mansion. Their parents—Ora in a light-blue sari, Inayat in an apricot-colored kurta—were waiting for them, standing proudly in front of a Christmas tree, the first at Fazal Manzil. The decorations dangling on the tree—fairies, deer, bells, angels—reflected the light coming from the tiny candles that were lit throughout the room. The children marveled at the tree and the candles and the decorations before returning to bed, their way guided by the kerosene lights that were brightening the stairwell and not really caring that, ordinarily, Sufis didn't have Christmas trees. The "incandescent glittering treasure," as Claire, Noor's sister, called it, had enthralled them, and that was all that mattered.

In the summer of 1926, Inayat announced that he was returning to India for a sabbatical. His declining health (he had suffered from pulmonary difficulties for several years), worsening relations between his brothers and Ora, and his annual swings through the United States and Europe had worn him down. He was also exasperated by followers who were determined to anoint him a Messenger of God or were pressuring him to make his organization less Islamic; Inayat had never hidden that he, and Sufism, had their roots in Islam. "My ancestors were Muslims," he said many times. For him, as for all Muslims, there was *one* Messenger—the Prophet Muhammad. To share that title was blasphemy. While Inayat had threaded Muslim terms and concepts throughout his writing and talks since his early days in the West, he had also reiterated many times that his spiritual home was everywhere: "I have no religion. All places of worship are one to me. I can enter a Buddhist temple, a mosque, a church or a synagogue in the same spirit. Spirituality is the tuning of the heart." In Inayat's heart, he was a Muslim—a *mystical* Muslim. To make inroads in the West, he had significantly softened Sufism's connection to Islam. But he could stretch his faith only so much.

Returning to India was overdue. "I'm often homesick," Inayat told friends. He missed India's traditions and rituals, its colors and its smells, and had never been completely comfortable in the West with all its rushing about and its hustle and bustle: "I would have been most happy sitting with my vina in my hand in some corner in the forest, in solitude. . . . But for my music, the soil of India was necessary."

Inayat planned his departure carefully. A few days before leaving, he initiated Vilayat, who was only ten, as his successor. Inayat's brother, Maheboob, would direct the Sufi order until Vilayat was old enough to lead it, or until Inayat came home. Inayat also laid down the rules for Sufi chivalry, a modern version of the gallantry Sufis had originated in the eighth century, a mode of living that required generosity, courage, ethics, and steadfastly ignoring the faults of others. Sufi chivalry championed a goodness and decency that never wavered, even when least expected. During the Battle of Khandaq near Medina in the seventh century, a son-in-law of the Prophet Muhammad was about to kill an enemy soldier when his foe spat in his face. Instantly, Ali ibn Abi Talib dropped his sword.

"What is wrong with you?" asked the soldier. "Why do you not strike?"

"Before you spat at me," Ali explained, "I was fighting for Allah. After you spat, I was fighting because I was angry, and a Muslim can only fight for Allah, never for his own ego."

And when King Richard I was sick during the Crusades in the twelfth century, he sent a message to Saladin, the general leading the Muslim armies that were fighting against him. Richard had heard that Muslim medicine was the best in the world and that Muslims were required to help anyone in need. Saladin sent his personal physician to tend to the king.

When Muslims conquered the Iberian Peninsula in the eighth century, their gifts to Europeans included mathematics and exquisite architecture.

Chivalry was another. Europeans turned chivalry into a formal caste, with kings bestowing titles ("sir") on knights and sending them on missions and pilgrimages. In the Muslim world, the reputation of a Sufi knight was the only title he needed. Knights in Arabia were known by their courage, their dignity, and their deeds, by who they were and what they had proven through their actions, not by a superfluous and often flowery title.

Each of Inayat's rules cultivated modesty, humility, empathy. A Sufi could not make false claims, speak against others in their absence, harm anyone for the Sufi's own benefit, or spare themselves in the work which they must accomplish. They did not boast of their good deeds nor challenge anyone who was not their equal. Nor could they influence anyone to do wrong or bear malice against their worst enemy. This was a chivalry of inner strength, of inner consistency. Weak Sufis vacillated, not sure of themselves or their purpose. Strong Sufis—as unchanging as the God to whom they had hitched their lives—maintained their faith and their word of honor, and they kept their "ideals high in all circumstance." For Inayat, duty was "as sacred as religion." This was a knighthood of conscience, spirit, and truth.

Noor was twelve years old when Inayat laid down his rules. They would guide her long after he left for India. A few years after he departed, she ruminated, much as her father had, on our duties and our obligations and how, while all of us "cause our own troubles," we should never judge anyone. Our messes and our predicaments are indispensable and invaluable lessons, *if* we know what to do with them. That qualifier goes for everyone. From the outside, we have no idea of the dynamics of someone else's life. What looks easy to us could be hard for someone else, almost a punishment. But its difficulty could be a way to better oneself by rising to the challenges of life. It all depends on the attitude we bring to every situation, on the price we are willing to pay to gain a lesson and better ourselves. In life, Noor wrote, "There is always a price to pay. The price is what we give in order to receive life."

In September 1926, Inayat sailed to India. He planned to return home in a few months. Before leaving, Inayat told his brother Piromia that if he returned he would change his way of spreading his message—spending less time traveling, more time writing books, and considerably more time at home with his family. In New Delhi, Inayat rented a house on the banks of the Jumna River. "He does not want to see anyone," a local paper reported. "He lives in seclusion." That was precisely why Inayat had come. "Solitude," he said, "away from the world is the longing of my soul."

There had been no solitude, no inner life on Inayat's tours through Europe and the United States and none in Suresnes, surrounded by four children, three brothers, one wife, a wealthy dowager, and students who clamored for his attention and advice. A holy man, Inayat had little time to be holy. But as soon as word got around Delhi that Inayat was back, he was swamped with requests to deliver lectures—sixteen years abroad hadn't diminished his fame. Giving in, Inayat spoke at several universities, attracting students who had heard about him from their parents, and scholars who had read about him, and ordinary Indians who had sat at his feet during concerts he had given a long time ago.

Quite possibly some of these people were disappointed. Inayat hadn't given a concert in years. "To serve God," he had concluded in the early 1920s, "one must sacrifice the dearest thing, and I had sacrificed my music, the dearest thing to me." While away from India, every soul had become "a musical note" to him. Now perceiving "all life" as music, he said that "if I do anything, it is to tune souls, to harmonize people instead of notes." Love and words were the only instruments he needed—"my heart," he said, "turned into my vina"—and there was no difference between his words and his music since music was *everything:* "architecture is music, gardening is music, farming is music, painting is music, poetry is music. In all the occupations of life where beauty has been the inspiration, there is music." Through music, Inayat declared, "the world was created."

These were different "concerts" than those Inayat had given before leaving India though to him they were as harmonious as when he had played his vina. All went well until Inayat contracted pneumonia. He died three weeks later. The last Noor heard from her father was a telegram he sent on her birthday, January 1, 1927: "Abba's love. 13 years old."

The Khan children were almost orphans in their own home. Their uncles (whom they sometimes feared) became their de facto fathers, and their mother became more of a recluse, protecting her privacy and herself and not sure if she had any allies at Fazal Manzil. Inayat's students gossiped that she had had a nervous breakdown. Little understanding for Ora came from her brothers-in-law, who sometimes treated her like a tenant in the house that was in her name and that of her children, often ordering her about like a servant: in the winter, they instructed her to carry heavy buckets of coal several flights from the basement. And behind her back, the brothers said to each other, "*Hazratki zindagi kotah kaddi*" ("Ora shortened Hazrat's life"). Meanwhile, the brothers were trying to position themselves as the stewards of Inayat's teachings and the only relatives who truly understood Inayat's mission in the West.

As Noor slowly took Ora's place, Vilayat, Hidayat, and Claire began to call her "Little Mother." Noor made sure the house was tidy, and that everyone did their chores, and that all the children were ready for school on time, and she sometimes woke Claire by singing a song from the opera *Faust*:

> *Lazy girl, who slumbers still!*
> *Already the day shines,*
> *. . . All of nature awakens to love*

When Noor's siblings climbed the steep hill near their house to play in Mont Valérien—the sprawling fort named after the prominent hill that overlooked Suresnes—Noor kept Ora company. When Ora refused to eat, Noor said she and the other children wouldn't either. And when Ora's spirits were down because some of her children had misbehaved, Noor wrote a poem of apology:

> *Forgive us, dear Amma,*
> *For often we lose our way,*
> *How oft' in this vast world,*
> *You kept us from going astray.*

And on Ora's first birthday after Inayat died, Noor, as always, wrote a poem, wishing that "little rays of dreams come true" and "sunny skies [would be] forever blue.

In July, Ora celebrated Noor's graduation from eighth grade with a poem of her own. Only six months after Inayat's death, the poem was as much about Noor's father as it was about Noor. Noor was "Father's pride"—"gentle," "graceful," "fair of face" and Inayat's "worthiest daughter by Allah's grace." Her virtues were similar to her father's—"deep in thoughts and wise in speech." And when Noor won first prize in music in school, Ora wrote that Inayat had "sent it from above" to Noor "with his deepest love." Half a year after his death, Inayat was still the center of life at Fazal Manzil.

Noor was entering a new stage—her life was harsh, her mother was frail, her father was gone, and her poems were more searching, less about fairies and Santa Claus and more about the frustrating riddles of life. She asked in one that the "mystery of the night . . . breathe out to me . . . your mystical secret."

A year or two after Inayat's death, Noor wrote "Song to the Madzub"— one of her more sophisticated, endearing compositions. The words and music encapsulated Noor's aching to be with her father—the "madzub," or enlightened master, of the title. Tired and lonely, Noor has "come to seek rest," sure that her broken heart will heal in the presence of the madzub and that her "yearning soul" will be purified in the "fire" and "rays" of his glance. Neither a dirge nor a celebration, "Song to the Madzub" was a stately, measured contemplation on loss and parting, emptiness and farewell—a slow, meditative declaration that the love, and the presence, of Noor's father remained.

As a cousin of Noor's later said, "What must have been a happy household at one time become [sic] unstuck." For now, all that Noor could conclude was that the world had become too difficult for her father: surrounded by his family and students, interviewed by journalists wherever he went, and deemed by many of his followers to have all the answers to life's difficult questions, he needed to "leave this world for the world of dreams. The great teachers of the world," Noor wrote, "all come to a certain stage when they must leave." Noor couldn't follow Inayat, not at the age of thirteen and not when her family needed her so much. So she remained behind, dreaming of her father's path and trying to sort out her own at an age when most girls fantasize not about leaving the world but about having fun and doing well in school, then college, then creating a life for themselves. In Noor's time, the future of most girls was ordained and circumscribed. Noor wanted to shape hers even as she was devoted to her faith and her family and the memory of her father. She would leave when the dreams called to her.

CHAPTER 3

"THIS IS NOT GOOD FOR YOUR HEALTH"

I n 1928, Noor and her family and uncles set out on a pilgrimage to Inayat's tomb in Delhi. This was nineteen months after his death. Sufis in the Chisti order—the order to which Inayat belonged—believed if you visit the shrine of a saint, the prayers you recite there will come true. Certainly, the Khans had come to pray, but the trip would be their chance to come as close as they could to saying goodbye to Inayat. The brothers also wanted Inayat's children to know more about India. So they visited the Ganges, and the tombs of other saints, and the house in Baroda where Inayat had grown up. Not coincidental to the trip was that the brothers wanted to fulfill Inayat's wish that Noor marry a cousin she had never met: Alladad Khan.

Alladad and Noor became fond of each other and Alladad's father proposed that all the Khan children come with him to Nepal, where he was part of the royal court. The Khan children could study at an English-language school in Kathmandu. Noor's brothers and sister would eventually return to Europe, and Noor would remain and marry Alladad. Inayat's brothers liked the offer: someday, Alladad would inherit the bulk of the wealth of the Khan family. If Noor married him, everything that became his would remain in their side of the family and wouldn't have to be shared with a wife from outside their clan. Ora refused to separate her family. By the time they returned to Suresnes, the rift between Ora and Inayat's brothers, already severe, had widened irrevocably.

Back in Suresnes, Noor, as always, put Ora's happiness before her own.

Her father, idealizing Ora's devotion to their children, had instructed them to show Ora their "gratitude in the smallest little way." In one poem after another, Noor, now a teenager, pledged her unwavering devotion to this woman Inayat Khan had left behind:

Although life gives us each our way,
And we grow older every day,
We will remain forevermore,
Your little children as before.

But Noor wasn't a child now. In 1931, she graduated from high school and enrolled at the Sorbonne, majoring in child psychology—a natural extension of her interest in children, and of her faith in them. For Noor, children possessed a wisdom that even their parents didn't appreciate. "It is wrong," Noor wrote, "to think of the little ones as mere children knowing nothing. . . . [Their] true knowledge and understanding . . . are hidden from our sight." If parents were less wrapped up in their careers and their livelihoods, in trying to get through every day and make an impression on the world and on themselves, maybe, said Noor, they could learn from their children about how to be more open, and more attentive, to everything going on around them.

When she wasn't studying, Noor taught. In the fall and winter of 1935, she taught Sufism at Fazal Manzil to the children of her father's former students. The classes met on Thursdays, and Noor took them quite seriously—they were her way to say to the children, "I would like you to know what my father taught me and what he taught your parents. This is important to me. It is important to them. Here it is." While one seven-year-old came primarily for the bonbons that Noor gave everyone as they left, Noor gave her students more than candy. Each week, she handed them lessons to study between classes. One assignment was to memorize "Moïse" by the poet Alfred de Vigny. Vigny's Moses wasn't the imperious, proud, triumphant Moses of the Bible. He was tired from wandering through the desert, from leading hundreds of thousands of Jews from slavery in Egypt while having no one he could confide in. Speaking to God, Moses asks,

. . . will it never end?
Where yet do you want that I trudge?
Shall I live ever in power and solitude?
Let me finally sleep the sleep of the earth.

Moses wasn't asking for heaven or for paradise. He wanted to sleep—to die—without being bothered by the responsibilities which had drained him for forty years. This was a very human Moses, one who complained that, even after doing everything God had asked of him, he was "sad and alone in this glory." Vigny's Moses was like Noor's father.

And on notes handwritten by Noor, she gave students a distillation of what her father had taught about being considerate and respectful toward others:

Share only your happiness with others. Never tell them about your poverty:
*   only God should know about that.*
Never contradict the elderly even if they are wrong.
Be polite in all circumstances.
Trust in God no matter how difficult your life may be.
Forget all the good you have done, but remember all your bad deeds.

For Christmas in 1935, Noor gave books to all her students—happy books, books with morals, books about history and justice and morals. One eight-year-old received *Uncle Tom's Cabin*—in French, *La Case de l'Oncle Tom.* Everyone received bonbons.

In addition to teaching these classes and attending the Sorbonne, Noor was taking music lessons at the Ecole Normal de Musique, the best music academy in Paris. Founded in 1919, the school had recently moved to a Belle Epoque mansion on Boulevard Malesherbes, a gift from a marquise who was devoted to the arts. Noor's classes at the école were probably demanding at more than a musicological level. Her primary teacher there was Nadia Boulanger. The legendary music teacher of the twentieth century, Boulanger's students would include Leonard Bernstein, Aaron Copland, Quincy Jones, and Philip Glass—notables all. But Boulanger's little secret, the one hardly anyone talked about, was that she was a staunch nationalist, monarchist, and closet anti-Semite. She also disliked democracy and women's suffrage. Boulanger was as much an autocrat in the classroom as she was in her politics.

Noor augmented her classes with Boulanger with private lessons from Henriette Renié, a former child prodigy who had elevated the harp from being hidden in large orchestras to an exceptional instrument for recitals and solos. Renié coaxed a disciplined dedication to craft from a roster of students that included Harpo Marx, who came all the way from Hollywood to study with her one summer. Renié insisted that Noor exercise the same discipline that she demanded from other students. Apparently, Noor rose to the occasion: in the late 1940s, Renié said that Noor was "a very gentle girl . . . [who] studied so hard that I thought she must have an inner fire which her quiet manner hid." Possibly Renié had helped ignite that fire—she sensed that Noor's spiritual bent was similar to her own. "It is necessary," Renié believed, "to be very advanced in supernatural and mystical ways to find God in each moment of life, to serve Him and please Him with 'holy practice.' . . . Just as we do not see the air that fills our lungs with breath, the Divine being circulates in us, made more active and more perfect through each one of our acts."

At home, Noor had her own harp—an Erard model no. 4649 with a raised, sculpted grapevine curling around its five-and-a-half-foot-tall column. Several saints were carved around the crown. Two dogs were carved around the base. Their "job" was to "protect" the harp. One of the more expensive harps in Europe, an Erard's thin, tapered soundboard created a loud, bright sound that projected exceptionally well in concert halls. The music Noor played on it had a layering of arpeggios and glissandos in different harmonies, with themes of nature that imitated the sounds of wind and water. With Vilayat (on the cello), Hidayat (on the violin), and Claire (on the piano), Noor often performed pieces Mozart had written specifically for such ensembles. Though the concerts helped ease some of the tensions at Fazal Manzil, the siblings never fulfilled Ora's wish that they succeed the Royal Musicians of Hindustan, the quartet in which Inayat had performed when he first came to the West. As musicians, Noor and her siblings were good. By contrast, their father was formidable.

At the Ecole Normal de Musique, Noor met Elie Goldenberg, a pianist

Noor cherished her Erard harp, an instrument prized
by professionals.

On her vina—a rarity in Europe—Noor played
Indian melodies her father had made famous.

who everyone agreed was a better musician than she was. Elie's openness, attentiveness, and musical abilities impressed Noor; her kindness and beauty impressed him. Tall, with black hair combed almost straight back and a lean face and fine posture, Goldenberg had moved from Romania to attend the music school. His mother, who had moved with him, worked in a laundry to help pay his expenses. Though the Goldenbergs had a hard time scraping by, Elie was a dapper dresser, often sporting a white handkerchief in the breast pocket of his suit jacket and making sure the cuffs of his shirts extended the proper distance beyond the end of his jacket sleeve. Elie and Noor made a handsome couple: both were slim and dark-complexioned and carried themselves with a formal, slightly removed air—elegant, stylish, and graceful.

Soon, they were dating steadily and Elie moved from Paris to an apartment at 11 bis Rue Diderot in Suresnes, a short block from the Seine. Only a twenty-minute walk away from Fazal Manzil, he could see Noor more frequently now, often climbing the steep hill to her home to visit her—and to try to mollify her family, which was not happy about him. He was Jewish; Noor was Sufi. He was poor; she had access to resources considerably greater than his, especially through her father's more affluent students who treated her (and Inayat's other children) almost like their own. Worse, Elie was lower-class; Noor was a princess.

To prove his sincerity, Elie became a Sufi and changed his name to Azeem. Yet his influence on Noor, and the influence of Paris, where she went almost every day for her studies, continued to unsettle her family, especially her uncles, who wanted her to be proper, restrained, and modest. Noor started wearing what by Indian standards was high fashion, sometimes a lengthy black coat with a fur collar or dresses with floral prints and hats tilted rakishly to one side of her head. Just as upsetting, she began wearing makeup. Paris was the world's center for cosmetics and perfume: a chemist had recently invented a lipstick that didn't leave a mark after a kiss, and perfume was being mass-marketed for the first time. France had long been Europe's pioneer in haute couture and womanly beauty. This was difficult for Noor to resist as she tried to strike a balance between being French and living with her rather conventional, often hardheaded uncles.

Inayat's brothers were especially furious about an incident outside a café in the ninth arrondissement of Paris, where the uncles saw Noor and Azeem

Noor in her twenties: her new sophistication rankled her uncles.

strolling by with Noor's siblings. Wearing light makeup and a fashionable dress, Noor was absorbed in conversation with Azeem. Vilayat and Hidayat spotted their uncles. The uncles brushed them off. They were too angry with their free-spirited nephews and nieces to speak.

In the mid-1930s, Noor and Azeem began talking about becoming engaged. In their minds, they were *almost* fiancés. But first, they needed the approval of their elders. Noor's uncles saw Azeem as a stray Noor had taken in: he was taking advantage of Noor's innate kindness, her desire to help others. Their marriage would be a *mésalliance,* a mismatch that violated the accepted social order. Even Ora opposed the marriage. Two decades after she had married Inayat over her brother's objections, she seemed to be as rigid about matters of class and status as Pierre Bernard, her bogus yogi of a brother.

With Noor often crying herself to sleep and her poetry taking a melancholy turn—"Who has heard my painful cry / Who has heard my sigh"— Vilayat began taking her on vacations every summer, hoping that these would cheer her up. In 1935, they traveled to Spain to see Vilayat's cello teacher, who arranged an audience for them with Pablo Casals at the famous musician's beachfront villa south of Barcelona. Using his celebrity as leverage for his principles, Casals had recently announced that he would not perform in Germany until the Nazi rule ended. "I detest living in a time when the law of man is killing," he explained. For Casals, an artist "is under an obligation to take sides, whatever it means, if human dignity becomes involved."

Casals would have enjoyed the company of Noor's father had Inayat still been alive. Both believed in what Casals called "the perfectibility of man"—perceiving, as Casals said, "the good in you and obeying it," and seeing the holy in the ordinary and the mundane: "In music, the sea, a flower, a leaf, an act of kindness. In all those things," Casals continued, "I see the presence of what people call God." Casals urged every individual to be faithful to our common destiny: "An affront to humanity is an affront to me. . . . The main thing in life is not to be afraid of being human." Yet, we act like barbarians, "fearing our neighbors, we arm against them, and they arm against us. . . . When shall we become accustomed to the fact that we are human beings?" Casals took "pleasure in the natural and quiet and simple things of life. Each second we live in a new and unique moment of the universe, a moment that never was before and will never be again."

For Noor, talking with Casals may have been like talking with her father.

The next year, Noor and Vilayat went to Milan. At a performance of *Rigoletto,* Mussolini walked in, someone in the audience yelled, "Il Duce," and the crowd went wild. "In a second," Noor wrote, everyone in the theater "was in a fever" and the musicians almost dropped their instruments. Finally, "a profound sigh of joy rose from the whole crowd" and the opera resumed, with Mussolini "a simple spectator amongst the crowd." Noor didn't comment on Il Duce's fascism, or about Italy's invasion of Ethiopia, then in its second year, or about Mussolini's alliance with Hitler. Italy and Germany, Mussolini had recently declared, had a "common destiny." Noor's silence about politics was not surprising. She didn't belittle politics. She simply paid little attention to it. For her, the life of the spirit and the arts was the only life worth living.

In 1937, Noor and Vilayat went on the last of their summer adventures, renting a chalet in the Swiss village of Champéry for three months. On long hikes on mountain trails or drives in Vilayat's MG, they explored the countryside and thrilled at the mountain ridges, a rolling succession of peaks that were often lost in clouds or fog or whose cliffs spilled straight down toward valleys of the richest, densest emerald green. Their one disappointment was that the bicycles they had brought with them were useless in the Alps.

Though Vilayat was younger than Noor, he tried to give her a more informed view of the world. He kept up with the news; she barely did. He explained jokes to her; Noor had trouble understanding humor and jests. And on all their trips, Vilayat tried to persuade Noor to break up with Azeem. "This is not good for your health," he told her. Ignoring Vilayat, Noor wrote to Azeem several times a week, sighing "I kiss you with all my heart," and confessing that while she was in Barcelona she had heard his voice "in my heart" while reading all the letters he'd sent her, and relieved as her trip was ending that she would soon hear his "voice in reality and I will be so near to you. . . . See you soon, my beloved. I cannot contain my tears of joy."

Noor and her fiancé, Azeem. For both, a lengthy engagement. For Azeem, a name change and a faith change (Judaism to Sufism).

Every year, Noor and Vilayat returned to Suresnes, and every year Noor returned to Azeem. As the decade proceeded, Noor became more passionate, more certain of her love for him—"My dear Azeem, I hope this delivers to you all my affection, joy, commitment and happiness." In one poem, her most assertive declaration of her love, a male asks his beloved to lay her head on his heart as their destinies unite. Together,

We will see the years pass . . .
You will be, to me, the companion of my life.

Noor was so devoted to Azeem that when she performed in a recital organized by her harp teacher, Henriette Renié, she was the only student who played a piece by a barely known composer. Other students performed compositions that had become recital standards. Three played pieces by a composer who was present at the recital—Mlle. Renié herself. Noor played a piece entitled "Romance." The program listed its composer as E. Goldenberg. Sufis knew him as Azeem.

CHAPTER 4

THE ROAD IS WEEPING

As Noor and Azeem were sorting out their lives, and as her family was trying to keep the two of them apart, the world was haunted by war, and sorrow, and tumult. There was an unrelenting sadness to the 1930s: the worst depression in history; conflict in Spain, Ethiopia, Manchuria, Brazil, Albania, Tibet, the Philippines; show trials in Moscow; concentration camps in Germany. Saner voices were trying to convince death to keep its distance. They were not successful.

After meeting with Hitler at Munich in September 1938, Neville Chamberlain famously vowed there would be "peace for our time." Less is heard about France's premier, Edouard Daladier, who was also at that meeting with Hitler. In the official photo of the conference, Chamberlain looks starchily resolute. Hitler appears cocky and smug, maybe because he was silently rehearsing what he'd soon be telling his friends: "Our enemies are worms. I saw them at Munich." Mussolini looks insecure, his black eyes darting to his right as if he's searching for the nearest exit. All the while, Daladier—the shortest man in the foursome—looks tired and unhappy. He had every reason to be that way: letting Hitler annex Czechoslovakia didn't guarantee peace. It only postponed war. Returning home, Daladier was afraid that the large crowd waiting for him on the tarmac near Paris would jeer him. Astonished by the warm reception, Daladier announced he had come home with "the profound conviction" that Munich was "indispensable to the peace of Europe." On the drive into Paris, he leveled with an aide: "The imbeciles—if only they knew what they were acclaiming." France's parliament ratified the agreement (574 for, 75 against), *Paris-Soir* applauded "Peace! Peace! Peace!," *Le Matin* thundered "Victory! Victory! Victory!" and some very foolish people thought Munich had ended their problems with Hitler.

By the next summer, Hitler was eyeing Poland. For the annual Bastille Day in Paris, fleets of mobile "bomb shelters" (armored trucks sealed against gas, with room for fifty people) clattered down the Champs-Elysées and thousands of French and British troops marched smartly, saluting Daladier, the hero of Munich. "We menace no one," Daladier proclaimed soothingly from the podium. "We dream of no conquest. We desire only peace and . . . that spirit of human collaboration which alone can save civilization."

Six weeks later—the day after Germany and the Soviet Union signed their nonaggression pact—350,000 French reservists were called up, 31,000 children were evacuated from Paris, the Ritz Hotel put the finishing touches on a new air-raid shelter with fur rugs and Hermés chairs, and the *Mona Lisa* was wrapped in velvet, packed in a crate, and trucked to a château in the countryside for safekeeping. Daladier's "spirit of human collabora-tion" was over and people were looking for solace where they could find it. Astrologers, tea-leaf readers, and Tarot card prognosticators confidently predicted that Poland would crush Germany, Italy's king would dismiss Mussolini, Hitler would be locked up in an asylum, and French interven-tion would end the civil war in Germany that would follow the Fuehrer's downfall. From his synagogue, the chief rabbi of France promised that rea-son would prevail, and the world would emerge from the crisis more sane and more united. And Cardinal Jean Verdier—a fierce opponent of fascism who would soon declare that "no other war has had aims that are more spiritual, moral and, in sum, more Christian"—asked the twenty thousand parishioners crammed into the Sacré-Coeur basilica in Montmartre to be confident, stay hopeful, and not let their faith flag. The large mosaic under which the cardinal was speaking bore this inscription: "To the Sacred Heart of Jesus, France, fervent, penitent and grateful." "Grateful" had been added after France defeated Germany in 1918. With the Germans about to attack again, no one was sure whether gratitude or penitence would be the appro-priate next step.

. . .

On September 1, war was finally declared and half a million Parisians poured out of the city. Trains were free and nine hundred extra carriages were pressed into service. Cars clogged roads leading to the coast, the mountains, the south—any place where there weren't Germans. Blackouts were enforced, a new law extended the death penalty to anyone who robbed an apartment that was empty because its residents had left during an air raid, and waiters asked customers to pay as soon as their food was served. They were tired of being stiffed when customers ran off to bomb shelters.

For nine months, there was an eerie calm and many Parisians returned home. This wasn't really a war. It was too quiet, too still. The French called it *la drôle de guerre,* "a funny sort of war." The Germans dubbed it *Sitzkrieg,* the "sit-down war." The British anointed it the "phony war." The lull gave Noor time to get her life in order. She ended her romance with Azeem, writing to him that she was worn down by years of arguing with her family about him and, anyway, now that she'd earned her Red Cross certificate, she wanted to devote herself to the war, maybe as a nurse on the front. Noor was afraid that if she was still committed to Azeem, she might care more about returning to him than about giving the troops the attention they deserved.

In May 1940, war—the real war—broke out. Within weeks, the Maginot Line was easily overrun, 1.3 million French soldiers were running from the Nazis, half of Paris was joining them, and Noor and Vilayat withdrew to the Oriental Room in Fazal Manzil—the room their father had reserved for his most solemn moments. There they had the most serious discussion of their young lives. The Germans had already bombed Suresnes's railroad station and its airplane factories and an air-raid shelter. They had aimed at a factory, and hit a house. Two bombs fell on a cemetery, killing one man. Another bomb landed on a hotel, killing no one. The Germans strafed streets—Bartoux, Michelet, Keighley, Carnot, Verdun—less than half a mile from Noor's home. Three people were killed. By the middle of June, at least twenty-eight bombs had fallen on Suresnes, troops were abandoning the giant fort near the top of the hill where Noor's home was located, and the army was setting fire to a large fuel depot so it wouldn't fall into German hands. Plumes of black smoke filled the sky for days. Sixty-two soldiers had died in the local hospital, and local churches were holding Sunday mass as German planes circled over-head. Meanwhile, three million Parisians were joining more than six million refugees already on the roads from Belgium, Holland, and northern France. The migration was so immense—so biblical—that it earned the name *l'ex-ode.* Half of Europe, it seemed, was running, stumbling, falling, sprawling, tripping—anything to gain distance between them and the Germans. One Luftwaffe pilot called the scene below "desolate and dreadful." To the novel-ist Antoine de Saint-Exupéry, it was like an episode from a children's book: "Somewhere in northern France a boot had scattered an anthill, and the ants were on the march."

But this was no march. It was a rout, and Noor and Vilayat had to make an important decision. Until recently, Noor had played her vina and her harp in the Oriental Room. Her instruments were silent now as she and Vilayat discussed whether to stay in Suresnes or somehow get to England and fight the Nazis from there. Their mother, never strong since Inayat's death, stayed upstairs, and since in recent years Noor and Vilayat—especially Noor—had been making their family's more important decisions, the two of them retired to the Oriental Room by themselves to determine their next move. Noor and Vilayat had pledged themselves to their father's message of respecting, as Vilayat put it, "all religions, all races, the divinity of man. But now came the test: were these just words or were we going to stand up with our lives for what we pledged ourselves to?" Though he and Noor had heard about "the dis-mal cruelty and abject contempt of the most elementary dignity of the human person in [the Nazis'] concentration camps," Vilayat worried about the best way to proceed. "If you counter violence with violence," he asked Noor, "are you participating in the very violence you purport to oppose?"

Sufis weren't pacifists, but they had an aversion to violence that Noor didn't want to abandon. Hearing the blasts from the bombing that Suresnes had suffered, knowing of the killings that had already occurred, and sure there would be more, Noor thought of Gandhi. She admired the mahat-ma's passive resistance and his certainty that it could stir the decency he believed everyone possessed. But Gandhi's almost willful ignorance about conditions in Europe was troubling. In 1938, American Methodists meeting with Gandhi had pleaded that he denounce Hitler and Mussolini—two dictators, they told the mahatma, who lacked a conscience and were "impervious" to world opinion. Gandhi scolded his visitors: no one, not even Hitler or Mussolini, was beyond redemption.

Passive resistance worked—sometimes—against the British in India. But Gandhi couldn't admit that some profoundly distorted people courted Satan more than they feared God. So he told the people of Czechoslovakia to respond passively when Hitler annexed the Sudetenland, and he told the Jews of Europe to pray for Hitler and resist him with nonviolence, though that would not let them escape what even Gandhi called their "massacre." Their sacrifice would redeem them: "German Jews will score a lasting victory over the German gentiles . . . [and] convert the latter to an appreciation of human dignity." And during England's darkest days—France had fallen, the blitz had begun, and America was captive to isolationism—Gandhi would urge the British to lay down their arms and invite Hitler and Mussolini to "take your beautiful island with your many beautiful buildings. You will give all these, but neither your souls, nor your minds." If the Germans and Italians did not give the British free passage out of their isle, the English should let themselves—every man, woman and child—"be slaughtered" while retaining their honor: "you will refuse to give allegiance to them."

Gandhi's response to Hitler disappointed the British and the Jews and, surely, it disappointed Noor. The viceroy of India spurned Gandhi's offer to mediate between England and Germany: "We are engaged in a struggle. As long as we do not achieve our aim, we are not going to budge." From Jerusalem, the Jewish philosopher and mystic, Martin Buber, tried to explain to Gandhi that where there are no witnesses (because the Nazis had killed them), there are no martyrs; and with no martyrs, pacifism was an empty and useless gesture. Buber also sought to impress upon Gandhi the realities of Hitler's Europe: "Do you know, or do you not know, Mahatma, what a concentration camp is like, and what goes on there? Do you know of . . . its methods of slow and quick slaughter? . . . An effective stand in the form of non-violence may be taken against unfeeling human beings in the hope of gradually bringing them to their senses; but a diabolical universal steamroller cannot thus be withstood."

Muddling Gandhi's perception of Hitler was his unfamiliarity with any nation beyond India other than South Africa and England. Moreover, Nazism was so mindbogglingly inconceivable, especially from 7,000 miles away, that it beggared the imagination. As a sympathetic biographer of Gandhi wrote, the Indian didn't lack sympathy for the Jews. He "simply did not have, and could not have, any imaginative conception of their plight. In the quiet of the ashram, the even greater quiet of the gas chambers was inconceivable." Gandhi would go on to volunteer to mediate between the Allies and Hitler, who was "not a bad man."

Though Gandhi was not a reliable moral compass, Noor still had vague plans to go to India after the war and help gain the independence of her father's country. Fighting the British as a pacifist made sense. Fighting Hitler as a pacifist was suicide.

Meanwhile, Vilayat was growing impatient as he sat across from Noor in the Oriental Room. They were running out of time. The Germans had mounted machine guns on the bridge connecting Suresnes with Paris, the French government was shutting down, and many of Noor's and Vilayat's neighbors were packing up, not sure where to go.

"Right at our door," Vilayat argued, "people are calling for mercy. They are being tortured, treated like dogs. . . . If an armed Nazi comes to your house, and takes 20 hostages and wants to exterminate them, wouldn't you be an accomplice in those deaths if you had an opportunity to kill him and prevent these deaths, but didn't because of your belief in non-violence? Can we stand by and just watch what the Nazis are doing?" As "millions of Jews" were being exterminated, Vilayat asked Noor, "How can one preach spiritual morality without participating in some sort of preventive action? Spirituality in action—that was the real teaching of our father."

Noor agreed. They had to do something. Their father had taught that the world would be a better place "if revolvers or swords were never used." Yet he accepted that such weapons were the reality of this existence while hoping that "in the future man may evolve." Until it did, "we were obliged to defend ourselves, and defend our country if it treated every individual justly and with respect regardless of their belief or their station in life. At the same time, Inayat had cautioned, "Never think that this means standing up for war."

Noor didn't want to stand up for war. She was averse to violence. Yet she couldn't help thinking about the *Bhagavad Gita*. She and Vilayat were discussing war. The *Gita* was about war and about spirituality ("kill with the sword of wisdom the doubt born of ignorance") and about discipline ("the ruler of his soul . . . rests in the joy of quietness") and about love (see yourself "in the heart of all beings" and "all beings in your heart"). In the *Gita*, Arjuna, a soldier, tells Krishna, a god, how much he fears killing others in battle. Krishna assures Arjuna that after death there is life and there is honor and, even in war, there can be compassion if soldiers are motivated by love and by selflessness. Arjuna didn't have a choice. He *had* to fight. That was a warrior's duty and he came from a family of warriors. Fighting was his dharma—his destiny—and killing, if it wasn't motivated by pride or ego, was his path.

What the *Gita* and Noor's father taught about being a good citizen was convincing Noor that fighting Nazis was spiritually permissible, even spiritually redemptive. But Noor hadn't finished her own reflections, despite Vilayat's impatience. Needing time to think this through, she remembered Joan of Arc, who paid with her life while fighting the English who had invaded France. And she remembered that chivalry required her to turn away evildoers and defend the innocent and the weak. And she remembered what Plato, whom Muslims called Aflatun, had taught: do good though you gain nothing but trouble. The trouble will pass away and the good will endure.

For the first time in her relatively cloistered life, Noor was about to invite trouble. In England, Noor and Vilayat could enlist in defensive roles, maybe on the front lines. Their father would have approved. "The essence of spirituality and mysticism," Inayat taught, "is readiness to serve the person next to us."

Inayat had also known that wars are notoriously unpredictable vehicles for good. During the Great War, he had prayed that it would "awaken man of today to think, which he did not do before." But after the guns stilled and the armistice was signed, nations still argued and hate and nationalisms still festered, and Inayat had lamented that the "drunkenness" of the world had descended to an historic low and the "great bloodshed" was not over. Noor's father had been right. The world still wasn't sober.

. . .

Noor and her family carried some of their valuables to the homes of neighbors who weren't leaving. Manuscripts, letters, photos, paintings, and Noor's
harp and vina would be safe there until they returned. In the best of all
worlds, it would have made sense for the family to seek refuge with Inayat's
brothers—Noor's uncles—who were now living in The Hague, only three
hundred miles north of Suresnes. But to get there, they would have to go
against the thick tide of the millions of people from the north who were
fleeing the Nazis. And they'd be heading directly into the path of the invading German armies.

Instead, the family separated. Noor's younger brother, Hidayat, drove to
southern France with his wife and infant. Even if they reached the channel,
Hidayat was afraid, no boat would have room for everyone. The rest of the
family planned to take a train from Paris to the coast, then cross the Channel on a ship. But after hearing about the panic and the crowds in every
train station in France, it made more sense to drive some distance from
Suresnes, then board a train in a station that was reasonably calm—if they
could find one. The only way to get to that possibly mythical destination
was in Vilayat's MG—a great car for a jolly picnic in the country. Not for
fleeing from the Nazis. An open-air British sports car, MGs were made for
auto aficionados, or car rallies, or flirting with girls in Piccadilly or at Ascot.
They weren't intended for joining a long line of refugees who were escaping to the coast while the Germans strafed them from the air. The car was
lightweight (slightly over two thousand pounds), had little ground clearance,
and boasted a top speed of seventy-five miles an hour. The Khans wouldn't
get close to that, as they would soon discover.

Vilayat and Ora sat up front, Noor and Claire in the jump seat. Soon after
leaving Suresnes, they turned onto roads filled with broken-down cars and
broken-down people, and with infantrymen humiliated by their rout
and horses lying in ditches, and thousands of people on bicycles, weaving in and
out of the rabble, and farm wagons piled high with tables and chairs and suit-
cases, and a grandmother being pushed in a wheelbarrow. There was a man
carrying a cat, a woman carrying a bird in a cage, mothers pushing babies in
prams, children carrying toys, dolls, blankies, and everyone, it seemed, was

carrying pots, pans, or a suitcase or two. Cars overheated or crept along: the flood of humanity was too dense for the autos to move any faster. And everywhere you looked, mattresses were lashed to the tops of Renaults and Citroens and Mercedes. On the top of one car, the body of a grandmother who had died en route was tied to a mattress because her son could not bear to leave her alongside the road. So many mattresses were roped to cars that a French writer, Léon Werth, observed, "One would think this is the land of mattresses, that a mattress is the Frenchman's most precious possession."

The MG maneuvered around large stones that had been thrown on the road—fruitless attempts to block German tanks—and drove by fields of wheat that the Germans would soon seize for themselves and send back to their homeland. Germans in Messerschmitts and Heinkels circled above, unsure whether to strafe the refugees or let them collapse in exhaustion. The refugees begged farmers for fresh milk or eggs or for a few feet in a barn where someone from Paris or Belgium or Holland could sleep on a pile of straw for the night so, if all went well, they would have the energy to stagger a few more miles the next day and collapse in another barn. People talked, if they talked at all, of French victories that most likely had never occurred and of German defeats that, in the narrator's imagination, were worse than what had actually happened. If, indeed, they had happened at all.

This was not the neat, orderly France that had entranced Mark Twain when he traveled here seven decades before, convinced that France's "bright green lawns" were "swept and brushed every day and their grasses trimmed by the barber," and that the symmetry of hedges was "preserved by the most architectural of gardeners." In Twain's France, there was "no dirt, no decay, no rubbish anywhere." Everything was "charming to the eye. . . . All is clockwork, all is order."

No more. Jean-Paul Sartre summed up the France the Khans were lumbering through in an incongruous British sports car—a "black congestion of pedestrians . . . dead with fatigue." The only sound was "the scraping of boots and shoes over hard earth," and the only smell was the "hot stale stench of human beings, the sweet acrid stench of destitution, the unnatural stench of thinking animals."

Almost overnight, the population of Chartres had dropped from 23,000 to 800, of Lille from 200,000 to 200. All the inhabitants of the village of Bosselange

As the Germans marched into Paris . . .

. . . Noor and her family were stalled on the roads in what the French called
l'exode—the exodus.

left except one family, who committed suicide. As the refugees swallowed up entire cities (Pau swelled from 38,000 to 150,000 residents, Brive from 30,000 to 100,000, Bordeaux from 300,000 to 600,000), Nazi flags were flying farther north, especially in Paris (though the one the Germans tried to fly from the Eiffel Tower was so immense it blew away a few hours after they hoisted it; they raised a smaller one). At Versailles a motto that had seemed timeless when it was carved over a doorway long ago—"*à toutes les gloires de la France*" ("to all the glories of France")—was lost in the shadow of a flag with a massive swastika. If Hitler had his way, all future glories would be his.

Leaving the MG in Tours with a Sufi who had studied with Inayat, the Khans found seats on a train—in Noor's words, noisy and crowded, full of "frantic young mothers with tear-stained eyes carrying their sleeping youngsters. They knew not where [they were heading], just running toward freedom if freedom was to be found. . . . For the little ones, France should be saved from enemy hands at any price. I have wiped the eyes of some, given water to others. . . . The distress of a human being is impressive, indeed, but the distress of a whole nation? Those whose hearts have not beaten and suffered with this cannot know what it means."

The writer Léon Werth was also grieving. "If someone said to me," Werth said, "'the road is weeping,' I would have believed it. I'm weeping for France in this landscape I'm unfamiliar with, that I have not learned to love—a flat landscape with too much sky."

Noor and her family got off the train in Le Verdon, a small port where ships, yachts, fishing boats, and *schuyts*—flat-bottomed boats from Holland—were evacuating troops and refugees. This was Operation Ariel. Two weeks before at Dunkirk, 861 vessels had ferried 338,000 soldiers to England over nine days; Ariel saved about 200,000 soldiers, mostly English and Polish. At Dunkirk, Hitler had inexplicably held back his air force; during Ariel, he unleashed his bombers, fighters, submarines, destroyers, artillery. Yet the boats from England and from other ports in Western Europe kept coming.

Le Verdon was overflowing with parents, children, soldiers, all pushing, shoving, yelling for space on anything afloat. Anyone who got on a boat tried not to think about those who were left behind, stranded on docks that were crowded with thousands upon thousands of people standing tightly, and miserably, together.

With luck, the Khans found a hotel room. Noor didn't stay long. Hearing about a disaster near Saint-Nazaire, Noor wanted to put her Red Cross training to use. Claire, who also had a Red Cross certificate, insisted on tagging along.

Boarding a bus, the sisters passed through towns that had been strafed and bombed. Many were in flames. The worst was Saint-Nazaire. The day before, 9,000 passengers had been loaded onto a British ship. The *Lancastria* was anchored four miles offshore. Its draft was too deep to let it enter Saint-Nazaire's harbor.

The *Lancastria*'s capacity was 2,200; its captain had been ordered to load as many passengers as possible. Around 4 p.m., a Luftwaffe pilot scored four direct hits on the *Lancastria*. Men who could not swim clung to the hull, singing "Roll Out the Barrel" as the ship rolled over on them. German planes strafed survivors floating in the oil-slicked mess, setting the water on fire and incinerating everyone trapped in it. Several men held a baby aloft as the child's mother slowly sank below the surface. One soldier, Stanley Rimmer, jumped into the water without a life jacket. Clinging to two corpses that were held up by life jackets, Rimmer floated to safety.

Almost 2,500 people were rescued. Still, there were over 6,000 fatalities—the worst loss of life in British maritime history and more than the *combined* losses of the *Lusitania* and the *Titanic*. For months, corpses floated ashore, sometimes hundreds of miles from where the ship had sunk. In Saint-Nazaire itself, Noor wrote that "noises ceased. Movement stopped. The town was stunned stiff. . . . Throats were choked. . . . A silent rage stirred the crowd." A fisherman was crying. A few Englishmen consoled themselves with that old bromide that had comforted millions of British in the past—"There'll always be an England."

Such consolation was for another day. For now, the Nazis were in Paris and, Noor wrote, the Tomb of the Unknown Soldier—France's memorial to its dead from the Great War—was "being guarded by the enemy. God! It was worse than death!" Somehow she was hopeful as, above her, a dogfight broke out between the Luftwaffe and the few planes left in the

French air force: "Can the will of a nation be crushed? Perhaps suppressed momentarily. . . . Of all with whom I have come in contact, not one is ready to submit."

Noor and Claire turned back to Le Verdon from Saint-Nazaire. The town was too much of a madhouse for them to figure out how to put their Red Cross training to use. German strafing had wrecked the few buses that had been running the day before and the young women had "no bread, nothing to eat and no chance to sleep," Claire would recall. "We just walked and walked, and tried to find our way by asking people. . . . It was wartime and nobody knew what was going on. . . . At night, all was black."

The blackness gave Noor and Claire cover from German planes and snipers. When they found Vilayat and Ora in Le Verdon, Vilayat was furious. He had found space for all of them on one of the few boats left in the harbor—a twenty-two-year-old Belgian freighter, the *Kasongo*. If Noor and Clair had returned any later, they would have missed the boat. France was about to be handed over to the Germans.

The Britain to which Noor was fleeing was different from what she had known as a child. During the Great War, her father had asked Noor in a letter from northern England to pray that bombs from German dirigibles didn't land on him. Aerial warfare was crude and primitive in those days, and there was little chance a bomb would hit him, even by accident. But it was

The freighter that took Noor to England in June 1940: battered, bug-infested, and sunk by a German sub eight months later.

already apparent that this new war—Hitler's war—was different: airplanes were faster, bombs were more accurate, and the old-fashioned and very gentlemanly distinctions between civilians and the military were blurred, if not entirely erased. No one was safe, whether you were in uniform or not: the first German bombers—120 Junker JU87s—had hit England three days before Noor had boarded the *Kasongo,* killing nine people in Cambridge. Bombs had also been dropped on the London area, though Hitler had supposedly put the city off-limits.

June 19, the day the *Kasongo* left Le Verdon, was clear and blue—"beautiful and summery," remembered one passenger—with calm, dazzling water. At night, "the moon shone far too brightly for the boat's safety." A few ships were visible in the distance: a liner that had been pressed into service; a ship with a yellow cross painted on its side; a destroyer whose presence cheered everyone. At night, the *Kasongo*'s deck was covered with passengers wrapped in coats and blankets: no one went belowdecks—the cabins were swarming with bugs. In the moonlight, the passengers looked like corpses, only occasionally moving to pour tea from insulated flasks. The Khans didn't care about the discomfort or about the beetles. They were out of France.

Four days later, the Khans reached Falmouth. Whitewashed cottages spilled down hillsides toward the sea. Sailboats bobbed in the harbor. English accents were chirping in the air. Lovely as it was, there was little time for repose or reflection. The docks were almost as crammed as those in France and fear of a German attack was palpable and not unreasonable. A green bus drove the *Kasongo*'s passengers to a large building—a theater or a concert hall: the newcomers weren't sure amid the confusion. After officials processed the refugees' papers, they were ushered into a garden. Ladies in greenish-gray Harris tweed uniforms—members of the WVS, the Women's Voluntary Services, which helped the needy throughout England—offered lemonade and sandwiches of cold meat and cheese, and sympathy framed in genteel British formulations: "What an *awful* time you must have had." That was true though many refugees were not ready to talk about it. After standing for too long in too many queues, Noor and her family boarded a train for Oxford, three hours away: Vilayat was familiar with the town. He'd attended the university there a few years before. A bed-and-breakfast took them in. The Khans had no idea what to do next.

The day after Noor landed in Falmouth, Hitler toured Paris. The Fuehrer's procession of black convertibles prowled the empty, early morning streets, sped down Rue La Fayette to the Opéra de Paris, the largest theater in the world; then on to the Eglise de la Madeleine, a magnificent Roman Catholic church built as a tribute to Napoleon's armies; and after that to the Champs-Elysées where Hitler, grabbing the windshield of his Mercedes, stood up to survey the vista. Ordinarily teeming with cars, cyclists, and pedestrians, the wide boulevard was deserted. As the convoy swept past the Arc de Triomphe, Hitler got out and posed for a photo with the Eiffel Tower in the background. Looking slightly upward and toward his right, with the tower over his left shoulder, Hitler evinced no pleasure in the photo. Only a

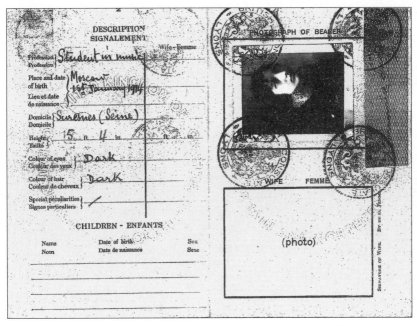

Noor's passport, stamped with a visa from the British consulate.

stolid, blank presence. Crossing the Seine, Hitler paid a brief tribute at Napoleon's tomb, then cruised through Montparnasse and the Latin Quarter, and Ile de la Cité and Notre-Dame, and scanned from the highest point of Montmartre the city that was at his disposal. On his return flight to Berlin, Hitler told Albert Speer, his favorite architect, "It was the dream of my life to be permitted to see Paris. I cannot say how happy I am to have that dream fulfilled today." He never returned.

Noor *would* return. The young woman who had written poems about fairies since she was a child would attend to less fantastical matters that she had barely known existed. A recent poem of Noor's had ended with an admonition to herself to

> *not covet foolish things . . .*
> *And never try to touch . . . [fairies'] shining wings.*

That was the last time Noor wrote about fairies.

PART TWO

"OUR CHEERS ARE GOING ALL OVER ENGLAND"

Only that which is done not for fame or name,
nor for thanks from those for whom it is done,
is love's service.

—HAZRAT INAYAT KHAN

CHAPTER 5

THE BLOODY WORLD'S ON FIRE

Noor settled in Oxford with her mother and sister. The university town was teeming with refugees from the Continent and from some of the more endangered cities in England itself. Vilayat settled in London, where he waited to be called into the Royal Air Force. Visiting him a few times, Noor made some new friends, impressing one of them—an aspiring writer—with the quiet and smallness of her personality, one, Noor's friend wrote, that did "not obtrude . . . and had to be sought." Noor's eyes also impressed her new friend: "eloquent," "timorous," and "trusting," "they made me think of a deer." But "most singular" about Noor was her voice: "exceedingly gentle, high and faint; it trailed in a curious way and might change pitch several times upon a syllable, quavering as though it were about to die out—and indeed sometimes it could scarcely be heard. It was the thinnest little pipe . . . such a voice as creatures of fairyland might be expected to use for it had no 'body' at all. . . . There was something elfin about her; it was as though the vibrations of her personality were so graduated as to pass almost unhindered through those around her."

The young woman who was meeting Noor for the first time was also affected by Noor's insisting that she could have been of greater service had she remained in France and joined the partisans organizing there. Now that she was in England, maybe the British should send her back to France as some sort of liaison? If she was caught, her appearance was so unique—she wasn't really British or American or Indian, and her skin was more tan than white and more light than dark—the Germans wouldn't know what to make of her. If Vilayat "becomes a fighter pilot," Noor told her friend, "he will be risking his life every day. Nursing seems so little in comparison."

For now, Noor expressed her solidarity with France by pinning to her dress a Cross of Lorraine—a vertical line crossed by two horizontal bars, the top one shorter than the other. The cross was a fairly accurate representation of the one on which Jesus was crucified. The Knights Templar had fought under the Cross of Lorraine during the Crusades and Joan of Arc had fought under it three centuries later. When Germany annexed Lorraine in eastern France after the Franco-Prussian War, the Cross of Lorraine was a rallying point for France's intentions to recover its lost province. Now the Cross was the emblem of the Free French, the government-in-exile that Charles de Gaulle, a barely known French colonel, had announced on the BBC on June 18. Hope was not dead, de Gaulle declared. With its overseas empire behind her, France could fight alongside Britain, which controlled the seas, and, like Britain, France could "use without limit the immense industry of the United States," *if* it ever entered the war. "This is a world war," de Gaulle continued. "The fate of the world depends on it. . . . Whatever happens, the flame of the French resistance must not be extinguished, and will not be extinguished."

German bombing of England intensified. Starting with the second half of July and the rest of the year and a good part of the next, waves of bombers darkened the skies—247 one night; 400 another. One hundred and seventy-nine civilians were killed in one assault; 450 in a subsequent raid. Hospitals, schools, homes were demolished. Docks burned for days. "The whole bloody world's on fire," a fireman told headquarters. St. Thomas's Hospital in London was bombed three times in six days. After burning for two days, the House of Commons was still smoldering. Even Buckingham Palace was hit. In Chislehurst, the children's ward of a hospital was moved to a colossal cave where dances were held for adults and church services offered on Sundays. All over the country, the air in shelters was dank, the power erratic, and tempers short. London's most notorious shelter—the Tilbury in Stepney—was jammed with whores, seamen, crooks, and peddlers hawking greasy, cold fried fish. And one night in 1941, Ken Johnson started singing

"Oh Johnny (How Can You Love)" in the Café de Paris—ads crowed it was "the safest and gayest restaurant in town, 20 feet below ground"—when two 110-pound bombs penetrated the ceiling and exploded in front of the stage, instantly killing Johnson and thirty officers and their dates. Young men in uniform, weeping, carried out the bodies of their girlfriends.

From Buckingham Palace, the queen wrote to her mother-in-law, "The people are marvelous and so full of fight," while an ordinary Londoner confided in his diary, "If we are saved, we shall be saved by our optimism." Maybe so, but humor and good cheer were rare. One exception was the time a man strolled about in Pimlico one night to check on the latest commotion—a bomb had exploded a block away. Feeling "a queer sensation," he suddenly felt the cold pavement beneath his feet. Looking down, he discovered that his slippers had disappeared in the blast. Otherwise, he was fine.

Hardly anyone mentioned that Britain had only fifty tanks when the war started. Or that downed German pilots were kicked and beaten, sometimes shot by civilians. Or that looters slid rings from the fingers of the dead and unclasped necklaces from around their necks. In Cardiff, even fruit trees were stolen. And then there were the Jews. Some residents of London's East End claimed that Jews demanded full rent for any bomb-damaged property they owned, and that they controlled the black market and refused to volunteer as air raid wardens or firemen. George Orwell took on the bigots: "Because two days ago a fat Jewess grabbed your place on the bus, you switch off the wireless when the announcer begins talking about the ghettos of Warsaw." Orwell was correct and he was decent, but that made no difference. The anti-Semitism continued.

Nevertheless, Vilayat stayed in London. He had friends there. They did their best to keep each other cheerful despite the bombs. Ora worked in a mental hospital in Oxford—the town was never bombed during the entire war. Claire served as a nurse in a military hospital not far away, wandering one day into a ward where soldiers with severely burned faces were awaiting treatment. Her "heart sank . . . I turned white . . . I was so sad I became useless as a nurse." And Noor lasted six weeks in the Fulmer Chase Maternity Home, a hospital for the pregnant wives of army officers on a sprawling Tudor estate once owned by a cigarette magnate. This wasn't how Noor had hoped to contribute to the war. Luckily, she had a life beyond the hospital, often going to London for movies, theater, or museums or to enjoy tea with friends at the Tottenham Court Corner House, where the waitresses were called "Nippies" and wore prim black dresses with white Peter Pan collars and served the best rum baba in town. Even bombed-out London was a welcome distraction from boring hospital work and from being repeatedly turned away by the military: since Noor was born in Moscow, she was not a British citizen. Still, she insisted she had the right to wear a uniform—her passport said she was a "British Protected Person," a status granted to Noor becaue her father was Indian, a colonial in the vast scheme of the British Empire. While a "protected person" didn't have all the privileges of a British citizen, Noor argued, she had the right to serve in His Majesty's forces. She was right.

On November 19, Noor joined the Women's Auxiliary Air Force. A branch of the Royal Air Force, WAAFs eavesdropped on German radio messages and studied radar screens, telling British pilots where the Luftwaffe was flying over England. Noor—#754197 Aircraftwoman 2nd Class—was assigned to Harrogate to learn how to operate a wireless telegraph. On her identity card, she was "N. Inayat-Khan," but she preferred being called "Nora." This was more British and less exotic than Noor.

Harrogate was a spa town in the north. Its posh hotels were filled with government offices that had evacuated from London. Other hotels in town were used for snazzy barracks for airmen. WAAFs squeezed into Quonset huts, twelve to twenty-three in a room. They slept on straw mattresses thrown on top of iron bed frames, and wore shoes that were almost impossible to break in and underwear that often dated back to the Great War. Their pay was two-thirds what men got; their food ration four-fifths; and what passed for food was often indigestible. One disgruntled WAAF too vividly described it as "lumps of grisly meat and soggy vegetables floating in greasy gravy followed by stodgy spotted dick." (Spotted dick was a traditional British pudding made from suet and dried fruit.) About the only advantage women had over men was their uniform. Men's uniforms were made from a coarse, itchy wool. Women's uniforms were made from a finer, more comfortable wool, and consisted of a straight skirt that finished sixteen inches from the ground, a blue-gray shirt accented with a black tie, a tunic fastened with buttons, a belt that buckled slightly above the waist, and a cap with a patent leather peak and a brass RAF badge. Noor was proud of her uniform.

WAAFs got three weeks of basic training: physical fitness, dental checks, a string of medical injections, lectures on first aid, and marching everywhere in groups, all day. "The constant marching and drilling went on and on," recalled a WAAF, "until I thought the idea was to march into Germany, fetch old Hitler out, and then have a go at him." Some WAAFs cried themselves to sleep. Others were stunned at the intimacy of the war: at an airfield in Kent, a WAAF regularly heard a German pilot banter with her in English on his radio: "Would you like me to drop a bomb on you? Wheeeee . . ." One day, British Spitfires shot him down. The German couldn't bail out and the WAAF "listened as he screamed for his mother and cursed the Fuhrer. I found myself praying, 'Get out. Bail out. Oh, please, dear God, get him out.' It was no use. We heard him the whole way down . . . I was sick. . . . In part, I was his executioner."

In December Noor was transferred to Edinburgh for advanced training on wireless telegraphy. Scotland was no safer than England. By the end of the war, air raids would kill 2,298 Scots. Edinburgh was bombed eighteen times; twice while Noor was there. In 1941, 528 people were killed in one raid on Clydebank, 617 injured, and only seven of the town's twelve thousand homes escaped damage. Peterhead, about one hundred miles north of Edinburgh, was the second most bombed place in Britain, not because it had any strategic value, but because it was the first city German pilots saw as they flew into the United Kingdom from Norway.

The radio telegraph that Noor was learning how to use required dexterity, both physical and mental—Noor's fingers had to move fast on the key, and her mind had to move equally fast through codes. And just being in Edinburgh required endurance: the winter Noor was there was the worst in Scotland for a century—more than two feet of snow fell in one day, with drifts higher than fourteen feet in parts of the country. The chilblains Noor contracted made her hop more than dance when she joined folk dancing lessons in a small hall at Edinburgh Castle.

The WAAFs were trained on the wireless in a basement across from Hollyrood Palace, the official residence of British monarchs while they were in Scotland. Each WAAF had her own desk with a telegraph key on it. The long days of cultivating a feel for the key—determining the best pressure to exert on it for the fastest, most accurate transmission—were broken up by the blast of the cannon that was fired from Edinburgh Castle at precisely one o'clock every day except Christmas, Good Friday, and Sundays. The daily concussion, dating back to 1861, had originated to help ships in the Firth of Forth, a nearby estuary, set their maritime clocks so they could accurately navigate the high seas. Some traditions were too embedded in British life to be ignored, even during the war.

Learning how to use the wireless telegraph was consistent with Noor's promise to Vilayat back at Fazal Manzil: she would fight the Germans as peacefully as possible, with little chance of violence and even less of death. This would let her remain a good Sufi, and a good daughter. If you're "in tune with the universe," Noor's father had taught, you "become like a radio receiver through which the voice of the universe is transmitted." *Everything,* he said, vibrates: trees, flowers, rocks, us; our bodies, our thoughts, our feelings exist "according to the law of vibrations." In fact, said Inayat, inter-fering with vibrations can make us sick or depressed since we *are* vibrations. Every time Noor pressed her telegraph key, she was sending vibrations—the foundation of Inayat's spirituality—into the universe.

Noor had never missed one of Ora's birthdays. She would now. She made up for it by sending Ora a birthday poem on May 8, the most patriotic poem she ever wrote:

> *Our cheers are going all over England . . .*
> *Three cheers by wireless from Scotland,*
> *Three cheers from the RAF planes!*

Despite these reminders that Noor and Vilayat were being trained for war, everything in the poem was as normal as could be. Ora was "cute." She was Noor's "May queen." And she deserved every kiss Noor sent her. "So dear-est," Noor urged, "cheer up, it's your birthday." For Ora, alone in Oxford as Claire did secret medical research that she could never talk about, and with two of her other children in the military, and her other son, Hidayat, not heard from since he sent a telegram from a village near Limoges in 1940, it must had been a sad birthday, indeed.

. . .

In June 1941, Noor was assigned to an air-force base near Abingdon, a small town in central England best known as the headquarters of the MG motor car company. Abingdon was also the home of a lesser known, but equally venerable tradition—tossing a bun from the top of Abingdon's town hall. The rite had originated three centuries before as Abingdon's version of donating bread to the poor. Over time, the bread was replaced by cinnamon buns thrown only on festive occasions—coronations, royal birthdays, the end of a conflict. Food rationing during the world war suspended bun throwing, and Noor missed all the fun.

Noor and another WAAF shared a room on the top floor of an old house in Boars Hill, an eight-hundred-year-old hamlet midway between Oxford and Abingdon. Many homes in Boars Hill had thatched roofs, and most of the roads weren't paved. Noor and her roommate decorated their room with travel posters and flowers. Renting a radio, they listened to music on the BBC and to Morse code beamed in from other countries. They realized they'd overdone their training when they started mumbling Morse in their sleep. They also read a lot and discussed their lives after the war, with Noor dreaming of a quiet marriage with several sons and daughters and a successful career writing stories for children.

For Noor, the chief advantage of living on Boars Hill was that she could bike four miles to the base in Abingdon or slightly less than that the other way to visit Ora, who still lived in Oxford. While pedaling along, Noor often sang "Heidenroslein," Schubert's merry adaptation of a poem by Goethe. There were two interpretations of the poem: it was either about a young man who plucks a bright rose from a bush or it was about the rape of a woman who was strolling alone through the countryside ("I will prick you"). Biking alongside houses that were centuries old, with bright green English hills all around her, Noor must have trusted in the first, more lighthearted interpretation.

At Abingdon, Noor helped pilots prepare for bombing runs over Germany and Italy. On some days, these flights seemed to do no more than scare chickens and geese on nearby farms although it was hard to forget that Boars Hill was right in the path of the training circuit of some of the pilots Noor was training. The hill's sudden three-hundred-foot elevation matched the angle of climb of the RAF's underpowered Whitley bombers. Two Whitleys crashed into Boars Hill while Noor lived there.

Inspired by Noor's "mouse-brown hair, her tiny voice, her shy ways, and her timidity," the men nicknamed her "the mouse." She'd had another nickname in Scotland—"Bang Away Lulu," inspired by the racket she made tapping on her telegraph key. Neither nickname stayed with her for long. She was too conventional and slightly formal for such familiarities to stick.

After almost a year at Abingdon, Noor was transferred to an RAF base in Compton Bassett. Discipline was strict, tougher than at most RAF bases, with frequent drills and inspections for personal appearance and living quarters. More isolated than Abingdon—forty-seven miles from Oxford, almost one hundred miles from London, and with few distractions—Compton Bassett was an ideal place for WAAFs to master codes that were more advanced than what they already knew. This, in fact, was the only reason the base existed. There was no airfield here—only bleak rows of wooden barracks with bare lights dangling from the ceilings and even more boring buildings where the WAAFs tapped away on their telegraph keys for hours every day. Aside from that, there wasn't much to do: Noor could ride her Raleigh bicycle three miles from the base to the Cherhill White Horse. (The massive horse outlined on a hillside in chalk dated back to the eighteenth century. Deemed a folly when it went up, the horse was declared a national treasure by the time Noor arrived.) Or she could go to the Astra, a small movie theater on the base that changed its program four times a week. Otherwise, social life centered on three pubs—the Black Horse, the White Horse, and the Strand.

Noor's course lasted seven weeks. When possible, she took the train to London (each way: seven shillings, sixpence), often staying with a friend who lived a few doors from Noor's mother. Both Noor and her friend had a similar interest in mysticism and the occult. When Noor's friend wasn't reading her palm (Noor had a "generous, but reckless character") and Noor now wasn't holding her friend's Tibetan prayer wheel ("there is such peace in it"), they spoke about literature. Having just finished Milton's *Paradise Lost,* Noor now planned to read a modern German novel to help improve her command of the German language. This would help the work she was doing in the military. Surely, her friend said, the people who were training Noor could provide her with an instructor. No, Noor replied. They did not consider how this could be relevant to her work. It was her idea, not that of the agency that was training her.

On all her trips to London, Noor visited Vilayat, who was studying nautical navigation. Poor night vision had disqualified him from serving in the air force. Volunteering for the navy, he had requested a commission for which he would not have to kill anyone, fulfilling the pact he and Noor had made as the Germans were pouring into France. His assignment would be entirely defensive though far from safe: he would command a mine sweeper.

One afternoon, Vilayat took Noor to see *Fantasia*, Walt Disney's experimental melding of animation and high culture. Mickey Mouse talking shop with Leopold Stokowski, the superstar conductor of the day, did not impress Noor (though Mickey respectfully called him "Mr. Stokowski") any more than the hippos who pranced around to Ponchielli's "Dance of the Hours" did. Especially offended by the lambs gamboling to Beethoven's *Pastoral* Symphony, Noor bristled that Disney was smothering Beethoven's genius in kitsch. The *London Observer*'s music critic agreed, sniffing that, in *Fantasia*, Beethoven's Sixth was "exciting because it is excitingly played."

Another day, Noor and Vilayat went to the London zoo. Noor was so enchanted with a deer that Vilayat almost asked a zookeeper if he could give his sister one of its fawns if it ever gave birth. Vilayat liked to compare people to animals, and Noor's fascination with the deer reinforced how he saw her. "Noor is a deer," he told a friend. The comparison would have pleased their father who had said that deer "live in this world only out of love." They don't ask others to serve them, and they are not attached to the world. Rather, deer declare, "I do all things for you, but I will not be bound to you."

Noor hoped that her training at Compton Bassett would help her earn a commission. With that, she would have a higher rank, greater responsibilities, and more substantial pay, which she would use to help her mother, who was always financially strapped. Wanting to look prim and proper when she appeared before the commission board in August 1942, she borrowed a pound from Vilayat for a permanent. "A lady-like hair style," she told him, "is the first condition for being well-kept and well-bred." Other than wanting to look good, she wanted to show how much she knew about codes and the wireless radio and how much she hated Nazis. That part went well. But there was a line of questioning she hadn't expected: her attitude toward Indian independence. The question was inevitable. Her father was Indian, her passport labeled her a "British *Indian* protected person [italics added]," and her skin was darker than the average European's. To the commissioners, she *was* Indian.

Britain and nationalists in India had been arguing about India's role in the war since it started: would England treat Indians as equals if they fought for the Empire? Or would they be treated as second-class citizens and called "coolies" and worse? And maybe more significantly, did the war have anything to do with Indians, many of whom had been fighting for their own independence from England for decades?

England had expected Indians to fight for the Crown. They had done this during World War I and all had gone well (if you could overlook the seventy-four thousand Indian fatalities). But that was before Gandhi preached the purity of *satyagraha*, passive resistance, and before more militant nationalists tried to jostle him out of the way. When war broke out in 1939, wealthy princes—hoping to curry favor with England—promised men, money, and matériel for Britain. Nationalists protested, demanding that Indians not contribute to the war in any way. Some of them even cozied up to Hitler. Every night on the radio from Berlin, Subhas Chandra Bose told the world that India's "natural friends"—Germany, Italy, and Japan—"have nothing but sympathy and good will for India and for Indian independence." And when six hundred thousand refugees flooded into India after the Japanese conquered Burma, the preferential treatment Britain gave whites infuriated Gandhi: "Hundreds, if not thousands, perished without food and drink, and wretched discrimination stared those miserable people in the face. One route for the whites, another for the blacks! India is being ground down to dust and humiliated. . . . And so one fine morning I came to the decision to make this honest demand: 'For heaven's sake, leave India alone.'"

Noor liked the nationalists' idea of a Home Guard in every town and village in India. The Guard would be administered by India's minister of defense—not by Britain. Armed with weapons powerful enough to stall a Japanese invasion, the Indians would hold out until better-equipped British forces arrived on the scene. "At present," Noor told friends, "we have to depend on the British to protect us. That is humiliating, apart from causing delay."

Straining to explain this to the board that would decide on her commission, Noor attempted to draw an equivalence between a possible Home Guard in India and the Home Guard that was already operating in England. One would defend India from the Japanese; the other was ready to defend Britain from Nazis. Arming Indians, Noor persisted, would signal how much England respected Indians, increase Indians' loyalty to the Crown, and create a friendlier, more relaxed atmosphere in which to negotiate India's future.

The board was offended. India was the crown jewel of the Empire. India's treasure helped make Britain great. Britain's greatness helped "civilize" India. Anyone favoring independence was a traitor. Noor slowly got angry, her voice rising, her face reddening until a board member asked, "If Indian leaders take measures embarrassing to Britain, will you support them?"

"My duty is to support the measures of any responsible Indian leader."

"Is that inconsistent with your oath to the Crown?"

Noor retreated slightly. As long as the war continued, she would be loyal to Britain. No one, not even Indian nationalists, was safe as long as the Nazis were in power, steamrolling over countries and slaughtering millions. If India's situation didn't improve after the war, she might support the nationalists.

Sitting down with Vilayat that night, Noor was sure she wouldn't get a commission. Hotheads didn't get promoted. "I should like to have appeared deliberate and cool and well balanced," she told her brother. "But I got angry. I could feel my face flushing. I gave the impression of being emotional, and that's no good."

Calm down, Vilayat told Noor. The board would respect the strength and integrity she'd shown. They probably didn't often meet such stubborn, principled women. "You'll get your commission," Vilayat assured Noor. She was sure he was wrong. Returning to training pilots at Abingdon, she tried to forget about her clash with the board.

Noor did this reasonably well until she was asked to come to London for a meeting—4 p.m., November 10, 1942, in Room 238 of the former Hotel

Victoria. When it opened in 1887, ads boasted that the Victoria—then one of the most elegant hotels in the city—was "completely lit by electricity," had "passenger lifts [that went] to every floor," and served dinners that were the "best in London." But that was another era. Noor had no idea that two years before, the War Department had requisitioned the Victoria for a new secret agency. Room 238 was where the Special Operations Executive interviewed possible agents. Instead of granting Noor a commission, the board had told the SOE about her "linguistic qualifications which might make her of value for operational purposes."

Noor, like almost everyone in England, had never heard of the SOE nor knew that Germany had already caught, tortured, and killed dozens, maybe hundreds of agents, all of whom could be shot as spies since they didn't wear uniforms. But Noor knew none of this, and she showed up at the Hotel Victoria promptly at 4 p.m. on November 10. Noor had rarely been late for anything in her life, and she didn't want to be late now.

CHAPTER 6

A THING NO HUMAN COULD FACE WITH ANYTHING BUT TERROR

He was cranky, crusty, and cantankerous. Always was and always would be, with no apologies for his ways or his fondness for alcohol (morning, afternoon, or night) or his rudeness that didn't distinguish between friend or foe, family or heel. And now that his years in the wilderness, as he called them, were over, Winston Churchill was in fine fettle. On his shoulders rested the future of Britain, the fate of Western civilization, the destiny of humanity—Churchill didn't mince words and he didn't like humility. He had no doubts he was up to the task. In Churchill's mind, he had been born for this moment.

Churchill promised the British they'd fight on the beaches and in the fields. Yet the first phase of the war for his beloved island was fought in the air (against the Luftwaffe) and in the seas (with ships and subs playing cat-and-mouse in two oceans). The beaches and the fields were quiet. That was good. Fighting there would mean the Germans had arrived.

For the first years of the war, Churchill wasn't sure England could beat Germany. Britain was on its own, a lone outpost against the Nazis. But ignoring Hitler would let the Fuehrer tighten his grip on Europe while demoralizing the millions who were suffering under him. Churchill had to create the illusion that he was Germany's match while also forcing Hitler to worry about the internal security of his new empire. That meant being clever, a proud family trait: during a battle in the War of the Spanish Succession in the seventeenth century, the Duke of Marlborough, Churchill's distant cousin, sent "deserters" to tell the French he was retreating the next day.

Instead, the duke attacked, and won. Churchill also had to be shifty: he had seen this work in 1895 while visiting Cuba, where a few thousand guerrillas were pinning down 250,000 men from the Spanish army. "Where are the enemy?" Churchill asked a Spaniard. "Everywhere and nowhere," the officer replied, alluding to insurgents who came out of nowhere, fought like hell, then melted away as if they'd never been there. Above all, the illusion Churchill wanted to create required courage, a quality that was almost sacred to him. Courage advanced humans through their worst quandaries, their most harrowing and frightful dilemmas. Lacking courage, we are nothing, and we deserve to be nothing. As Churchill wrote in the early 1930s, courage is "rightly esteemed the first of human qualities because . . . it is the quality which guarantees all others." Courage makes us human, and it preserves our humanness. The spine of our morals and our scruples, it keeps us upright.

At midnight on July 16, 1940—five weeks after Dunkirk—Churchill instructed Hugh Dalton, his minister of economic warfare, to create a secret agency that would spread fear and chaos among the Germans who were occupying Europe. British agents would sneak into Europe and blow up bridges, trains, factories, and power stations; cut telephone and telegraph wires; organize local resistance; send intelligence back to London; and kill Germans and collaborators when the opportunity presented itself. On D-Day, whenever that might be, the SOE and the entire Resistance—the homegrown movements in France that fought against the Occupation—would rise as one and do their damndest to blow up the Nazi war machine. If the new agency was successful, Hitler would never have a good night's sleep, and Germany would never be smug about taking over someone else's country.

The agency would be independent of the established armed forces and Britain's intelligence services. And it would operate entirely differently. Traditionally, spies were silent and invisible. Churchill didn't want spies and he didn't want tradition. By making a ruckus—helping the Resistance and dynamiting anything of strategic value and making all-around nuisances of themselves—Churchill's new agents would give Nazis the military equivalent of a nervous breakdown. Until England was strong enough to fight the Nazis head on, sabotage was the game.

Churchill called his agency the Strategic Operations Executive. The name was about as bland as English porridge. The eleven syllables could never be uttered in or out of the organization. It was so secret that even the cover name had a cover name—the Inter-Services Research Bureau. Most agents who served in it wouldn't even know that. They called it "the outfit," "the firm," or "the racket." Privately, Churchill had a more colorful name for it—the Ministry of Ungentlemanly Warfare.

Hugh Dalton accepted Churchill's challenge—a great chance, he wrote, to "smash things up." Turning to leave after his late-night meeting with Churchill, Dalton was almost at the door when the prime minister called out a line he remembered from *The Four Just Men*, a detective thriller by the British writer Edgar Wallace. "And now," Churchill instructed Dalton, "set Europe ablaze."

B y the time the SOE interviewed Noor, the agency already had a checkered history. In Holland, Germans had caught SOE agents as soon as they parachuted in and forced them to radio to London for large drops of arms and for more agents. Fifty-four agents had ended up in Nazi prisons. Forty-eight had been killed at Mauthausen. In Norway, an attempt to sabotage a hydroelectric plant the Germans were using to manufacture heavy water for an atom bomb had failed miserably. But the SOE also had pulled off some spectacular victories. Its second attempt to sabotage the hydroelectric plant was one of the great successes of the war—six agents squirreled their way into the plant, destroyed 350 kilograms of heavy water, then eluded the twelve thousand German soldiers who were looking for them. Around the same time, agents blew up a viaduct in Greece that was critical for the supply line between Germany and Rommel's army in North Africa. Forty-eight trains, each carrying hundreds of tons of weapons, crossed the viaduct every day. For the six weeks that trains couldn't cross the bridge, Rommel was deprived of more than two thousand trainloads of supplies.

All this was top secret. At her meeting in the Hotel Victoria, Noor sat on a wooden folding chair in a small, blacked-out room, totally unaware that the man sitting across from her had argued with several layers of the government to even be allowed to talk with her. The author of more than a dozen detective novels (with titles like *I Met Murder* and *Keep Murder Quiet*),

Selwyn Jepson's fertile imagination helped him appreciate, as he said, that women were "better than men" for the SOE. Agents had to be shrewd and decisive and able to tolerate operating alone, with nothing to guide them but their wit, their instincts, and their intuition. Women were perfect—brave and resourceful and armed with what Jepson called a "cool and lonely courage." Men, he complained, couldn't "work alone" and "tend to be always in company with other men." Women blended in more easily, especially in France. With two million Frenchmen in POW camps, women were biking everywhere, and doing what ordinarily was men's work. Women could also charm the Germans with their good looks (which many of the agents had). Even Nazis were susceptible to a pretty face.

Ordinarily, Jepson met with possible agents three or four times, sizing up their personality, skills, and character, and switching from English to French. Agents had to be as fluent in French as he was. Being fluent meant more than knowing French. Agents had to know about recent news and scandals and rumors in France, about French nursery rhymes, songs, proverbs, about French sports figures or writers, and class and regional distinctions and manners in France as well as which wine went with which dish in which province. Overall, agents had to behave as though they'd been born in France and swaddled in French culture since they were babies. If they couldn't pull this off, locals *and* Germans would know they didn't belong. Jepson also had to figure out agents' motives. There were several theories about this. One psychiatrist said SOE agents were trying "to give worth and meaning to their otherwise futile lives." A writer from South Africa claimed they were "truants from the obligations of life and society." And one agent said—almost quaintly given the degradation which much of humanity sank into during the war—that he and others in the SOE were defending "human decency." Most of all, Jepson didn't want a "hero." They were too rash and too impulsive and usually the first to be caught or killed. For Jepson, "hero" was another word for "show-off."

One interview with Noor was enough for Jepson. She had, he said, "an intuitive sense of what might be in my mind for her to do" and she "stood out as almost perfect" to operate a wireless from France—"careful, tidy, painstaking and [she] possessed all the patience in the world." Jepson also sensed that he could confide in her, something he usually delayed until his third or fourth meeting with a possible agent. "I realized it would be safe to be frank with her," he said some years later, "that her 'security,' as we called it, would be good, that if she felt unable to take it on, she would not talk about the reason she had been called to the War Office. . . ."

Leveling with Noor, Jepson told her, "I have to decide whether I can risk your life and you have to decide whether you're willing to risk it." Most wireless operators didn't survive more than six weeks in Europe. The Germans knew that radio operators were the indispensable link in the SOE's chain—more valuable than the couriers or organizers in what the SOE called a "circuit," or cell. As a Gestapo agent told British investigators after the war, "My object was always to break up the [radio] liaisons, even more than arresting the [other] chaps. What could they do without communications?" Jepson warned Noor that if the Germans caught her, she'd be up against "a thing no human could face with anything but terror"—whips, chains, electric shock, rubber hoses, rifle butts, burns from cigarette butts. She might be injected with concoctions that had been whipped up in the next room.

Jepson paused, contemplating an asset of Noor's that had nothing to do with how well she spoke French or how easy it would be for her to get around Paris: her beauty. Noor had been turning heads for years. One line of thinking in espionage circles was that ordinary, unassuming women made the best agents: they didn't draw attention. The other line—Jepson's line—was that good looks and a refined personality made agents seem like they were part of the moneyed, leisured class. Germans didn't like stopping someone like that—even Nazis were intimidated by the rich.

What Jepson said next contradicted his duty to the SOE—finding the best agents for the hardest jobs. But, he rationalized, "Since we were undoubtedly going to win in the end, it could be excused, perhaps." Sensing a "natural feeling of kinship" with Noor—they were both writers—Jepson advised, "You could be justified thinking you can be more valuable to humanity by surviving the war and using your skills as a children's author to help shape the minds of the youngsters who would be inheriting a partially destroyed world. They will become the men and women who will have to rebuild it."

Noor thanked Jepson. This was kind of him and there was a certain logic and caring behind his offer. Still, she tentatively turned him down. She wanted to serve in the SOE *if* she passed the training. There was little doubt about that, Jepson assured her, though he may have been concerned about a misunderstanding that he wasn't aware had surfaced fleetingly between them: Noor had assumed he was referring to London's subway system when he said she would be operating "underground."

Buoyed by Jepson's confidence that she would pass the agency's training, Noor was on the verge of accepting his offer—*if* she could dispel her mother's worries about her doing anything dangerous. Even Noor's safest assignments bothered Ora. Visiting Ora that night, Noor was sketchy and vague, telling her mother that a group she called the "Special Services" might send her abroad. She gave Ora no details and no specifics, only a vague intimation that this might not be what Ora wanted for her daughter. Ora's response by letter a few days later was as predictable as it was maternal: "I wish you would decide to remain where you are. . . . I am certain you are less exposed to the trials of life for which you are not strong enough. Do consider my judgement a little bit, won't you?"

Noor had not considered Ora's judgment. She had already written Jepson—the day after their interview, in fact—that she was "gratefully accepting the privilege of carrying out the work you suggested." Her biggest worry—aggravating her mother's anxieties and nervousness—were now "more or less wiped out." "In time," Noor continued, her mother would "get used to the idea of my being overseas." Having her SOE salary sent directly to Ora would help her finances considerably. And "besides," Noor added, brushing aside all her reservations about Ora and the dangers of being in the SOE and the quiet, writerly life she'd always planned for herself, "family ties are petty when winning this war is at stake."

CHAPTER 7

"I AM A BUSY
LITTLE GIRL NOW"

Noor returned to her RAF base near Abingdon, training pilots while
MI5, England's domestic intelligence agency, checked if she had ever
been arrested or joined the "wrong" organizations. On occasional
trips to London, she began researching what she hoped would be her next
book—a collection of folktales from Poland similar to her adaptations of
Buddhism's traditional jataka stories, each about a different incarnation of
the Buddha. Noor's *Twenty Jataka Tales* had been published to good reviews
in England and the United States in 1939. "If I begin collecting the material,"
Noor told a friend about her new project, "I shall have some notes to start
from after the war."

In January, the SOE sent Noor her orders: report on February 8 to Room
238 in the Hotel Victoria. In the same room where she had met Selwyn Jepson, Noor signed the Official Secrets Act, promising not to reveal any code
words, passwords, sketches, plans, models, articles, notes, documents, or
confidential information to an enemy, a foreign power, or anyone not authorized to receive it. If Noor violated these terms, she could be jailed for up
to two years. And she began wearing the uniform of a FANY, the First Aid
Nursing Yeomanry. The SOE used FANY as a cover for women who were
no longer in the branch of the military in which they had actually enlisted.
Noor's schedule was now so full that she only had time to say this in a letter to Vilayat: "I am a busy little girl now, and life is just full of activity and
interest. I feel like I am making up for all the time lost in Abingdon."

The SOE's training lasted two to four months, depending on how soon agents were needed in the field and how much training they required. A crash course in ingenuity and self-preservation, it enabled candidates to learn how to take care of themselves in a totally alien environment. Some of this was practical and simple, like not telling anyone more than what that person needed to know or remembering to relieve oneself in a lavatory before a long surveillance. Some of it was sneaky, like encouraging local women with venereal disease to have sex with Germans as a way to infect the enemy. And much of it was violent, like learning that the best way to kill a sentry with a knife was to approach him from the rear, smother his mouth and nostrils with your left hand, and drag him downward while thrusting your knife firmly into his kidneys. If his belt or jacket blocked the knife, slide it farther forward and shove it into his abdomen. If that failed, slash his hamstrings at the back of his knees. If none of this worked, as one trainer loved to yell at the end of his lectures, "then kick him in the testicles."

Noor didn't want to slash or kick anyone. But her father had taught that if avoiding conflict was impossible, then you do "not turn your back [on it]. Life is a struggle and we must be ready to struggle." Inayat's mysticism wasn't ethereal or gauzy. It was a mysticism of messy hands.

The SOE's training was hand-tailored for every agent. Since Noor wouldn't do any paramilitary work, she wasn't sent to Arisang in Scotland where, on several estates, agents were learning how to destroy bridges, jump off a train moving at forty miles an hour, and break someone's neck. Noor also didn't go to the SOE's school in clandestine printing near Manchester—she wouldn't be printing propaganda when she got to France. Nor did she go to an airfield near Manchester to learn how to parachute. And since Noor wasn't going near the water, she didn't need to know about the one-man submarine the SOE had invented that could attach explosives to German ships from three hundred feet below the surface, or about its twenty-eight-pound "amphibian breathing apparatus"—an early version of a scuba tank.

Instead, Noor had four weeks of basic training at Wanborough Manor, an Elizabethan country house in Surrey that dated to the sixteenth century. Until the SOE came along, Wanborough was posh, reserved, hushed. Now there was a constant racket from pistol practice. (An ad for the manor's sale a few years before the war touted "first-class shooting over the estate." SOE agents continued that tradition though not for the game and sport that had made Wanborough's reputation.) Guards patrolling the estate's 280 acres told curious neighbors that "commandoes" were being trained there. Some local residents had already guessed that whoever was being trained at Wanborough would be sent behind the lines in Europe. But most neighbors ignored the tumult coming from the estate: with thousands of Canadian troops training at other estates in the area, the SOE barely stood out.

Since most agents were men, Wanborough was full of bankers, schoolmasters, journalists, insurance agents, boxers, pimps: men from men's professions. There was an ex-head waiter. A former chef at a golf club. An actor who had starred in musical comedies. Some men drank too much. Trainers watched them carefully to make sure they could hold secrets while they were holding their drinks. Or bought them drinks to find out how susceptible they were to free booze. Over drinks, trainers talked with them about their personal lives or about politics, government, religion, or the progress of the war—conversations designed to test agents' ability to keep their feelings and thoughts to themselves, and see if liquor loosened their tongues.

On many evenings, the recruits gathered in Wanborough's parlor. Often, attractive women joined them for what the SOE called its "honey-trap test." The women's job was to coax secrets out of the men or see if they would boast about how brave they were. If the men took the bait, they were too weak for the SOE. The agency soon dropped the test. Too many truly brave and painstakingly trained young men were succumbing to the tempting women.

Noor's group—six men and four women—arrived on February 16, 1943. About all they had in common was a command of French and an unerring contempt for Nazis. After the war, Vera Atkins, the second in charge of F Section, took this one step further. "Bravery," Atkins said. "Bravery was what they had in common. You might find it in anyone. You just don't know where to look."

One agent in Noor's group had been born in Petrograd a few days before the Russian Revolution broke out. Another, a native of Chicago, was the son of a naturalized American citizen who had immigrated from Germany. A forty-seven-year-old Belgian interior decorator was the oldest member of the group. Besides Noor, the women included Yolande Beekman, who had worked in children's fashion in London before the war. With a Dutch mother, a Swiss/French father, and an education in Paris, London, and Switzerland, Beekman's pedigree was almost as international as Noor's. Though Beekman didn't impress all her trainers—"fit for no more than darning men's socks," said one—another trainer, Jaap Bateman, fell in love with her and they married. Bateman hoped the marriage would prevent his new wife from being sent to France. It didn't.

Then there was Cecily Margot Lefort, a British citizen who had married a wealthy French doctor. Both proficient sailors, Lefort and her husband moored their yacht in a little-known cove along the northern coast of Brittany. Lefort's husband insisted in 1940 that she return to England. While at Wanborough, Lefort heard that the SOE needed a safe beach in France for landing agents and picking up downed airmen. She offered her cove in Brittany, and lent the agent running the operation an antique ring that he could show the caretaker of the villa to prove she was letting him use the inlet. From here, over 102 aviators were smuggled to England in 1943 and 1944.

And, finally, there was Yvonne Cormeau. Her husband was sent home to recuperate after being wounded in France. He was killed when a bomb fell on their house. Yvonne was saved because a bathtub fell upside down on her. Before leaving for Wanborough for her SOE training—her proficiency in French and German appealed to the agency—Yvonne left her two-year-old daughter with nuns at a convent in Oxfordshire.

The routine at Wanborough was rigorous and demanding. After waking up at 6:30 in the morning, the recruits went for a run, usually to the top of Hog's Back, a five-hundred-foot-high ridge about two miles away whose view—"sheer perfection"—had impressed Jane Austen more than a century before. At breakfast, as at all meals at Wanborough, only French was spoken: students' fluency determined if they went on for further training. A French chef prepared all the meals. In the mornings and afternoons students shot pistols, threw hand grenades, read maps, detonated explosives, learned self-defense and leaping from a sturdy branch of a tall tree about fifty yards from the manor house for the initial stages of parachute jumping.

At night, students occasionally marched through the woods or dirt roads with only a compass to guide them. More often, everyone gathered in Wanborough's parlor for games designed to sharpen their perception, like being given a glimpse of a tray littered with a variety of different items, then asked to recite exactly what they had seen. On warm nights, some students played tennis or relaxed around the swimming pool in the manor's garden. Unlike how male agents were enticed with beautiful females, the women weren't tempted with handsome men. Traditions had been bent so the SOE could recruit them, yet the women were still accorded the dignity England liked to believe it had always bestowed upon females.

Surprisingly, Noor wasn't hesitant about firearms. In an essay she wrote while training, she said that the instant when you held your breath and squeezed the trigger and prayed you had done well and you had done it precisely, with no mistakes and no remorse—in that moment— you can discover your true reason for being, one that could guide you and sustain you and provide a thrust and a direction to your life that until then had maybe stubbornly and persistently eluded you. "The act of shooting," Noor wrote, "is significant of focusing one's mind in a certain direction, and thus is symbolical of concentration, and meditation." Noor recalled a guru in the Hindu epic the *Mahabharata* who instructed his students to shoot a bird who was flying above them, then asked what they saw the moment they released their arrows. All except one said they had seen their teacher, and trees, and everything around them. Arjuna, one of the heroes in the epic, said he had only seen the bird's eye. "This," commented Noor, "is the meaning of discipleship," of subjecting ego to guru and teachings and love. It is what occurs when we "only see the purpose toward which one aspires," when we perceive only "pure essence and not the surroundings."

This was the Sufi in Noor speaking, the Sufi whose father had taught her to defend the world when, indeed, defending was needed.

One trainer who first sized up Noor as meek and timorous came to respect her: "A person for whom I have the greatest admiration. Completely self-effacing and unselfish. The last person whose absence was noticed. Extremely modest, even humble and shy. Thought everyone better than herself. Very polite. Takes everything very literally. Is not quick. Studious rather than clever. Extremely conscientious." Others commented that she was "slow to get the hang of map reading," had "no aptitude" for writing reports, and could "not express herself on paper." One instructor called her clumsy three times in a single report. From the outset, Noor's small build—barely one hundred pounds and slightly over five feet tall—had made her an unlikely candidate for the SOE. Yet she carried on, despite the fact that her innate awkwardness was a drawback when dealing with explosives, demolition, or simply running.

Noor wasn't at the top of her class but she was far from the bottom, and the head of Wanborough let her go on to the next level of training. "From a shaky start," wrote Major R. C. V. de Wesselow, Noor had "developed a certain amount of confidence." Her "earnest intentions" outweighed her "timid manner." The major was sure Noor would "come up to scratch when the occasion arises."

At another manor house that the SOE "borrowed"—Grendon Hall in Aylesbury—Noor studied codes that were more sophisticated than those she'd used while training pilots at Edinburgh, and she learned how to operate a portable wireless the SOE had recently invented. The 3 Mark II was a receiver, transmitter, telegraph key, earphones, and a few spare parts crammed into a small suitcase. Its signal strength of twenty watts gave it an impressive range of five hundred miles in good weather. But the radio had two major problems: it weighed thirty pounds, and operators had to find someplace to stretch its seventy-foot antenna. Agents disguised antennas as vines growing on trees or braided them into the rope of a clothesline. When the antenna was fully stretched, agents had to send messages quickly, preferably with a gun ready in case the Germans broke in. And they could not keep written copies of their messages or codes "unless absolutely unavoidable." If the Germans got hold of the messages or codes, they could use them to send fake messages to London. This was the opposite of what Noor had learned as a WAAF. Then she had been instructed to save *everything*—all her codes, all her documents, all the messages she received and sent. This distinction between saving and discarding would haunt Noor while she was on her eventual mission.

The SOE called radio operators "pianists." Operators' dexterity on the telegraph key vaguely resembled a musician's ability to achieve a tone and a cadence that was identifiably theirs—almost an extension of their person-ality. An operator's touch on the key—their "fist," it was called—was as individual as a fingerprint, with dots that were quick as a flash (or not), and dashes that lingered (or not), and hesitations between letters or words that were more or less predictable, agent to agent. Even in the field, agents' fists stayed consistent, regardless of the tensions of the moment. Their fist was their telegraphic DNA: their imprint, their stamp. Experts in England who listened to incoming messages were attuned to the subtleties of an opera-tor's fist. Their job was to confirm that messages had truly come from the agent and not from German impostors who had acquired one of the SOE's radios and the codes that had been assigned to the agent who was supposed to be using it.

The SOE also began giving radio operators "security checks"—intentional mistakes that agents could insert into a message, like misspelling every tenth or twentieth word. If that word was spelled correctly, London knew its operator had been arrested. When the Germans figured out what the British were up to, the SOE gave agents *two* checks: one they could pass on, more or less safely, to the Germans and one that they actually used in their messages to England. The problem was that most agents were usually so rushed (and scared) while coding and transmitting that their messages were full of mistakes. One expert figured that up to twenty percent of the SOE's radio traffic couldn't be decoded because of agents' errors. To some extent, this glut of mistakes made security checks moot.

Sending a message on a Mark II was no different from the radios Noor had used until now: she was still tapping out messages in Morse code. But first—and this was the part that was new to her— she had to convert the message into Playfair, an encryption system Britain had been using since the Second Boer War. Playfair's inventor, Charles Wheatstone, boasted that it was so simple that anyone could get the hang of it. While trying to persuade the British Foreign Office to adopt Playfair in the late nineteenth century, Wheatstone wagered that three out of four boys in a nearby school could master it in fifteen minutes. "That is very possible," responded the under-secretary of the foreign office, "but you could never teach it to attachés." Wheatstone was never given the chance.

Noor had been sending messages in Morse for a year and a half. She knew her way around dots and dashes. And from her start in the RAF, she'd had an advantage over other radio operators. Her fist was well-tempered. As an experienced musician, she had a keen sense of timing and rhythm. That helped her maintain a regular tempo on her key. Noor now had to adjust that pulse and speed to accommodate Playfair, a fairly simple system compared to most codes, but trickier and more time consuming than the straightforward Morse. Playfair was so adaptable that it was widely used: if it was good enough for Lawrence of Arabia during the Great War and for Americans now that they'd entered the Second World War (a message in Playfair would tell the US Navy that John F. Kennedy's PT 109 had been sunk in the South Pacific), then it was good enough for the SOE. Playfair required stripping a message of all spaces and punctuation, then substituting the same letter, usually an x, for letters that were repeated after each other. These adjacent letters were then grouped into pairs. Next, the text—preceded by a pre-chosen word (such as "hello" or "victory")—was inserted into a 5x5 square grid, with one letter in each square of the grid. To confound anyone trying to break the code, letters were occasionally moved to the next square in the grid or to the square immediately below it. Further confusion could be sowed by substituting a letter for one in the opposite horizontal corner from it. Samuel F. B. Morse, who had given his name to the code he invented in 1838, sought clarity and speed. Charles Wheatstone, who invented Playfair sixteen years later, sought mystery and inscrutability.

Noor was warned that the Germans had trucks that could pick up radio signals within twenty square miles. Disguised as ambulances or delivery vans, the trucks patrolled suspicious neighborhoods. Once the Gestapo narrowed its search, it switched off electricity, block by block, as a radio was transmitting. The Germans then focused on a particular block if a signal they were tracking suddenly stopped. Supplementing the trucks were fat men in raincoats who walked around the streets slowly and deliberately, peering intently at their wristwatches as they went. The "watches" were small dials connected to miniature radio detectors strapped to their waists, hence, the fatness. To frustrate the Germans, the SOE's newest radios had six-volt batteries. When the electricity stopped, SOE agents switched to the radio's battery. If they did this fast enough, there was only a brief, barely detectable break in a transmission.

. . .

Midway through Noor's training, one of her teachers expressed relief that she hadn't joined the SOE to recover from a broken heart (Azeem was "old history," an SOE report stated) or to kindle "any romantic ideas of the Mata Hari variety." Still, he wasn't happy with Noor's overly "vivid" imagination and her eagerness "to please everyone and adapt herself to the mood of the company or the tone of the conversation." He even faulted her integrity—a quality that would have been honored in almost any other situation. Noor had a hard time being "two-faced." To her, the trainer noted, this implied "cultivating friendly relations with malice aforethought."

And yet, to be a good agent, Noor had to bend one of her father's cardinal principles: never lie. The heart, Inayat had said, "always tells the truth. . . . True religion is the sea of truth. What begins in deception ends in deception." Could anyone, he asked, with "any sincerity in his nature . . . experience daily the insincerity, falsehood and crudity of human nature and avoid suffering?" Maybe not, but the SOE was based on insincerity and falsehoods. Mendacity was an agent's stock in trade. Agents couldn't be honest or truthful. Without deceit and guile, an agent was a dud. Probably a dead dud.

A few years before, Noor had celebrated what she called the "joy of sacrifice," the thrill of sacrificing her life for a good person or an honorable cause. This was noble and worthwhile. But Noor hadn't anticipated that joy and sacrifice would require distancing herself from what her father had sanctified as "the light in which the true nature of all things manifests"—the truth.

Early in the war, the SOE had barely trained its radio operators in security. The thinking was that they would have one job to do when they got to Europe—set up their radios, remember their codes, and send and receive messages. Other people would protect them. But as the SOE began to lose operators, it realized radio operators were a danger to the rest of their cells. So operators received additional training, this time at Beaulieu, the SOE's "finishing school" deep in the New Forest, an unspoiled stretch of pastures, heathland, and woods. In her letters to Ora, Noor couldn't reveal any details about Beaulieu. Even if she could, they would have upset her mother. So

Noor limited herself to describing her surroundings and the general atmo-sphere at the estate. That calmed Ora, who in the best of circumstances worried about Noor. "Glad to know you are in such a lovely home hid-den away amidst the pines," she wrote. "What a charming atmosphere sur-rounded by Nature's beauty in which to write your pretty stories." But even the smallest details about life at Beaulieu, like Noor's rigorous schedule, alarmed Ora, who wrote, "I hope you retire no later than ten o'clock each night which gives you nine hours of rest."

At Beaulieu, Noor learned how to mix invisible ink. Or if someone she was following went into a café, she was taught to sit with the suspect's back to her and order "short meals and short drinks," anticipating his departure by paying her check straightaway. If she were being followed, she was to take a taxi (but not the first or second that came along), give the driver the wrong address in case someone overheard her, and change her mind when inside the cab. Take the cab to a store, a church, a park—an innocent place—that was in the direction of her destination, but not the destination itself. Leave the cab and try to throw off anyone who was behind her by going into a large store or getting lost in a crowd. Then take another cab, but get out before her final destination and complete the rest of her jour-ney on foot.

To disguise herself, Noor became skilled at rubbing black charcoal pow-der into her hair to darken it, applying a mild adhesive to her ears so they would stick closer to her head; brushing iodine on her teeth to discolor them, and making holes in two small nuts before inserting them into her nostrils to alter the shape of her nose while still breathing freely.

All this was fun, in the way that an Alfred Hitchcock film was fun. But training at Beaulieu could be frightening. Men wearing Gestapo uniforms woke up students in the middle of the night and marched them to a bar-ren room for interrogations. In this gentler version of what the Nazis could do to them, no one was tortured or whipped or had bones broken or was forced to watch someone else's being broken, as a Parisienne suspected of shooting a German was forced to watch the Nazis break every bone in the hands, arms, legs, and feet of a sixteen-year-old she knew. Then she was forced to watch the Nazis shoot her friend in the head. At Beaulieu, stu-dents "only" had to face blinding lights and endure endless questions while pretend "Germans" stomped around in heavy boots, waving steel rods and snarling "*Raus, du schweine!*"

These practice interrogations, Maurice Buckmaster, the head of SOE's F Section, wrote after the war, gave agents "some small idea of the rigours of interrogation. If they survived without cracking, their confidence would be greatly increased and they could face the thought of genuine German interrogation in the knowledge that they had already withstood a similar grilling successfully. . . . If they cracked badly under the strain, it was tolerably sure that we would not send them. A man who caved in when questioned by H.Q. staff . . . would be only too likely to wilt . . . [when facing the Germans]. We derived no pleasure, I need hardly say, from those occasions when our cruel jibes, our reiterated, shouted questions and our implacable persistence broke a man's spirit. But we could console ourselves with the fact that his cracking at a rehearsal might well have saved his life—and others'—by preventing the possibility of his doing the same thing with the enemy. We were not playing a game."

One officer who witnessed Noor's "interrogation" said she gave nothing away. At the same time, she "seemed absolutely terrified." Disoriented by the lights shining on her and the noise and the yelling, and confused when she was ordered to do something as simple as stand on a chair, Noor "was so overwhelmed she nearly lost her voice. As it went on, she became practically inaudible. Sometimes there was only a whisper. When she came out afterwards, she was trembling and quite blanched."

Yet, the SOE continued to train Noor.

One more exercise was on Noor's schedule before she was done: a practice mission that the SOE called a "scheme"—part initiation, part hazing, part test of everything she'd learned during training. For the four days that Noor would be on her own, she couldn't stray from her cover story. "This," she was told, "is the life which you lead and the story which you will tell about that life to account for your presence. Your ostensible present must be consistent with your alleged past." In the city of Bristol, Noor had to recruit contacts, scout around for places where agents could retrieve messages, find flats that would be safe for her wireless, and weather an "interrogation."

Bristol was one of the most heavily bombed cities in England. Almost 1,300 people had already been killed here and over 81,000 homes destroyed. The city was more rubble than habitable. Noor's cover name for her scheme was "Nora Kirkwood." Her cover story was that she had been a secretary for British Airways. Now an author, Nora was in Bristol to research children's impressions of the air raids for a book she was writing and for several scripts for the BBC. She rented a room in a boardinghouse run by a Mrs. Harvey at 30 Richmond Park Road. Noor deemed the boardinghouse "unsatisfactory" and Mrs. Harvey "frightfully conventional and police-minded." Noor remained there anyway: accommodations in Bristol were "scarce" and "landladies as a whole [were] uncongenial." Everywhere she went, she found Mrs. Harveys.

Once settling in, Nora met with a Mrs. Laurie, a government worker who screened the documents of travelers entering or leaving Britain. Nora told her she needed a job. The real intent was clear when Noor dropped a password into her conversation—the SOE was actually using Mrs. Laurie to test agents. The next day, Noor returned to Mrs. Laurie's office with a job application she had filled out. Quietly, she asked Mrs. Laurie to help with communications if the Germans invaded England. She agreed.

In her report, Noor called Mrs. Laurie "responsible, understanding, tactful, security-minded." Mrs. Laurie's report was less glowing about Noor. Mrs. Laurie called Noor uncertain, wary, and unconvincing. The SOE blamed this on Noor's nerves.

For her next assignment—finding someone with whom she could leave or receive messages—Noor chose a porter at Bristol University and a secretary who worked on Whiteladies Road, telling both that she was moving to Bristol and didn't have a place of her own yet. For a dead-letter box—a secure place where agents could drop or retrieve messages—Noor found a crack in the bombed-out steps of a church on Great George Road. For another dead-letter box, she chose a thin space behind the fuse box in a phone booth at the end of Queen's Road. The SOE rated these sites "very suitable."

Noor also had to select places and times to meet sources. For one source—the SOE said this had to be a "gentleman" with "the same social standing" as Noor—Noor chose meetings at the library of the University of Bristol between one and six p.m.; the entrance to Victoria Rooms, a Greek Revival building on the university's campus after eleven p.m.; and the Clifton Lawn Tennis Club on Beaufort Road before noon on a Sunday. For the other source—an "elderly working class woman"—Noor chose St. George's Church at noon on a Sunday; the waiting room for Platform 8 at Temple Meads train station after eleven p.m.; and the waiting room at a bus station in Knowle, a working class neighborhood, between one and six p.m.

Noor still had to find a safe house where she could use her radio and select two "cut-outs"—intermediaries who passed messages between agents but didn't know their identities. Noor looked at two flats at 9/34 Cornwallis Crescent. Rent was eighty pounds a year, and the "kindly" landlady, Mrs. Sutton, lived alone and was "very deaf, most helpful, rather half-witted." The electricity—210 volts—was perfect for a Mark II radio. A flat on the top floor had a window that led onto a balcony—ideal if an agent had to make a quick escape. The other flat—a cottage that was separate from the main house— was better. An agent could escape through either of its two doors (one toward the street, another toward the rear) and could string up a seventy-foot antenna in the garden next to the apartment. For cut-outs, Noor settled on T. A. Leach, the secretary of the Bristol University Union, who was popular with students, and two physicians who shared a medical practice on Clifton Down Road.

Noor's interrogation still remained. The SOE had arranged for local police to arrest her. Noor failed miserably, making what the SOE called "stupid" mistakes and "always volunteer[ing] more information" than necessary. This "could easily have been avoided by a little forethought," her SOE superiors scolded. "She must learn to be more discreet."

Apart from the police interrogation, the SOE considered Noor's "quite a good scheme." Bristol's police chief was less kind. Noor had almost fallen apart during her "interrogation" and, while biking one day through town with her Mark II radio, a policeman asked what she was up to. "I'm training to be an agent," Noor said, offering to show him her radio. "If this girl's an agent," the police chief told the SOE, "I'm Winston Churchill."

And still, the SOE continued to train Noor.

After four months in the SOE, Noor was still getting mixed reviews. Her speed on the wireless had improved, yet one instructor said she was still "a little nervous" on it. "With more experience, she should be able to handle

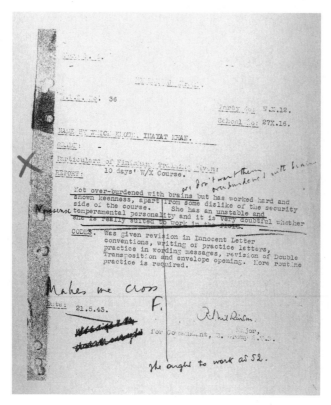

"Not over-burdened with brains" angered Buckmaster.

traffic more confidently." Noor's personality was of more concern. "Highly temperamental," summed up one SOE instructor. "Inclined to give in when confronted with difficulties rather than attempt to overcome. Take care not to give her any task which might set up a mental conflict with her idealism. This might render her unstable." Another officer, Frank Spooner, was more blunt: Noor didn't belong in the SOE. She lacked wit, wile, and cunning. Worst of all, she lacked the mental agility that was indispensable for a good agent—"Not over-burdened with brains. . . . She has an unstable and temperamental personality and it is very doubtful whether she is really suited to work in the field." Spooner's report outraged Maurice Buckmaster. Buckmaster scribbled on Spooner's report, "We don't want them overburdened with brains. Makes me cross." And no one, not even Frank Spooner, wanted to make Buckmaster cross.

. . .

Noor found time to visit friends in London, telling one that after the war she'd like to take up music again and learn Sanskrit so she could read the Hindu *Vedas* in their original language and do "so many things . . . I have been leading such a one-sided existence these last three years. I don't want to get to think there's nothing else in the world but [the] wireless and the war."

As always, Noor wrote a birthday poem to her mother, blending good wishes with nostalgia for a past that, Noor knew, would probably never return. The world had moved on, taking the Khans' innocence with it. So Noor asked her mother,

> *Do you remember when quite small*
> *We peeped behind the garden wall*
> *To watch the birthday man pass by*
> *And pull his bag and ask him why.*
> *We wish and if our dreams come true*
> *And if the ones we have for you*
> *Were in his knapsack tucked away*
> *To give to dearest on this day.*
> *He said that he had loads of love*
> *And joy and presents from above.*

The wall surrounding the garden was across from Fazal Manzil—now in occupied France. The birthday man was Noor's father—now dead. The knapsack was Inayat's trove of love and wisdom. Each was a memory from when the Khan family was together and the world was at peace and everything seemed as if it would forever remain complete, and intact, and one.

Ora couldn't wait for Noor's visits. She missed her so much that once she asked Noor to write to her every two days to set her "mind quite at ease"—"please try, won't you?" To distract her anxious mother, Noor told stories of her romantic life. There was the RAF airman who wanted to marry her.

Noor admired him; she didn't love him. She promised to think more seriously about his offer after the war—*if* they survived. He persisted. Noor, still uncertain, asked Vilayat to meet him. Vilayat liked him: the pilot was refined, sensitive, devoted to Noor. Noor still hesitated, explaining that an Englishman—any Englishman—would find it odd to marry into her family of mystics and seekers. One day, the pilot mentioned that Noor reminded him of a young woman with whom he had broken off a previous engagement. Noor asked for his former fiancée's name and where she lived. On her next leave, Noor visited the young woman and encouraged her to see the airman. Noor was sure he still loved her. Soon afterward, they reconciled and married.

Noor's next story about romance was more serious: she was engaged to an officer who had a British father and a Norwegian mother. Noor had met him a few months before. They had fallen instantly in love and planned to marry before either of them went overseas. But Noor's training with the SOE kept interfering with their plans and they moved the wedding to sometime after the war. Noor never gave anyone in her family the man's name or his address or any way to contact his relatives—perhaps he was just an amorous fantasy. Or maybe Noor deliberately kept that information from her mother, afraid Ora would intrude into this new romance as she had with Noor's with Azeem back in France.

One afternoon, a friend of Noor's named Jean came to visit her. Noor was staying for a few days at her mother's apartment at 4 Taviton Street in Bloomsbury, a few blocks from where Virginia Woolf had written her experimental fictions and where, a few decades before that, Gandhi had studied law at nearby London University. Ora's apartment was small and quiet—large trees across the street insulated her block from the sounds of the city and the thick walls in her almost hundred-year-old building muffled most sounds her neighbors might make.

When Jean arrived at Ora's, Noor made a cup of tea for her mother and her friend, then went to the chemists to buy her mother some aspirin, leaving her friend alone with Ora for the first time. Given what Jean had heard about Ora's preference for privacy, she was surprised at Ora's openness, particularly her concerns that she hadn't raised Noor well.

"She spends so much of her time doing things for me," said Ora. "I'm afraid I've done wrong in allowing myself to depend on her. She has no life for herself." Though both women agreed that Noor was happy, Ora wasn't sure she had been the right mother for someone like Noor: "I don't know why it should have been given me to have such a daughter."

Before Noor returned, Ora needed to get one more thing off her chest: was the military the best place for Noor? With Noor's sensitivities, maybe she could have better helped the nation, and herself, someplace else? "I thought she would meet a rough type of girl there," Ora said, referring to the WAAFs, "and she has always been so carefully brought up." Yet Noor's efforts to tell her mother as little as possible about the SOE, and to make whatever she said sound upbeat and rosy, had worked. Ora was relieved that Noor's current colleagues were, like Jean, genteel and ladylike.

CHAPTER 8

"I HAVE GAINED
MY SUBJECTS' FREEDOM"

The SOE was an experiment. A bold one. No country had ever relied on sabotage on such a scale. And no country, especially one as weak as England during the first years of the war, had relied so much on a force as unproven as the SOE to keep itself alive. As with every experiment, it took a while for the SOE to figure out what it was all about. The rules were being written as the game was underway, and the going at first was slow: in 1941, only one SOE agent was flown into France. In 1942, fifteen were flown in. In 1943—the year Noor was sent to France—102 agents left the SOE's secret airfields in Britain: a forty-seven-year-old woman with impeccable bearing and sharp intelligence; a thirty-year-old who used to work as a chef in Paris; a twenty-seven-year-old former conscientious objector; a twenty-four-year-old who had smuggled spies and POWs across the Spanish border, fled to England, then demanded to return to France with the SOE; and many more, all with varied backgrounds that had prepared them in no way for the sabotage they'd signed up for.

Three years into the occupation, SOE agents were boosting French morale; scaring German soldiers so much that they were sometimes ordered not to go out alone; and inflicting serious damage: a freshly overhauled German mine sweeper loaded with twenty tons of ammunition was sunk hours before it was scheduled to leave port; a single SOE "circuit" was derailing up to twenty trains a week; another circuit destroyed twenty-two transformers and a million gallons of oil in one night at the largest locomotive works in France; a third stopped the water traffic in northeastern France for six weeks by dynamiting the locks on canals.

Hitler was furious. Large yellow posters were plastered all over France—on billboards and public buildings, in town squares and in Paris's Metro:

All traitors working for the British will be shot.
All male relatives of these traitors between the ages of 1 and 65 will be shot.
All female relatives and children will be deported to Germany.

Until around early 1943, the Gestapo had concentrated on homegrown French resistance, and the Abwehr, Germany's military intelligence, had concentrated on the countries that were fighting the Nazis—Germany's external enemies. But with the Abwehr's enthusiasm for Hitler waning, the Fuehrer gave the Gestapo ultimate responsibility to quash the SOE. Lacking any moral restraint, and flush with cash with which it paid informers, the Gestapo was more effective, and more brutal, than the Abwehr. Arrests soared. SOE cells collapsed. Safe houses fell. Some agents bluffed their way through torture, then were killed. Some wouldn't talk, then killed. Some told the Germans everything they knew, then they were killed. The Germans had the same answer for everything.

In other words, Noor was finishing her SOE training just as the SOE was facing the greatest threat since its creation. But it was also the moment when, more than ever, the SOE needed effective, reliable communications. In France, letters were censored, enigmatic conversations that were overheard in restaurants aroused suspicion, phones were bugged, and most telephone exchanges were full of informers and German agents. Within France, the SOE relied on couriers to coordinate attacks. But to communicate with London, radio operators were indispensable. And with the Germans cracking down on the SOE even as the agency was expanding its operations—one agent established sixty cells in central France in eight months—the agency could barely turn out wireless operators fast enough.

So the SOE began taking shortcuts. Noor's training was abbreviated: the time in which she could have learned more sophisticated codes or other ways to blend into occupied France was abbreviated. And she received no parachute training. That meant when she was flown to France, a Lysander would have to land her in a field. Nor was there time for continued doubt about her abilities despite reports that she still suffered from a "lack of ruse." Another report stated that Noor "showed signs of being easily flustered when difficulties cropped up, especially if they were of a technical nature, and it is doubtful if she will ever be able to overcome this."

On top of all this, two agents staying with Noor at Beaulieu wrote about her to Vera Atkins, Maurice Buckmaster's right-hand person in the SOE's French Section. This was unprecedented. Agents did not tattle on other agents. But Noor's colleagues at Beaulieu believed this was urgent: Noor was too despondent, too blue to proceed with her mission. Atkins summoned Noor to London for a talk.

Vera Atkins was a force of nature in the SOE. Arriving as a secretary, she was soon promoted to confidante and top adviser to Maurice Buckmaster. "Atkins" was actually "Rosenberg"—the daughter of a wealthy Jewish shipping magnate, formerly of Romania. On her family's estate in Crasna, Vera had a pony, a sleigh, and her own boat; as she got older, she socialized with diplomats and powerful politicians—the prerogative of a child of affluence. Mounting extremism forced the family to move to London in the late 1930s. Everyone agreed that Atkins, tall, thin, slightly less than pretty, and highly intelligent, was F Section's "most powerful personality." But she wasn't the most popular, not with her penchant for sarcasm and being curt to anyone who got in her way. But she wasn't like this to those she cared about, and she cared about Noor.

Atkins had first met Noor when she reported to the SOE on February 8 at the Hotel Victoria. Atkins greeted all the new agents, and she seemed to know everything about them: their personal history, their family's origins, any special talent that had appealed to the SOE (their facility with language, skill with a gun, expertise on skis or piloting an airplane). Noor's sweetness appealed to Atkins, a quality heightened by Noor's high voice and the innate delicacy and precision with which she did everything. But missions to France didn't require sweetness and innocence, and Atkins's concerns about Noor expanded as reports drifted in from trainers at the SOE's "schools." Noor was "childlike," and she was clumsy, and her devotion to her mother and her close bond with her brother Vilayat could make her overly cautious when she was sent into France. Conceivably, agents who cared more about returning safely to their families split their loyalties between their domestic life and the SOE. The agency didn't have the luxury of dealing with such perilous ambivalence.

The letter about Noor that had come from the two agents at Beaulieu rekindled Atkins's apprehensions about her. She invited Noor to meet her at Manetta's on Clarges Street in Mayfair. Noor got there early. When Atkins arrived, they requested a secluded booth and settled into its well-padded red leather upholstery. Manetta's boasted it had "every modern convenience" which, in 1943, included an air-raid shelter. More to the point for lovers of good food was its *truite meunière*, for which Manetta's was renowned, and its Swiss wine, especially the Montibeux, which a guidebook rated as "rather sweet, but not without character." The floor in Manetta's had been settling for over a century—it was now so uneven that one wag claimed the restaurant was set "on a hill." The floor, the wine, and dancing in the evening to Sam Webber's Orchestra all provided "gaiety," to borrow an adjective from a wartime guidebook. And gaiety was in short supply after four years of war.

There was much for Noor and Atkins to talk about. Atkins hadn't called the meeting to convey *her* doubts about Noor. She didn't have any. She needed to air the doubts others had voiced. Above all, Atkins needed to hear that Noor hadn't lost confidence in herself and to assure Noor that she could back out of her mission gracefully, with no embarrassment and no mark on her record. "There is only one crime," Atkins told her. "To go out there and let your comrades down."

Noor was used to being underestimated. When her dander was up, and it was up now, she could be direct and forthright and no pushover. Noor made it clear to Atkins that she hadn't come this far to be turned back now. She had every intention of going to France, Noor firmly said. The SOE would be proud it sent her and she would surpass everything it expected from her. Together, they would beat the Germans.

Noor was as resolute as the best agents Atkins had sent to France. Her French was impeccable; her knowledge of France—and especially of Paris—commendable; her skill on the wireless incontestable. But when Atkins asked about Noor's gloom that the two agents had mentioned in their recent letter, Noor confessed she was worried, but not about her mission.

Saying goodbye to her mother would be the most painful thing Noor had ever done, partly because Noor would say she was going to Africa, not to a country in Europe occupied by Nazis. For Noor, lying, especially to her mother, was close to a criminal act.

Atkins asked how she could help. Simply bend one of your rules, Noor replied. The SOE's policy was to promptly inform the family when an agent was missing. Noor asked that bad news be passed along to her mother only if there was no doubt she was dead. That would relieve Noor's mother of needless anxiety—Ora had grown progressively weaker and more jittery in the sixteen years since her husband's death. Atkins promised to honor Noor's request. As Noor relaxed, so too did Atkins's concerns about her.

But not totally. In 2000, a journalist asked Atkins if it had been right to send Noor to France. Atkins hesitated. Finally, she answered, "There were questions about Noor, about her suitability. But she wanted very much to go." Atkins's response was annoyingly circular, in effect saying that Noor went to France because she wanted to. Not because the SOE was convinced she was right for the job.

Some of those concerns that Atkins referred to were sent to Leo Marks, the SOE's codemaster, in early June 1943—a few weeks before Noor was supposed to leave England. Late one night, Marks heard a knock on the door of his office. In walked Maurice Buckmaster. The canteen was closed and he was hungry. Marks handed him a sandwich his mother had made for him, then waited to hear what was really on Buckmaster's mind. With his mouth half full, Buckmaster blurted out, "Noor Inayat Khan." Marks had no idea what he was talking about. Noor, Buckmaster explained, had recently finished training at Beaulieu. The school "hadn't had to teach her a damn thing" since she'd been taught code by the Air Force, which was "damn sorry to lose her." She was scheduled to fly to France in ten days, but Frank Spooner, Noor's commanding officer at Beaulieu, had called her "temperamentally unsuitable" and a security risk. "Absolute balls," Buckmaster scoffed. "But what else would you expect from that mob of second-raters?"

Buckmaster railed at Spooner. The "damn busybody" had forwarded his "stinking" report about Noor to higher-ups. Noor's mission hung in the balance. She was already set to meet with Marks for the final briefing he gave every departing agent. Buckmaster wanted Marks to meet with Noor longer than usual so he could evaluate her more intensively. Fine, Marks said, but he needed to know more about her. Noor, said Buckmaster, was "sensitive, somewhat dreamy," and slightly absentminded. Despite the "mystical upbringing" she had received from her father—an "Indian prince"— she could be practical when necessary. She also "could think a damn sight straighter than Spooner." There was one more thing: Buckmaster desperately needed another radio operator in France. Noor was the only one available.

Reaching for his calendar, Marks changed the one hour scheduled for Noor to three. "Any longer than that," he reflected later, "and I might emerge as an Indian mystic."

Marks met Noor at noon on June 7 in a four-bedroom flat in Orchard Court, a short walk from the SOE's headquarters on Baker Street. The flat was another layer in the SOE's security: many recruits were often interviewed there so they wouldn't accidentally see any classified material that was lying around. And many agents leaving got their final briefing here— not at headquarters up the street—so they would have little up-to-date information about the SOE in case the Nazis caught them.

Marks had prepared carefully for the meeting, spending one of his lunch hours on the phone with Frank Spooner, the colonel who had written the devastating report about Noor. Though the SOE was now closely vetting Noor, Spooner wasn't mollified. Noor was a "potty princess." Her father was a "crackpot." "And do you know what the bastard taught her?" Spooner asked Marks. "That the worst sin she could commit was to lie about anything."

Maybe so, but Marks set out to learn as much as he could about Noor. One day he bought a copy of the book Noor had written a few years before— her adaptation of traditional stories about the Buddha's various reincarnations. These "jatakas," or birth tales—there are more than five hundred of them—signal that no creature was too small or too insignificant for Buddha to take on as a reincarnation: a rabbit, a fish, a woodpecker, a deer, a mouse. Anything that exists, the jatakas say, the Buddha was. Anything that will be, the Buddha will be, too. During the Buddha's many lives, he faced the same problems, the same vexations and annoyances as all the rest of us. This is the

Buddha as bodhisattva—an enlightened being who delays entering nirvana so he can relieve the suffering of others. This is the Buddha who appears in our lives and in our history. He is not a spirit, but flesh and body and blood. For Buddhists, jatakas aren't fanciful parables or tall tales. They are real and they are true and they teach that, despite all our setbacks and frustrations and thwartings in life, we can be kind and decent and caring, just like the Buddha. If we choose.

In her book, Noor adapted jatakas for children. Since some jatakas are not for the weak or the fainthearted—ogres kidnap children; a prince offers himself as food so a tiger and her cubs won't starve—Noor had to be careful not to scare her readers. And she couldn't dwell on the Buddhist theology that threaded through every story, subtly or explicitly. Her readers wouldn't understand it. She had to speak to children in the language of children.

After graduating from the Sorbonne in the late 1930s, Noor had had time to collaborate with a family friend on the jatakas. Noor would write the words; her friend would do the illustrations. Now in her forties, Henriette Willebeek Le Mair had been illustrating books since she was fourteen. She and her husband, a wealthy Dutch baron, were among Inayat's first students in the Netherlands. They had known Noor since she was a little girl. Noor visited them often, especially after her father died, sometimes riding one of the Le Mairs' horses on a wide, flat beach near their house, or spending hours in Henriette's studio, gazing at paintings Le Mair had done in Suresnes. Noor was especially drawn to one of Inayat knocking on the door of a sick neighbor's house. "It's beautiful," Noor reflected, "how this painting tells us the whole story."

Le Mair was an ideal partner for Noor on the jataka project. Her art delicately rendered relationships between people and nature, and between people and people (especially mothers and children), and its soft colors and precise lines possessed an almost maternal tone. Le Mair had illustrated dozens of children's books in the United States and Europe, and her work so enchanted A. A. Milne (the future author of *Winnie the Pooh*) that, when he was shown some of Henriette's canvases, he wrote an original story for each. Their eventual collaboration, *A Gallery of Children,* burst with a child's wonder at the closeness of family and the splendor of the most mundane of human acts: folding laundry, reading, feeding birds in the early fall—the everydayness of life that we take for granted, and which Noor's father had taught was as extraordinary as it was quotidian.

Noor and Henriette chose twenty jatakas for their book. Henriette worked on the illustrations at her home in The Hague; Noor rose at six every morning at Fazal Manzil to write in her room, enjoying the quiet before everyone was awake, then amending what she had written with new sentences, scribbled on stray scraps of paper throughout the day. Only Noor knew where they belonged in her text. Noor's quest was common to writers. *Good* writers. The better ones are prone to a nagging fear that their latest revision is only a temporary reprieve until the next brilliant idea comes along. Usually the writers who appreciate the role of stamina in their craft are more experienced, more senior than Noor was while struggling with her jatakas. Her effort reflected a mature diligence. *Twenty Jataka Tales* was published in 1939 in the United States and England. Throughout, Noor's prose was clear, meticulous: simple, but not childlike. In each jataka, there was a decision to put others before self. Often fatal, this was a deliberate end of one's physical being to help other beings.

Leo Marks found the jatakas so compelling that he read them twice. He was stunned by his reaction: "Oh Noor, what the hell are you doing in the SOE?"

Despite all his preparations, Marks wasn't ready when the day came to interview Noor. Marks prided himself on being detached and objective. After one glimpse of the "slender figure" waiting for him in the briefing room, he realized that "the only thing likely to be detached was one (if not both) of my eyeballs. No one had mentioned Noor's extraordinary beauty."

Marks got down to work: Noor had to compose a message of at least 250 letters and encode it for transmission. Without wasting a second, Noor wrote a message in French, spent five minutes coding it, then spent so much time reviewing it that Marks "suspected she'd written another jataka tale and had forgotten that she was supposed to encode it." Gently urging Noor back to the work at hand, Marks said, "London is on the air and would like to receive the message."

"Returning suddenly from a better place," Marks would write later, Noor began coding more rapidly than any agent Marks had tested. Believing she had finished, Noor picked up the paper on which she'd been writing, read it several times, and looked up. Marks told her she'd finished in under ten minutes, a record for one of Marks's briefings.

Picking up Noor's worksheet, Marks found several mistakes. "Fewer than most," he told her, "but those you have made are very inventive." As he went over them with her, line by line, Noor was almost in tears. Trying to lighten the mood, Marks brought up Noor's jataka about a monkey king who had stretched his body across the river to save his subjects from a human king who wanted to kill them so he could enjoy the mangoes in the tree they called their home. Almost all the monkeys crossed the "bridge." One of the last—a mischievous fellow—jumped so hard on the king's back that he broke it. The monkey king died, but not before telling the human monarch that he wasn't pained to leave this world—"I have gained my subjects' freedom"—and that all rulers should govern with love, striving only to bring happiness to their subjects.

"Coded messages have one thing in common with monkeys," Marks told Noor. "If you jump too hard on them, you'll break their backs. That's what you've done to this one. I doubt if Brahmadatta himself"—the human king in Noor's jataka—"could decipher it. I know my monkeys in the code room couldn't."

Noor's eyes grew larger. "You've read my book?"

"Yes. And I greatly enjoyed it. It taught me a lot."

"What?" Noor asked.

Pointing to one of her mistakes, Marks said, "You've told me a lie, Noor—and you've made the code tell a lie."

Marks knew he'd used a loaded word. Noor sprang to her feet.

"*I've what?*" she shouted.

"What else is a mistake but a lie?"

Totaling up Noor's mistakes—"Six lies and one half-truth"—Marks offered a way to improve her accuracy: "Your jataka tales could help you become a very good coder. . . . Every time you encode a message, think of each letter in it as a monkey trying to cross a bridge between Paris and London. If it falls off, it will be caught and shot. . . . If you don't help it by guiding it slowly and methodically, one step at a time, giving it all your thought and all your protection, it will never reach the other side. When there's a truth to pass on, don't let your code tell lies."

Trying again, Noor doubled her previous speed. Then without being asked, she coded another message, running her fingers across it when done. She handed both messages to Marks. They were perfect.

Marks addressed another concern: Noor's security checks. The checks proved that a message was coming from the agent who had been assigned the frequency on which a signal was being transmitted. Checks could take many forms. They could be a group of numbers inserted at a prearranged point in the cipher text. Or an *x* inserted in the code after a certain number of letters. Or a deliberate mistake inserted at predetermined intervals in a message. Whatever the form, they were safeguards against impostors and frauds.

Marks wasn't sure Noor would lie to the Nazis about her checks. "If you tell them what your 'true' check is, they'll pretend that their messages are coming from you. We won't know you've been caught. That's why you must lie to them."

"To stop them from lying to you?" asked Noor.

"Yes."

Noor had a better idea. "Suppose that I refuse to tell them anything at all—no matter how often they ask?" Recalling that the monkey in Noor's jataka had let his back be broken so his subjects could be free, Marks realized that Noor was offering to let her back be broken to avoid telling a lie. But he couldn't rely on her courage, not when she was up against Nazis.

"All you have to do," Marks told Noor, "is remember one thing. Never use a key phrase with eighteen letters in it. . . . If you use eighteen, I'll know you've been caught."

Eighteen was Noor's lucky number. She would have no problem remembering her security check.

By the time they were done, Marks didn't want Noor to go to France— she was too lovely, too ethereal, too out-of-her-league for this sort of danger. As a last-ditch effort to keep her in England, Marks told her to encode three messages by noon of the next day. Each had to have at least two hundred letters *and* Noor's security checks. The following day, Noor gave

Marks *six* messages. They were perfect. Marks reluctantly told Buckmaster that Noor was ready for France.

Noor spent her final leave in London. Visiting Vilayat, she showed him the cyanide pill the SOE had given her. No, he said. Not suicide. That's going too far. Don't go wherever these people want to send you. Noor wouldn't listen to him. After a tearful farewell with her mother, Noor's sister, Claire, walked her to a nearby underground station. Along the way, Noor warned Claire not to listen to the War Office if it asked her to join the FANY (the front the SOE used for female agents). As they descended the steps to the underground, Noor turned to Claire. Leaning over, she whispered, "Be good," and gave her a soft kiss.

Before leaving England, Noor mailed a letter to Claire: "My little sister [who] makes me laugh more than anyone can! . . . Wherever we go in the world and whoever we meet, you never can find a substitute for a brother or sister." And she mailed a letter to Ora: "Please don't worry, girlie when you don't receive any letters. We're not so far apart, after all." The next time they saw each other, Noor promised, she would be "bonny and beautifully well" and Ora would "be young and bonny, too" and they would celebrate with pink champagne.

To Vilayat went Noor's longest letter: "We will meet someday— somewhere—somehow . . . what a day it would be . . . and what a lot we would have to tell each other." For now, Noor imagined Vilayat standing on the deck of his ship in the Navy, "facing the wind with the same frown as in your little MG. . . . Every time the Navy puts up a good show, [I] feel terribly proud of my brother. Duty can pull us apart to different ends of the world, but it only strengthens ties and brother is dearer than ever. We'll carry on, old boy. Wish me luck, the same to you . . . and 'V' [for victory] very soon. Tallyho and all the love from . . . Babuli."

PART THREE
THE POWER AND
THE GLORY

If you will not rise above the things of
this world, they will rise above you.

—HAZRAT INAYAT KHAN

CHAPTER 9

THE BUSINESS IS UNDERWAY

Noor climbed into Frank Rymills's Lysander around 10 p.m. on the night of June 16. She shared the cramped passenger section of the Lysander with Cecily Lefort. They hadn't seen each other since their initial training at Wanborough Manor. After that, they had separated—Noor to learn about her Mark II radio, Lefort to be trained as a courier, messengers who traveled from circuit to circuit, acquiring intelligence about the Germans and passing it on to other cells or to radio operators to transmit to London. Noor was wearing a green oilskin coat. She would need it. Lysanders got chilly. The sky was clear; the moon was bright. That and a map and a compass were the only way Rymills could find his way. Noor was in good hands. In his first ten months ferrying agents to France, Rymills had flown sixty-five operations without a break, twice the usual number. He never lost anyone, going in or coming out.

Rymills was twenty-three years old. Tall, with fair hair and a casual manner, he was flying Lysanders almost accidentally. When he joined the RAF in 1939, he was assigned to massive Halifax bombers—forty feet longer than Lysanders, 34,000 pounds heavier, and with enough room for seven crew members and an arsenal of machine guns, four forward and four aft. Lysanders made Rymills laugh, especially after almost slamming into one while landing his Halifax. From high up in the Halifax, the Lysander looked like a scale model a boy scout had glued together from matchsticks and balsa wood. It moved about as slowly as a model, too, and could barely get out of Rymills's way as he hurtled down the runway.

Soon after that incident, Charles Pickard, the commander of a squadron of Lysanders, spotted Rymills in the crew room. Most likely, Rymills's cocker spaniel, Henry, was with him. Henry accompanied his master wherever he was allowed, and often where he wasn't. Pickard and Rymills relaxed over drinks while Pickard slowly brought their banter around to the real reason for his sudden interest in Rymills. Would he like to fly a *real* plane, one that required a *real* pilot? In a Lysander, you can sense the air currents around you half a mile up and land in a field in the middle of nowhere guided only by two or three men standing on the damp ground, holding a flashlight in one hand and a revolver in the other. And you almost flew on cloth: other than the cockpit and the hot areas around the engine, a Lysander's wooden frame was covered with specially treated cotton. With all that cloth, Lysanders were one step up from flying a laundry basket. Even better was that the pilot's seat was the highest of any plane in the air force. Getting there was like climbing the rigging on a square-rigged ship: you slipped your feet into toeholds here and there, swung from a series of struts, and when you reached the summit, squirmed your way into the pilot's seat. By winding a wheel next to your right leg, you cranked the seat so high that you could actually see over the nose of the engine. That oversized bomber which Rymills was flying, Pickard persisted, was essentially a tube made of steel and aluminum, and its crew, like studious accountants, calculated, every minute, the plane's allowable speed depending on the amount of gas left in its tanks. Flying a Halifax wasn't flying, not Lysander-flying.

Pickard, over six feet tall , was a great leader. When he looked you in the eye, it was difficult to look the other way. Knowing a good argument when he heard one, Rymills signed up with him before the night was up.

An officer who regularly prepared SOE agents for their secret flights said they had "a wonderful sense of humor and cheerfulness." There was no false bravado. "On the contrary, it was real wit that came through. No written word can recapture the warmth of the atmosphere. Whenever . . . a feeling of dread pervaded, someone in the small group would rally the spirits of the others. They had, too, an extraordinary humility and a religious faith which was exemplified in the way they prepared themselves for their missions, such as making their confessions to a priest who would come to the station especially for this purpose."

Pilots of RAF Squadron No. 161. Frank Rymills, far right, flew Noor into France.

The "reception committees" who were waiting in France for these flights had a slightly different reaction. They were not alone. They had comrades. The Nazis had not extinguished freedom. Beyond the occupation was a land of honor and dignity, a land very different from the Nazis' Greater Reich with its stiff-armed salutes to a false and very deluded messiah. The clatter of an approaching Lysander, said a *résistante* who greeted these planes, was "proof in ourselves and in the fraternity of combat . . . Those who haven't known it have missed something. Not the crushing occupation, but this refusal by everyone to be defeated [by] creating the victory. This breathes liberty."

When Rymills landed his Lysander near Angers in France, Noor and Cecily Lefort were handed bicycles. Pedaling about seven miles to the village of Ettriche, they then boarded a train for the two-hundred-mile-long trip to Paris. Lefort continued on to the Rhone Valley to join the circuit to which she had been assigned. Noor remained in Paris to meet the contacts that would take her to a cell being established in Le Mans, about 130 miles southwest of Paris.

Noor was no longer "Noor." To anyone in the SOE or the Resistance, she was "Madeleine." To everyone else—ordinary citizens and the Germans—she was "Jeanne Marie Regnier." Before leaving England, Noor had practiced writing these names so they would flow from her pen as automatically as "Noor" had since she was a little girl.

Some of Jeanne Marie's cover story overlapped with Noor's life. The rest was fiction, a pastiche of real towns and dates and imaginary lineages and careers. Jeanne Marie was born on April 25, 1918 in Blois, a small town along the Loire. Her father, a philosophy professor at Princeton, had been killed fighting in the Great War; her mother, an American, had moved to France in the 1920s. She fled to the United States just before the Nazis arrived. Like Noor, Jeanne Marie had studied child psychology at the Sorbonne. Unlike Noor, she had never written poetry or children's stories, or composed music, or fled to England as Paris was falling. Jeanne Marie was a less interesting version of Noor, shorn of her artistry and imagination. Hopefully, she was so bland a concoction that no one would think twice about her. Her story was the one Noor would tell everyone who was not in the SOE or the Resistance from the moment she landed in France. "Never," the SOE had told Noor, "come out of character. By this we mean not only from the clothes point of view, but from the mental." Noor had to bury herself in Jeanne Marie. Bury herself, and forget herself.

The orders given to "Madeleine"—Noor's other code name—were more exciting than the story invented for Jeanne Marie. As the radio operator for a cell named "Cinema," Madeleine would, if possible, transmit messages to London around 9:05 a.m. on Sundays, 2:10 p.m. on Wednesdays, and 5:10 pm on Fridays. In turn, London would broadcast to Noor every day at 6 a.m. and 1 p.m. (Around the middle of August, this seems to have changed to 3 p.m daily.) When she landed in France, the head of Noor's reception committee would tell her how to find the agent who ran her cell, a Frenchman named Emile-Henri Garry. If Noor had to find Garry on her own, she would proceed to his apartment on the eighth floor of 40 Rue Erlanger in the sixteenth arrondissement of Paris. He had two telephone numbers—AUTeil 62.35 and VAUgiras 86.55. Noor would sever contact with her reception committee as soon as possible. After that, she would try not to contact anyone who was not in her cell.

Noor and Garry had never met. Passwords were crucial for their first encounter. Noor's was "*Je viens de la part de votre ami Antoine pour des nouvelles au sujet de la Societé en Batiment*" ("I come on behalf of your friend, Antoine, for news of the building company"); Garry's reply was "*L'affaire est en cours*" ("The business is underway"). Unless Garry told Noor otherwise, she could only send messages that she got directly from him. If Garry "disappeared," Noor should wait for further instructions from England. And as Noor had been told throughout her SOE training, she had to "be extremely careful with the filing" of her messages.

Noor's orders covered numerous possibilities. If the Germans were looking for her as she was settling into Paris, she might have to stay in her flat for as long as six weeks, opening her door only to visitors who asked, "*Puis je voir Jeanne Marie, la fille d'Ora*" ("Can I see Jeanne Marie, Ora's daughter?"). She would answer with "*Vous voulez dire Babs*" ("You mean Babs"). If she couldn't transmit her address to London, she would mail a postcard to an address in neutral Portugal that the SOE had given her. The postcard would have her current address in Paris. She'd sign it "Madeleine." And if she had to escape to Spain, she should mail a postcard to the address in Portugal that she'd been using, write "*quatre*" and "Madeleine" somewhere in her message, and head for the British consulate in Barcelona. Once there, she'd identify herself as "Inayat Khan."

Noor couldn't contact relatives, friends, teachers—anyone—she had known before the war. She always had to look purposeful ("Do something during the day," the SOE told her. "Don't hang about"). If she ran into old friends and they called her "Noor," she couldn't respond. Noor also had to learn her way around this new Paris. This wasn't the city she had left three years ago. It was rife, according to Maurice Buckmaster, "with denunciations. You never knew if the young lady at the grocer's who smiled so sweetly as she detached the coupon from your ration book was about to inform the security police of her suspicion as soon as your back was turned. A knock on the door in the evening set your heart thumping." German soldiers were everywhere, often wandering around the Arc de Triomphe, pistols on their right hips, daggers sometimes on their left. Military bands played marching tunes on street corners. Posters appealed to Frenchmen to join Hitler's battle against Communism—"If You Want France to Live, Fight in the Waffen-SS

Against Bolshevism." Tobacco rations were cut by a third, taxes on bikes shot up forty percent, and food rations were slashed to the lowest in Europe—175 to 350 grams of bread a day, 50 grams of cheese a week, 120 grams of meat a month. Different Métro stations were closed every week to keep Parisians jumpy and offguard. On the subway itself, Parisians pulled away from Germans who were riding it, lowering their gaze to deprive the occupiers of what a Frenchman called "the joy of an exchange of glances."

Most taxis and cars had disappeared—only Nazis, black marketers, collaborators, and doctors (who were needed in medical emergencies, and there were many of them during the war) could afford gasoline. Everyone else got about on bikes, horse-drawn carts, and gazogenes (charcoal-fired autos that barely hit twenty-four miles an hour in top gear). One *résistante* said the city "now resembled Shanghai, with its thoroughfares thick with bicycles, tandems, and bicycle-taxis whose drivers, like Chinese coolies, got out of the way of the fast, powerful enemy cars with an enigmatic expression on the faces of their drivers." The mostly empty, comparatively quiet streets were disorienting at first. Once you got accustomed to them, you learned to use them: the quiet helped you hear if someone was behind you.

The unrelenting surveillance made everyone claustrophobic, especially the closer you got to Avenue Foch, Europe's most elegant boulevard, which the Nazis had turned into their own personal playground. Adolf Eichmann was planning the Final Solution at 31 Avenue Foch; the German police had their headquarters at 74 Avenue Foch; and the Gestapo had commandeered 19, 82, 84, and 86 Avenue Foch to house its men, torture prisoners, and plot how to tighten its grip on an unexpectedly querulous population. Shuttered mansions were scattered among these citadels of terror: Pierre Wertheimer, a Jewish partner in the prestigious house of Chanel, had abandoned 55 Avenue Foch for New York; Alfred Lindon, a Jewish diamond merchant, had fled 75 Avenue Foch for London. Baron Edmond de Rothschild had deserted 19 Avenue Foch. The broad avenue had been named after Ferdinand Foch, the French marshal who accepted Germany's surrender in 1918. Furious that the Versailles Treaty hadn't weakened Germany so much it could never threaten France again, Foch called it "an armistice for twenty years." He was off by sixty-eight days.

. . .

Before Noor left England, she had asked the SOE to mail a letter to her brother. Vilayat's twenty-seventh birthday was on June 19, two days after Noor landed in France. As close as they were, Noor knew she could not leave the country without making sure he would receive a birthday message from her. "I was so disappointed not to have been with you on your birthday," she wrote. "It is more than your birthday, anyway. . . . [It] is a day we shall never forget and never regret." On June 19 three years earlier, Noor, Vilayat, and their sister and mother had been on an ancient Belgian freighter—decrepit and bug-infested—sailing from Le Verdon to Falmouth. "And now," Noor continued,

> you will be in your uniform—I am longing to see you. When will that
> be, I wonder? I expect you are frightfully busy at present. I feel so awfully
> proud of you. I guess I will be quite conceited, soon.
>   Til we meet again, brother dear. Such a lot of things we shall have to tell
> each other. Good luck to you and tally ho!
>   Babuli

Military strategists like to say their plans are brilliant until they try them out. When Noor scrambled out of Frank Rymills's Lysander, she didn't know that the week before, a member of her reception committee—Henri Déricourt, who for months had been welcoming Lysanders and slipping agents in and out of France—had started feeding information about the SOE to the Germans. Or that in April the Germans had begun whittling away at Prosper, the SOE's largest and most powerful network in France.

Accompanying Noor on the train to Paris was René Clement, a member of the reception committee that had greeted her Lysander. "*Elle avait très peur*," Clement said later. "She was very scared." In Paris, Noor made her way to Emile Garry's flat. Overlooking an intersection at rue Erlanger and rue Molitor, the eighth-floor apartment had clear, unobstructed views in several directions. Garry's cell hadn't had a radio operator since he'd recently formed it. But after taking one look at Noor, he wasn't sure about Noor. Why, as the Germans were picking apart Prosper—the SOE's most effective network in Europe—was he stuck with this slip of a girl? Was this a joke? Or was the SOE so desperate it was sending him anyone who volunteered? Garry didn't know and he didn't have time to find out.

Noor couldn't have come at a worse time. Two months before, the Gestapo had arrested the sisters who had helped a top SOE agent, Frank Suttill, organize Prosper. A few weeks later, the Germans caught a Resistance leader, André Marsac, and two of the SOE's best agents, Peter Churchill and Odette Sansom. All three were tortured. Churchill and Sansom said nothing. Marsac talked, conned by a German officer who pretended he hated Hitler. Marsac's misplaced trust was part of the beginning of the unraveling of Prosper.

Garry and his fiancée gave Noor a good meal. She'd barely eaten for more than a day: the SOE hadn't told her how to use the ration cards it had given her and she didn't think it was wise to ask strangers about them. Garry and his fiancée liked Noor. She was sweet and endearing, open about how much she appreciated their company and how hard it had been to leave her mother. But she looked and acted like she was twenty. Twenty-one, at the most. Too young to be on the run from Nazis in Paris. And too tired on this, her first night in occupied France, to run from anything. Noor had been awake for more than twenty-four hours. She fell asleep in front of them.

On Sunday, June 20, another radio operator, Gilbert Norman, took Noor to an agricultural college twenty miles west of Paris. The Institut Agronomique Paris-Grignon had seven hundred acres of woods and pastures, and pigs and sheep, elaborate greenhouses and an arboretum with several hundred specimens of trees. The institute's main building was an elegant example of Louis XVII architecture, so serene that it was hard to guess its students and faculty had anything on their minds other than boosting the annual yield of crops or improving the health of livestock. This made it an ideal hub for the Resistance and the SOE. The future playwright Samuel Beckett liked visiting the college: its serenity gave him a break from the strain of fighting in the Resistance.

Gilbert Norman, Frank Suttill, and their courier—Andrée Borel, a young Frenchwoman—went to the agricultural college so often that it was virtually their second headquarters. Dinners there with SOE agents or with members of the Resistance were so relaxed that, for a few minutes, it was possible to forget there was a war going on. A lawyer before the war, Suttill was ordinarily cool and level-headed. But he blew up when Noor said upon meeting him at the college that the SOE had instructed her to go to a certain "safe house" in Paris. Suttill sent a blistering message to England, reminding his bosses that he had warned them in February that the apartment was no longer secure and that he had repeated this to their faces in May when he was in London. Had Noor gone to the apartment, Suttill's message continued, her stay there "would have coincided with one of the Gestapo's periodic visits to that flat! I hope I have made myself clear."

On the day Noor met Suttill in Grignon—barely seventy-two hours after arriving in France—she sent her first message to England. Her transmission was short and simple: she was safe. For that, Noor used Gilbert Norman's radio, which he had hidden in a greenhouse at the agricultural college. Noor was still waiting for her radio to be parachuted to her. There had been no room for it in Frank Rymills's Lysander. So when the BBC broadcast this message on June 21—"The commissioner becomes stockbroker"—Alfred Balachowsky, a professor at the college, drove to a nearby farm that was owned by a *résistante*. The message meant two radios and Noor's suitcase were being parachuted to the farm that night. The radios landed safely. The parachute with Noor's suitcase got tangled in a tree and all her clothing spilled onto the lower branches. Balachowsky and the two students who had come with him spent most of the night climbing through the tree, retrieving Noor's garments and throwing them into her suitcase.

Noor spent the next few days at Garry's apartment in Paris or with the Balachowskys in Grignon, practicing her skills on the wireless, enjoying good meals at the college, and telling any students she ran into that she had just enrolled as a student. Everything went smoothly until the next Friday, when Mrs. Balachowsky learned that the Gestapo had arrested Frank Suttill and two of his chief lieutenants in the Prosper network. Mrs. Balachowsky immediately telephoned Noor, who was in Paris. Noor radioed the news to London. On her next trip to Grignon, Noor and Professor Balachowsky buried Gilbert Norman's radio under a bed of lettuce in a vegetable garden, and the professor told Noor to leave immediately: it was only a matter of time before the Gestapo raided the college. In Paris, France Antelme, who ran another SOE cell, moved Noor to a possibly safer safe house at 1 Square Malherbe—the apartment of Germaine Aigrain, who ran a women's fashion shop on the Champs-Elysées. Four blocks from Emile Garry's apartment, Noor could easily go back and forth between the two flats.

A day or two later, Antelme ordered Noor to go back to Grignon to find out how the Balachowskys were doing. When she got there, they told her to stay away. It was too dangerous for Noor to be seen with them and, especially, for them to be seen with her: she was too new to the game of staying ahead of the Gestapo. They worried she would draw attention to herself. And that, in turn, would draw attention to them.

In less than a week, the Balachowkys and others had sized up Noor. She was earnest, innocent, delightful—and a risk. Returning home the first day Noor was visiting them, Professor Balachowsky found a briefcase in his foyer. It was Noor's. Inside was her radio code. Finding Noor, the professor pointed to the briefcase he was carrying. Almost livid, he told her, "I picked this up. Somebody else could have done so, too." Never, Balachowsky ordered, leave anything important unguarded anywhere. The Gestapo had friends everywhere. Even a house as presumably secure as his could be full of informers. Noor couldn't take anything for granted.

In the meantime, Mrs. Balachowsky was noticing that Noor had forgotten some of her French ways while she had been living in England. Some of these were small, like putting milk in her teacup *before* pouring in the tea. The French did the opposite: tea first, then milk. Such details were crucial: they could give Noor away. After Mrs. Balachowsky told Noor to be aware of such minor habits, two female *résistantes* who'd overheard the exchange took Mrs. Balachowsky aside and told her she had been too harsh with Noor. The poor girl would begin thinking she did nothing right. Not at all, said Mrs. Balachowsky. If Noor didn't learn all of this fast, she would be a danger to herself, and to everyone else.

Mrs. Balachowsky wasn't quite as forgiving when Noor handed her a sketch in the Luxembourg Gardens one day. The homemade map showed where a Lysander would make a parachute drop. Never, Mrs. Balachowsky chided, give anything like that to someone on the street. Police were everywhere, watching everything. Noor had to learn to be suspicious: anyone could be a Gestapo agent or a friend of the Gestapo. It didn't matter whether Noor was on the street or the Métro or in a restaurant. "It isn't written on them, you know," Mrs. Balachowsky told Noor firmly. "They look like anybody else. Suppose somebody had come over and asked to see what you gave me?" For the next hour, Mrs. Balachowsky reviewed how careful Noor had to be, stressing that if Noor had something sensitive to give someone, she should do it in the home of someone she trusted. Never on the street.

The SOE had told Noor to be independent and self-sufficient. She wasn't. Every day, someone was complaining that she was sloppy or careless. She had been in France only a few days and already she was forgetting one of the SOE's cardinal rules: security is "a frame of mind attainable through self-discipline and self-training that will make taking precautions a habit." Be "tidy." Be "methodical." Be "inconspicuous." Too many people were devoting too much time to ensure Noor's safety when they needed to attend to their own. France was not a school for beginners. Noor was a beginner in the wrong place at the wrong time.

Though the Balachowskys had told Noor not to visit them, she showed up again on June 30 to tell them she and Emile Garry were going to Le Mans. They would run their cell from there. After Mrs. Balachowsky served Noor tea to help her fight a cold, Noor said she was setting off to visit Garry at his apartment in Paris. Mrs. Balachowsky told Noor to telephone him first to make sure everything was all right.

"Everything was all right there yesterday," Noor said.

"That does not mean everything is all right today," Mrs. Balachowsky bluntly told her. "The situation changes very quickly now and there are arrests every day. Better telephone in case the Gestapo came during the night or morning." Noor began walking toward the phone in the Balachowskys' sitting room. Mrs. Balachowsky stopped her: "Not from here. The call could be traced and they would come here next." Noor should call from a pay phone in Paris. If someone answered whose voice she didn't know, she should say she was a "friend" of Garry's, assume the Germans were occupying the flat, and stay away.

Noor should have been aware of this danger. The SOE's handbook warned, "Always assume that telephone conversations are censored" and the "conversations of suspected people are often recorded automatically. Therefore, use public call-boxes."

When Noor dialed Garry's number back in Paris, the voice she heard wasn't his. As it turned out, Garry and his new bride had left for a brief trip to Le Mans, where they told an innkeeper they were happy honeymooners, one of the few cover stories during the war that was actually true. When they returned to their flat in Paris, their concierge stopped them before they could go upstairs—strange men were in Garry's flat. Neither Garry nor Noor went near the flat again.

On July 1, the day after Mrs. Balachowsky told Noor to stay away from Garry's apartment, German police discovered dynamite and submachine guns on the farm where Noor's transmitter and suitcase had been parachuted. A double agent working for the Germans had probably made the connection between the farm and the agricultural college. Not knowing this, Antelme ordered Noor to return to the college to find out from Mrs. Balachowsky who had called the previous week to warn her about Frank Suttill's arrest. It was good to know who your sources were. As Noor pulled up to the college on her bike, she sensed something was wrong. She was right. About eighty Gestapo agents and French and German police were inside, grilling the college's director, Eugène Vandervynckt. They were sure Vandervynckt had been present for a drop of weapons and that he knew where they were hidden at the institute. Though he belonged to Prosper, Vandervynckt could truthfully deny seeing the drop or knowing anything about the weapons. He had never stepped outside on the night in question. With the Germans focused on Vandervynckt, Noor quietly biked away.

The Germans marched Vandervynckt, several gardeners from the college, and most of its students in groups of ten to a quarry near the campus. Shouting "If you do not talk, another ten will be shot," they blasted a machine gun in the direction of their prisoners. Ten other prisoners were marched in. There were more shots, more threats, and some heroics—when it was his turn to be shot. Vandervynckt shouted "Long live France." Somehow, by the end of the night, everyone was still standing. The Germans had been shooting in the air all this time. The whole exercise was a waste of time. The Germans learned nothing about the weapons.

The next day, Balachowsky was arrested. The Germans had concluded he was part of Prosper. A week later, Vandervynckt was arrested when the Gestapo found eight parachutes and a radio transmitter at the agricultural college. Less than a month after Noor had jumped out of a Lysander near Angers, the Prosper network didn't exist. It had stretched from Le Mans in the West, Sologne in the South, Saint-Quentin in the east, and northward almost to Belgium. Its agents and *résistants,* maybe as many as a thousand, had wrecked factories, toppled power stations, derailed trains. They were the SOE's best agents in northern France. By early July, 1943, only one of the SOE's radio operators was still free: Noor Inayat Khan.

Noor and France Antelme holed up in Germaine Aigrain's apartment on Square Malherbe for fifteen days. When Noor could finally send a message to England that the Prosper network didn't exist anymore, Maurice Buckmaster ordered her home: Paris was "the most dangerous place" in all of France, "swarming with Germans and with security police of every description." A Lysander would bring Noor home. She refused. Leo Marks, the SOE codemaster who had screened Noor just before she left England, knew she wouldn't come back. "Laying low," Marks told a friend, straining toward a pun, "was as close to 'lying' as Noor would ever get."

Noor was one of the few SOE agents left in almost half of France. She told Buckmaster she would stay in Paris for at least a month, rebuilding Prosper maybe not to its former glory, but strong enough that it could hurt the Nazis. When Frank Suttill had flown into France in 1942, his job was similar to what Noor was proposing for herself: he needed to rebuild Autogiro, the SOE's first circuit in France, after the Germans had shattered it. By the time he was done, his new creation—Prosper—was bigger and tougher than Autogiro in its prime. Now it was Noor's turn to start a network from scratch.

Noor's idea didn't thrill Buckmaster. She was too new, still getting her bearings in France. But she was the only radio operator available, and she was already on the ground. When Buckmaster reluctantly agreed with Noor's idea, Colin Gubbins, who ran the entire SOE, noted that Noor had catapulted herself into "the principal and most dangerous post in France."

CHAPTER 10

THE JOY OF SACRIFICE

N oor knew that we pay a price in life: the price we pay to receive life. If paying that price was not, as she said, "the greatest joy, the highest and most inconceivable joy," then it was "not a willing offering." Giving, in fact, was so fundamental to Noor that she called it the "beginning of the inner path," and it was authentic only if we are primed to give our offering before it is expected or asked of us. The best and the truest giving was an anticipation of the other, a clairvoyance that sprang so reflexively from our depths and our marrow that it is shorn of artifice and free of ruse. For that to occur, Noor declared, it had to be genuine. "The heart," she wrote, "must be broken in order for the real to come forth"—an unadorned, unstained emanation of truth, and of love.

Until the middle of June 1943, the price Noor had paid in life—the gifts she had offered the world—were mostly her music and her stories and her love for others. In Paris that summer, hiding and on the run from the Germans, she was beginning to more fully appreciate that the most profound, the most prodigious gift was "expressed in sacrifice." Most sacrifices, she believed, were small, often involving wealth or material possessions. But "the greatest sacrifice," she said, was "the sacrifice of one's self," a sacrifice that "bathes" the world in a "love which purifies and heals the suffering of humanity." This was the "real religion"—faith "conceived through the heart and the mind, not through the mind only. And the question arises, Noor continued: which is the way toward that faith? The answer," she asserted, was through meditation that guides us "toward the real imitation, the imitation of God." To do this, Noor had to reach for a part of herself that she hadn't ignored, but which she had been content to leave fallow during most of her fairly protected life—courage. Her father had called courage "the light of the soul," a beacon that lets "us see life more clearly and gives us the power to surmount our difficulties." Fear, its antonym, erodes "as soon as one touches the barrier which keeps souls apart."

A tonic and an invigorator, courage isn't static. Even Shiva—a god!—understood that courage has to be continually flexed and exercised: as a measure of moral fortitude, it could neither slacken nor relax. Which is why Noor's father had admired the classic image of Shiva standing with a snake around his neck, a sign to Inayat that the Hindu god was "not afraid of keeping the enemy he has conquered curled around him. That is bravery."

Noor's enemies were curled around her in Paris. She had not conquered them. There was a good chance she might not. But with the world more broken than ever, she had to determine the extent of the sacrifice she was willing to make, and the fullness with which she would abide by her father's vision about fate and destiny and purpose. Sacrificing yourself for someone you love and respect, Inayat had said, "raises you higher than the standard of ordinary human beings." Those who do this—"awakened souls," Noor's father had called them—view humanity "without thinking they are German or English or French. They are equally dear to him or her. The awakened soul looks at all, full of forgiveness. . . . To a soul which is wide awake, Judgement Day does not come after death. For that soul, every day is a Judgement Day."

Before the war, Noor had biked everywhere. She still did, though an SOE agent with whom she was close warned her that it was "not advisable" to ride a bike in Paris. Bicyclists, Noor's friend said, were stopped "as many as ten times a day." After Noor biked to the agricultural college in Grignon while the Germans were raiding it, a more experienced agent told her to stop "such child's play." After what he deemed to be her sheer foolishness, the agent refused to work with Noor, even if that meant "doing without radio." That didn't discourage Noor from proceeding with her tasks for the SOE. Several times a week she retrieved from dropboxes messages that she would transmit to England or she met with other agents (museums, parks, homes, and Catholic churches were the best meeting places; hotels, railway stations, and post offices were the worst) or she got advice from her new friends in the Resistance about a safe house where she could move to next.

Noor carried her radio wherever she went. She didn't want the Germans to find it if they raided her flat while she was out. But even when Noor was not in her flat, she was in danger, like the time two soldiers approached her from the other end of a Métro car. There was no way for Noor to get away: the train was between stations.

"What have you got in that case, mademoiselle?" a soldier asked, pointing to her radio.

"A film projector," Noor answered.

The soldier ordered her to open it. Unclasping the locks, Noor raised the lid slightly. As the Germans peered in, she realized they had no idea what they were looking at. "Well, you can see what it is," she snapped at them through her fear. Pointing at several vacuum tubes, she added almost condescendingly, "You can see all the little bulbs."

After more peering and much confusion, the Germans let her pass. "Excuse us, mademoiselle," they apologized. "We thought it was something else."

The SOE must have primed agents with fibs in case the Germans stopped them while they were carrying their radios. When another agent was asked what was in her "suitcase," she calmly said, "A portable X-ray machine." The German didn't dare ask her to open it.

Every day, agents had to be ready for the unexpected or the unknown. In mid-1943, a German soldier standing next to Eliane Plewman on a train asked her for matches for cigatettes. Reaching into her purse, Plewman took a deep breath and handed the German one of the two boxes of matches she was carrying. She didn't know which box contained a message from a *résistant*. Upon reaching her safe house, Plewman rummaged through her purse for the remaining matchbox. As it fell to the floor, a small, twisted piece of paper with the message fell out. She, and the *résistant*, were safe. A few months before, another agent, Odette Sansom, had some time to kill in Marseille before meeting her French contact. As she walked toward the box office, some German soldiers standing outside began laughing. Sansom learned why when she handed a fifty-franc note to the cashier. "This cinema is for German forces only," the woman scolded. "Can't you read the sign?" Walking away, Sansom chided herself. Taught by the SOE to be inconspicuous, she'd had now done precisely the opposite.

By the evening of her encounter with the Germans on the Métro, Noor had begun to think the incident was amusing. "The great thing," she told a friend, "is not to lose one's head if anything like that happens. I knew that only somebody who was familiar with a wireless set would be sure what it was. . . . [One of the soldiers] thought it was a transmitter, but he didn't know what it should look like because he had never seen one. Then he didn't like to expose his ignorance, and my bluff succeeded."

Noor didn't like the SOE's orders not to contact anyone she had known before the war. Largely on her own now, and with few people to turn to, she kept stretching the constraints the SOE had placed on her. Most of these had to do with finding a safe place where she could extend the antenna for her radio. Ideally, Noor would have access to a yard or a tree or a balcony. At Germaine Aigrain's (where she was mostly living now), there was no yard, no tree, and no space for a seventy-foot antenna. Desperate, she began to think of anyone she knew from before the war who might help her. The first person she visited was Henriette Renié, the harp teacher with whom she had studied a few years before. Noor hoped Renié knew of a room she could rent. Noor hadn't seen Renié for nine years, but she knew she could trust her. Renié had always been fond of Noor, and she hated the Germans.

Renié was stunned when she opened her door. Noor was one of the last people she expected to see. "I have come to Paris to establish a wireless post for transmission to England," Noor explained, matter-of-factly.

"But you run the risk of death if you are discovered," Renié responded, trying to talk some sense into her former student.

"I know I risk my life," Noor replied. "That is how most people end who do this work."

Renié knew of no rooms to rent and Noor refused to stay with her: she couldn't risk bringing reprisals on the elderly woman. After giving Renié a farewell kiss, Noor hurriedly told her, "I must go away at once. I am afraid of having been followed, . . . and I would not for the world bring you into any trouble."

Some days, Noor pedaled down the Champs-Elysèes—one of the streets in the city that retained some of its élan from before the war. Noor would zip along next to other cyclists who were proud of their bikes' gleaming handlebars and shiny bells, and glide past cafés full of patrons enjoying their coffees while pretending to ignore the Germans sitting near them. One day, Noor heard someone shout her name. Jamming on her brakes, Noor turned and saw a neighbor from Suresnes—a Madame Salmon. Motioning her toward a side street, Noor explained why she was in Paris. She also pleaded for Madame Salmon to only call her "Jeanne Marie" if they ever met again.

Madame Salmon apologized: "It seemed so natural to see you cycling along that I momentarily forgot you had ever gone away. I called out before I ever suspected why you must be here." Looking carefully at Noor, Madame Salmon offered what she meant as a compliment. "You haven't changed at all."

But Noor *had* changed. She was wearing a light summer frock and sunglasses, and her hair was set in small, tight curls and dyed red. Noor would never have dared to look like this at Fazal Manzil. Such an appearance would have displeased her mother and, especially, her uncles. She looked too casual, too contemporary, too *French*. Madame Salmon was looking at one of Noor's first attempts to use a formula the SOE had given her to dye her hair. To make their hair lighter, agents were told to mix Bitza (a commercial dye available in France), peroxide, and Max Factor hair whitener; to make their hair darker, work charcoal powder into it with a brush and comb and their fingers. These tips were cheap and simple. Sometimes they actually worked. But it took Noor a while to find a color that worked for her: her new red hair clashed with her olive skin.

Like Henriette Renié, Madame Salmon didn't know of a room for Noor. But since she belonged to a Resistance group that printed anti-German propaganda, they agreed to meet occasionally at a café near the Champs-Elysées. As a security measure, neither gave the other her address.

. . .

Noor was dyeing her hair a different color often, sometimes every week. And she kept changing her style of dressing, or used no makeup for a few days, then too much the next three, or lisped for a week, then spoke normally the next. And almost every day she rode her bike through the middle of Paris, the outskirts of Paris, towns and villages not far from Paris, doing everything she could to keep the Germans off her trail as she searched for an ideal spot for her antenna. Sometimes friends in the Resistance drove her to semirural suburbs—Montrouge, Levallois, Noisy-le-Sec—then parked next to a field. Hopping out, Noor threaded her antenna through the trees or through the high grass, then sent messages from the safety of the car.

The *résistants* who helped Noor called her "Rolande." Regardless of her name, their first impression of Noor never changed: "A little dark girl, always carrying her . . . [radio] with her and always out of breath."

Wherever Noor went, she lugged her "suitcase" radio to communicate with London.

Some *résistants* had recently lost two of their radio operators. They asked Noor to send messages to de Gaulle's headquarters in London in exchange for driving her out of Paris so she could transmit her own messages. Noor agreed.

In the middle of July, Noor visited the doctor who had been her physician before the war. Dr. Jourdan didn't know of an apartment or house anywhere in Paris with a yard that suited her, but he offered his country home in Marly-le-Roi, twelve miles west of Paris. It took Noor about an hour and a half to get there from Germaine Aigrain's apartment: she walked a few blocks to the train station, rode the train for roughly forty-five minutes, then walked to the doctor's home. It was worth the trip. Noor could drape her antenna from several trees in the garden in the rear of the house. Approaching the house, she was thrilled that the front was ablaze with pink climbing roses: the maturation of a small rosebush Noor had given the Jourdans when she was a little girl and a reminder of the life she used to have.

Noor was breaking two SOE rules by going there: wireless operators were encouraged to always have someone with them—a lookout for the vans the Germans used to detect outlawed radio signals. And involving the Jourdans, however peripherally, violated the SOE's axiom that "a chain is as strong as its weakest link. Everything depends on the individual. We must have the best for the particular job to be done." Noor didn't know how strong the Jourdans were, and it was wise that she didn't find out.

Noor visited the Jourdans' apartment in Paris more frequently than she went to their country home. The visits were a caesura from reality: Noor had known the Jourdans since she was a child and she could pretend, while visiting them, that it was almost like the good old days. "My only good moments are those I spend here," she told them. "Everywhere else, I feel like I am being watched and must hold myself ready to escape if the Gestapo should knock on the door." Sometimes, Noor brought flowers; once she brought a model airplane that another SOE agent had made. While waiting for the Lysander that would fly him back to England, the bored agent, Noor told the Jourdans, made "these little things so he had something to do."

. . .

Noor couldn't keep wandering around Paris, lugging her thirty-pound radio wherever she went, endangering friends and trusting her intuition to warn her if the Nazis were nearby. Another SOE agent, Julienne Aisner, found a place for Noor—a small, ground-floor apartment at 3 Boulevard Richard Wallace, opposite the Bois de Boulogne and slightly upstream along the Seine from Suresnes. For the first time since Noor had come back to France, she had her own flat and her own phone number: SABlons 80.04. The previous tenant had been eager to sublet: she was moving to the unoccupied zone. She also wanted to sell her furniture. So overnight, Noor had a furnished apartment plus a new cover story, one that no one in London had thought about dreaming up for her: Aisner's boyfriend visited Noor often to make her neighbors think he was her boyfriend. To the other residents of 3 Boulevard Richard Wallace, Noor was just another Parisienne with a handsome beau.

The problem was that most of Noor's new neighbors were Nazis: the SS, the shock troops of the occupation, had taken over almost all the apartments in the building. Every day, Noor brushed by the SS in the hallways of 3 Boulevard Richard Wallace, drawing in her breath as they approached and exhaling with relief as they passed.

The new apartment was too small for Noor to spread out her radio antenna. But one night she had to send a message to London immediately. With no time to go elsewhere, Noor tried to hang the antenna from the branches of a tree in front of her building. Suddenly, she heard someone call "Mademoiselle." Turning around, Noor froze. An SS officer stood a few feet away from her.

"May I help you?" he asked.

"Thank you," answered Noor, as calmly as she could. "I would be glad if you did." Handing the officer the antenna, she retreated a few steps as he stretched it across several branches. Finishing his task, the officer bowed slightly toward Noor, bid her farewell—"At your service, mademoiselle"—and turned into their building. When she recovered, Noor returned to her room to start her transmission to England.

A few weeks later, Noor told this story to Raymonde, one of her best friends in Suresnes. Raymonde was incredulous. "Why did he help you? Why didn't he arrest you?"

Noor shrugged. "He must have thought I was using my radio for entertainment."

"But people aren't allowed to use a wireless," Raymonde said, "not even for entertainment."

"I know," Noor agreed. "I expect some people *do* despite the regulation. He probably thought I wanted it just to listen to music or even to listen to the BBC. He decided to be sporting about it. After all," she added, reasoning this through, "he would never think I could be an agent transmitting to London in such a place and in such a manner."

Raymonde pleaded with Noor to move. "You can't stay there after such a thing. Maybe he is only giving you rope to hang yourself and now he'll watch everything you do."

Noor laughed at Raymonde's idea. She had become comfortable at 3 Boulevard Richard Wallace. Raymonde was perplexed.

Madame Jourdois, the concierge at 3 Boulevard Richard Wallace, also couldn't figure out Noor. Her new tenant didn't have a job; men were always leaving letters or packets for her; and whenever Noor came or went, she was always in a hurry. Friendly though quiet and private, Noor never talked about herself, her family, her past, her present. Yet Madame Jourdois was certain that Noor was a "nice" girl with good morals and no bad habits. Eventually, she realized that the men who were leaving letters for Noor or picking up messages for themselves all had English accents, and that Noor, too, had a distinct accent. At that point, her husband advised, "These people are working for *us*. The best we can do is see nothing, hear nothing, understand nothing—and let them get on with it." And so they did.

On July 20, France Antelme (with whom Noor had briefly shared an apartment in Paris) flew back to London. Constantly on the run since the Prosper circuit had collapsed, he needed a respite. Since Noor had arrived in Paris, Antelme had hovered over her—keeping her safe; finding her new apartments; telling her how to act, talk, dress; giving her money for expenses, a total of 51,000 francs in three installments. To acquire those funds, Noor had been instructed to go to Café Touret at the corner of Rue Pergolese and Rue Weber, ask for the proprietors by name, and respond to their password *"Connaissez vouz les banlieues Parisiennes?"* ("Do you know the suburbs of Paris?") with *"Oui, surtout la banlieue Ouest"* ("Yes, mostly the western suburbs"). Next, she would ask for "Monsieur Charles" and a meeting would be set up for the transfer of monies.

The contacts Noor still had in Paris took her under their wing, guiding her, tutoring her, trying to keep her safe: a radio expert fixed her set when it went on the fritz; a lawyer helped her with logistics; a businessman who the Nazis were convinced was a German sympathizer introduced her to politicians who were planning for the France that would emerge after Liberation. Other than these few, Noor was mostly on her own until Nicolas Bodington arrived on July 23 on one of the SOE's flights, a flight that Noor arranged on her radio and that landed on a large field near the village of Soucelles, about 173 miles southwest of Paris. One of the top officers in the SOE, Bodington had told Maurice Buckmaster he wanted to personally assess the damage from Prosper's collapse. Buckmaster liked the idea. Slightly bald, with a round, cerebral face and the sort of glasses favored by students and writers, Bodington was smart (he had attended Oxford), knew French (he was born in France to a French mother), knew Paris (he had been a Reuters correspondent there before the war), and was as close to an espionage savant as the SOE had: he was working simultaneously for the SOE *and* the British spy agency MI6—two rivals that rarely got along. While it was difficult to find anyone better suited for Bodington's mission, Buckmaster seems to have overlooked something fairly important: Bodington knew all of the SOE's secrets. If he was caught, and if he talked, the SOE was history.

Once in Paris, Bodington realized there wasn't much he could do. "The entire Prosper organization," he told London, "is destroyed . . . no element should be touched. . . . Prosper should be considered dead." But Bodington wanted to use his time in Paris as best he could. For that, he needed a radio operator. The Germans had caught his first choice. His second choice was hiding after the rest of his family had been deported to Germany. That left Noor.

Noor introduced Bodington to Robert Gieules, her radio repairman (and a *résistant*). Gieules agreed to find other *résistants* who could help the SOE organize cells in the northeastern corner of France. Noor also traveled with

Bodington to the estate of Robert Benoist in Auffargis. About fifty miles west of Paris, with barely several hundred residents, Auffargis was one of those French villages that the Germans admired for their beauty and dismissed for their remoteness. They should have paid more attention to it. In France before the war, Robert Benoist was a hero after winning four Grand Prix and the grueling twenty-four-hour race at Le Mans. In 1940, he escaped to England, joined the SOE, and parachuted back into France two years later. The Germans saw him as no more than a famous racing car driver who lived in a large château in a small town. The British saw him as a director of the Bugatti auto company and the owner of a small transport firm who had access to trucks and had the permits to drive them at night. The Resistance used the trucks to move weapons the English parachuted into France.

At Gieules's estate, Bodington and some Resistance leaders laid the groundwork for reviving the SOE in France. When their meeting concluded, Bodington asked Noor to telegraph London that there *would* be a new version of Prosper, with better security, and maybe fewer agents, but as lethal and dangerous as the previous version—exactly what Noor had told Buckmaster she'd do when she refused to fly back to England the month before.

Bodington had two more things to do before going back to London. One was to purchase Chez Tutelle, a café at 28 Rue Saint-André des Arts to use as a contact point for SOE agents, escaped POWs, and downed pilots, or as a dropbox for agents who wanted to get messages out of France or to other agents who were there. With five exits, including one that was underground, and a room that could double as a bedroom in an emergency (presumably for an agent who was on the run), the Tutelle was ideal. Even a possible drawback—it was near the Nazis' headquarters—was an advantage. Some agents preferred working near the enemy, the least-expected place for them. Bodington was strict about how the Tutelle would be used: black-market drinks or cigarettes were off-limits and agents had to leave immediately after arranging flights back to England or leaving or picking up messages.

Bodington stressed that the café couldn't be used as "a general meeting place." And not just anyone could go there and arrange a flight. Agents had to pay for their drinks with a fifty-franc note or something higher. In the top right corner of the note, they'd write in pencil the number of the day of the year that they were there, say "4" if it was January 4 or "365" if it was December 31. In the top right corner of the note that they'd get as change, the bartender would write the first letter of the French word for the day of the week on which they were making this transaction, say "L" for "Lundi" or "J" for "Jeudi," followed by a number corresponding to the number of the current week of the month. Having established their bona fides, the agents would ask for "*le patron*," actually an SOE operative who used the cover name of "Claire" and was at the Tutelle from four to six p.m. every day. During those two hours, Claire would accept or pass on messages or make arrangements for agents to leave France. The café didn't do much business. It did help many spies, agents, and soldiers get out of France.

Bodington's last goal before flying out was to convince Noor to leave. France was too dangerous. If the Gestapo could catch Frank Suttill, the SOE agent—one of its best—who had organized the massive Prosper network, it could catch Noor. She had already exceeded the average life span of a radio operator in France—six weeks. And since arriving she had lived in four safe houses, barely escaped the shootout at the agricultural college in Grignon, forgotten about too many security measures she'd been taught in England, contacted the kind of people—old friends—the SOE had told her she should never go near, dyed her hair so badly it was almost an invitation for the Germans to arrest her, and was living in a building swarming with SS. (Noor wasn't the only agent who disregarded the SOE's rule about contacting old friends. Soon after arriving in France in 1942, Frank Suttill had visited Nicholas Laurent. They had known each other since childhood. Laurent and his wife, Maud, agreed to let Suttill use their home at 75 Boulevard Lannes as the base for some of his operations.)

Noor refused to leave Paris. London still hadn't sent anyone to replace her, and she had barely begun building new cells to fill the vacuum left by Prosper. She was convinced she was needed where she was.

Bodington flew to England on the night of August 16/17. Noor could have been squeezed onto that flight: only three agents, including Bodington, were on it. In a pinch, a Lysander could carry four passengers: one on the floor, two on a seat, and the fourth on a shelf at the rear of the cabin. Three nights after Bodington flew back, ten more agents returned to England on a larger plane—a Hudson—despite the mist and the cattle on the field near Angers where the pilot had landed. Essentially, the SOE was evacuating all its agents from northern France.

Noor was now the only SOE agent in half of France. Before leaving for London the previous month, France Antelme had told a friend, Noor "is really wonderful. In the whole of Paris, she is the only operator working, and all the [SOE's] arrangements . . . have gone through the Poste-Madeleine. Nobody here is able to understand how she keeps up." What Antelme couldn't know was that soon after he left, Noor arranged for all the flights SOE agents would take to England, ensuring their safety while deepening her solitude in the French capital.

CHAPTER 11

"I NEED TREES"

Then one day, the Gestapo raided the Benoist family's estate in Auffargis. They were led there by Maurice Benoist, the younger brother of Robert Benoist, the Resistance leader with whom Nicolas Bodington had recently met. Maurice had been in Robert's shadow before the war. Both brothers raced cars, but Robert was considerably more successful. Maurice remained in his brother's shadow during the war: Robert didn't trust him with secrets or with significant assignments against the Germans. Maurice resented this. A few hours after the Gestapo arrested him in late July, under torture and pressure, Maurice took them to Auffargis. The Gestapo arrested his wife, his father, and all the family's servants. The Germans also found papers and notes lying around that were from some of the radio transmissions Noor had made while she was briefly there with Bodington. They were signed "Madeleine." This was the Gestapo's first inkling that someone named "Madeleine" was sending messages to England. That's all they knew about her—not her appearance or her nationality or if she was good at her job, or if it was even worth making the effort to catch her. All they knew was that the SOE was short on radio operators and that "Madeleine" was probably one of its few agents still communicating with England. Maybe its only one.

The Gestapo had arrived in Paris secretly in 1940, with twenty agents hidden among the tens of thousands of soldiers who were occupying the city. Wearing the uniforms of military police and driving light vehicles with almost no armaments, they drew little attention, not even from other

Germans who were goose-stepping their way into the French capital. The furtiveness was the idea of Heinrich Himmler, Hitler's security maestro and a former chicken farmer. Army generals (some of whom were still delusional about the true nature of their Fuehrer) had complained to Berlin about the Gestapo's behavior in countries the Germans already occupied. Smuggling the Gestapo into France let Himmler establish a beachhead for his own men, and on his terms. By the time the army became aware of Himmler's scheme, it was too late to argue with Berlin.

While training Noor, the SOE had hinted at how the Gestapo operated. If it had been too specific, Noor might have stayed in England. The Gestapo hadn't taken torture much beyond what was practiced during the Inquisition. No sane person would want to go up against that.

And the SOE definitely didn't tell Noor about the Gestapo's version of "honor." Sufi honor rested on compassion, truth, courage, on appreciating the sacredness of life. Anyone who didn't manifest those qualities, Noor's father had said, "lives, but his soul is in the grave." By Inayat's standards, Gestapo agents were already in their graves. Their "honor" relied on power and strength and on their devotion to Hitler, who had announced a few years before that it was time to "defend the strong against the weak," to stop all the "crocodile tears for the poor and the humiliated," and to "free mankind from the yoke of reason which weighs upon it, from so-called conscience and morality."

The Nazis had their honor. Noor had hers. Noor's emanated from service and selflessness: "Harm no one for your own benefit." "Have regard for the feelings of every soul." "Extend your help willingly to those in need." By swearing "My honor is my loyalty"—loyalty to Hitler—the Gestapo's "honor" emanated from fear and hate, barbarism and atavism. These two visions had been colliding since Noor jumped out of a Lysander the previous June.

As summer in Paris wore on, the Nazis tightened their dragnet, looking in every nook and cranny of Paris for the woman they only knew as "Madeleine." Meanwhile, Noor sought out old friends in Suresnes, hoping they could help her with the albatross the SOE had bequeathed her: the seventy-foot antenna for her radio.

. . .

Noor returned to Suresnes on a Thursday morning in early August. Not long after the occupation began, a Swiss writer lamented, "I no longer recognize the face of France." Now, Noor tried to recognize the village where she had grown up. Horses the Germans used for patrols were tied up in front of the mansion of a prosperous wine merchant. Some buildings were camouflaged with dull green paint to deter bombs or strafing from the Allies. Soldiers patrolled the shopping area along the Seine and they patrolled the train station, which was mostly empty, and the hospital, which was mostly full: people didn't stop getting sick during a war. Curtains were drawn at night because of the blackout and the curfew, which was strictly enforced—usually 8 or 9 p.m., depending on the time of the year or if the Germans were uneasy about "local terrorist action," otherwise known as the Resistance.

Resistance here was subtle, persistent. Under a bridge, a father of two hung the French flag. On another bridge, a twenty-year-old pulled down a Nazi flag in the middle of the night. A high-school girl regularly took the train to Paris, filled her schoolbag with copies of *Défense de la France,* the newspaper of one of the larger Resistance groups, and slid them into the mailboxes of her neighbors. Her greatest pleasure was stuffing them into the mailboxes of collaborators. A few miles to the north, Marie-France Geoffroy-Dechaume hid downed Allied pilots in her home in Valmondois. When the coast was clear, she drove the pilots to the coast, where dinghies ferried them to a British ship waiting offshore.

Noor didn't know that the Gestapo and the German army and police were occupying 180 homes and apartments in Suresnes, and that the first neighborhood in Suresnes that the Germans had occupied was hers. She was also unaware that the Germans had taken over Mont Valérien, the sprawling fort near Fazal Manzil where her brothers and sister had played while growing up. For the last two and a half years, Jews, Communists, and Resistance fighters were executed in a copse inside the fort. Down a slight decline from the rest of the fort, the execution pit was surrounded by hillocks. These muffled the executioners' rifles so civilians living nearby weren't disturbed by the killings that were going on almost in their backyards. The executions

When Noor returned to Suresnes, she had no idea Germans were executing resistance fighters in a fort half a mile away.

began in September 1941, when thirteen hostages were killed as reprisal for an attempt to kill a German officer. When more German officers were attacked in December, forty-four prisoners were executed. They were given sauerkraut for their last meal.

The pace soon picked up. A few months before Noor returned to Suresnes, forty-six Frenchmen were executed at Mont Valérien, in revenge for a bomb thrown into a theater in Paris that killed one soldier and injured thirty others. Around the same time, seven Resistance fighters—all eighteen years old—were executed for attacking seventeen German soldiers and derailing trains that were taking soldiers home on leave. The teenagers sang "La Marseillaise" before the Nazis fired. The priest who administered last rites said he had seen many Frenchmen die, "but none so well as these."

By the end of the war, 1,014 Frenchmen would be killed at Mont Valérien. During August 1943, when Noor returned to Suresnes, Joseph Axelrod was executed and Marcel Couillant and Jules Godfrey and Jules Gillian and

Michel Legois and others. The next month: Abel Blanchard and Marcel Ber-
naud and more. And more after that. D-Day was still a year away.

Nor did Noor know that Fazal Manzil, her family's beloved home, had
been turned into the local station for the German police—the SD—and
that twenty-eight officers were living there.

Noor had a tough climb to her old neighborhood. The steep hill from the
village near the Seine winded most people; Noor had the additional burden
of a thirty-pound radio. Turning right onto Rue de la Tuilerie from the
side streets she had walked from the village, Noor turned left in two more
blocks onto Rue de l'Hippodrome. On her right was a long section of the
wall that encircled Fazal Manzil. Her home was on the other side of the wall.
The last time Noor was there was when she squeezed into the jump seat of
Vilayat's MG to escape the Germans.

Noor knocked on the door of the first house on her right—29 Rue de
l'Hippodrome: a narrow white home with shutters; long, tall windows; and
a steeply pitched, tiled roof. The woman who lived there, Madame Pinchon,
had to open the door to learn who her visitor was: the lower two-thirds
of the door was wood; the top third was opaque stained glass with lead
muntins and blue diamonds at the intersections. Noor was disguised that
day with sunglasses, newly dyed blonde hair, and bright makeup. Only when
Noor gave Madame Pinchon a little wave and greeted her former neighbor
with her high, suddenly familiar voice, did Madame Pinchon gasp, "Babuli."

Standing on the front steps, Noor blurted out that she had come as an
agent of the British War Office. As liaison between London and the Resistance, she was helping to prepare for what everyone called "the invasion."

Madame Pinchon gasped again. This time, an unbelieving "You?" came
out. Madame Pinchon invited Noor inside so no one passing by would over-
hear them. Walking toward Madame Pinchon's living room, Noor explained
that she needed a house with a garden where she could spread out her
antenna. Pointing to her radio, Noor almost boastfully said that the device
was disguised as a suitcase. Madame Pinchon immediately rejected Noor's
idea. It was ludicrous: her house was surrounded by Germans—they'd

taken over Fazal Manzil as well as the larger house up the hill at 22 Rue de l'Hippodrome, where Sufis used to stay when visiting Suresnes for classes with Noor's father. Noor pleaded that she could string up her antenna so inconspicuously that no one would see it. Impossible, Madame Pinchon said. Fazal Manzil's windows looked directly over her garden. German soldiers would see Noor.

Noor asked if she could look at her home through one of Madame Pinchon's rear windows. That was not wise, Madame Pinchon said. Soldiers might wonder why Noor was staring at them and come to Madame Pinchon's house and ask about her. Noor implored so achingly to see her home that Madame Pinchon finally agreed. Almost hidden by a curtain, Noor gazed at Fazal Manzil until Madame Pinchon lured her away. Over tea, Noor asked Madame Pinchon to promise that, if Noor was killed, she would never tell her mother that she had come to Suresnes. Noor worried that Ora would conclude that Fazal Manzil had pulled her back to Suresnes and placed her in danger. Noor did not want a shadow cast over the one home her family had truly enjoyed. Madame Pinchon promised.

Relaxing slightly, Noor showed Madame Pinchon the forged identity card the SOE had made for her, almost as though she were showing off after an especially good day at school. Bearing the name of "Jeanne Marie Regnier," it stated she had been born in Bordeaux. That made Noor uneasy. Now that she had an apartment of her own on Boulevard Richard Wallace, she might have to register with the authorities. But she'd never been in Bordeaux, and it might be a good idea for her to visit the city to be prepared if officials asked about it when she registered. In that sense, the apartment was a liability even as it relieved Noor from constantly relying on others. Otherwise, the apartment was good for everything but using her radio. "I need trees," Noor sighed to Madame Pinchon.

With that, Madame Pinchon repeated how foolish Noor had been to come to Suresnes. Everyone here knew her and the town was full of soldiers. Noor didn't mind the soldiers. Most, she said, weren't hostile. She did mind the Gestapo. They were her worst enemy.

If Noor insisted on remaining in Suresnes, Madame Pinchon suggested that she try another neighbor—Madame Prenat, who lived a few doors up the street. That thought had already occurred to Noor. She was old friends with the Prenats. Leaving Madame Pinchon's a few minutes later, Noor first stopped briefly at the home of one of her oldest friends, Geneviève Vanlaere. Unfortunately, Geneviève was away. Continuing up Rue de l'Hippodrome, Noor unknowingly ran a gauntlet of homes—numbers 2, 6, 14, 19, 21, 24, 25, 27—occupied by a total of thirty-three men from the same SD unit that had taken over Fazal Manzil. The unit was also occupying seventeen homes on Rue de la Criola two blocks away.

Noor strolled into the Prenats' home on Rue de l'Hippodrome as though she were still living around the corner, announcing with no fanfare to Madame Prenat that she would like to use their home to send messages to England. Madame Prenat, the only person home at the time, readily agreed. It was as if she had intuited that Noor—the best friend of her daughter, Raymonde, since elementary school—would walk in one day and, instead of gossiping about boys or complaining about schoolwork, say she was working for the British. In this war, anything was possible.

Noor had spent much time at the Prenats when she lived around the corner. She and Raymonde were the same age, in the same classes at school, and had a tradition of baking cakes and writing poems for each other's birthdays. In those days, Raymonde looked to Noor for creativity and Noor looked to Raymonde for courage. While walking home from school one day, several girls were followed by a dubious-looking stranger. The other girls were ready to run away when Raymonde, turning toward the man, asked what he wanted. Stunned at her boldness, he backed away as Noor, wide-eyed at Raymonde's audacity, repeated admiringly, "Oh, Raymonde! Oh, Raymonde!"

That was almost two decades ago. Today Noor was going through the Prenats' home with Raymonde's mother, trying to figure out the best room for her radio. They finally settled on the dining room. Without wasting a moment, Noor asked Madame Prenat for some clothespins so she could string up her antenna in the backyard. Anyone seeing her would think she was setting up a clothesline.

Noor and Madame Prenat next plotted the best way for Noor to sit in the dining room, slowly opening and closing the curtains until they determined the narrowest slit through which Noor could see the front gate of the house while using her radio. Madame Prenat told Noor to run out the back door if she saw anyone coming toward the house and not worry about her radio. Madame Prenat would hide it somewhere. With that, Noor began typing on her telegraph key. Madame Prenat heard the racket in another room. Noor's fist was as noisy as when she had gotten the nickname "Bang Away Lulu" during her training in Scotland. The SOE had never figured how to dampen the sound of the telegraph keys its operators used. Madame Prenat could almost imagine that the soldiers who were housed in half the homes on her long, steep street were hearing every dot and dash that Noor was radioing toward England.

Somehow, Noor found time to write to her mother, sending letters via outgoing Lysanders that were vague and cheerful and gave no sense of where she was or what she was doing there:

> Mother dearest,
>
> If only I could describe to you the lovely spot I am in—simply marvelous. Of course there is such a lot to do that very little time is left to contemplate the scenery. I feel I would like to bring you round here on a holiday tour after the war—who knows?
>
> . . . Mother please don't worry if my letters are long reaching you. You see, it is rather difficult at time being in reach of a post. I think there has been some difficulty about your letters reaching me. I am afraid they have been following me around. I'm so longing to receive them! Cheerio and a big kiss.
>
> Babuli

CHAPTER 12

A DATE AT LE COLISÉE

Raymonde Prenat wasn't home the first time Noor radioed messages from her home on Rue l'Hippodrome. When Noor returned to Suresnes a few days later, the two young women were delighted to be reunited. They talked about old friends and poems and mischief and dreams, and wondered what happened to former schoolmates and neighbors, and what the world would be like after the war. Madame Prenat got into the habit of leaving the dining room when Noor was using her radio. The time for sending and receiving messages was short and fairly well regimented—with several hundred secret radios all over Europe, there would be chaos if operators didn't respect their scheduled transmission time. Raymonde usually stayed while Noor tapped out her messages, impressed with how well Noor had mastered her codes and with the radio itself—how much was squeezed into its tiny space and that messages were actually traveling from the Prenats' dining room in Suresnes to the SOE in London. One Sunday, Noor explained her code to Raymonde and asked if she would like to help her decipher a message. They did that together several times. It was almost like when they were schoolgirls doing their homework together. Raymonde never understood the meaning of the messages or learned who they were intended for. Noor didn't know, either: everyone had a code name and a cover name. Sometimes, Noor had to remind Raymonde of the importance of these names: if the two of them were ever outside together, Raymonde *had* to call Noor "Jeanne Marie." The names were also another wall of security between Noor and whomever a message was intended for. Not only did Noor rarely meet anyone for whom a message was intended, but she left most messages she deciphered in a drop box somewhere. Coupled with cover names and code names, drop boxes were a close-to-foolproof ploy to ensure secrecy and anonymity.

All these precautions made Raymonde worry. Most of the French she knew were miserable under the Germans. Some kept quiet about it. Others grumbled. Too many tried to reach some sort of accommodation with the Germans that was tolerable, maybe honorable. Only Noor, Raymonde's timid, quiet friend whom she had known her entire life, was actually resisting the Nazis. Most of all, Raymonde and her mother were terrified that, if Noor was caught, the Germans would torture her. Noor discussed this frankly with them. She knew she would suffer. The Germans might strap her into an ice-cold bath for an unendurably long time. They might do something worse. No matter what happened, Noor promised she wouldn't reveal anything. The Prenats—aware of the depth of Noor's convictions—believed her. Still, they urged Noor to be more cautious, echoing what Madame Pinchon had said when Noor asked her for help a few doors down on Rue de l'Hippodrome: Noor had been foolish to come to Suresnes. This wasn't the place for her: shopkeepers, families, kids—*everyone*—knew her. Noor agreed. She *was* known. But no one, she was sure, would betray her.

Though Noor felt safe in Suresnes, she was careful when traveling there from Paris, improvising a different route on almost every trip to shake off anyone who might be following her. Sometimes she used tricks the SOE had taught her: Melt into a crowd. Walk up an empty street or enter a café or small store and see if anyone was tracking her or standing nonchalantly outside. Leave an item, like a newspaper, in a store, walk away, then turn around suddenly and go back to retrieve it. Take advantage of street noise, like a car backfiring, as an excuse to look around to see if anyone suspicious was behind her. If Noor was sure she was being followed, she could run to catch a bus or train or enter a big store with many exits that she could use, or just act completely normal—innocently converse with innocent people or go to a movie and hope whoever was following her lost interest in the pursuit.

Noor told Raymonde and her mother about another trick, one that the SOE hadn't taught her: she had a sixth sense that warned her when she was in danger. She had first been aware of this when she biked to the agricultural college in Grignon in June and sensed that something was wrong though everything looked fine from the outside. Since then, she had depended on her intuition to warn her when she was in trouble. Right now, it was telling Noor that Suresnes was as safe a place as she was likely to find near Paris.

On Rue de l'Hippodrome—the Prenats' street—Noor could imagine, if only for a few hours, that there was no war, that the Germans were in Germany, and that the normal rules of friendship and decency still prevailed. She wrote a letter to the Jourdans, the physician and his wife who had let Noor use their country house for her radio. The Jourdans were on vacation in southern France and Noor hoped the "frightful rain" that was drenching Paris wasn't ruining their trip, too. Noor had another reason to write: she didn't want Madame Jourdan to worry about her:

> I am very well . . . and you will find me looking much better on your return. I hope to see Françoise [the Jourdan's daughter] with beautiful cheeks. Give her a kiss for me . . .
>   P.S.—I shall have a lot to tell you when you come back!

One reason Noor was looking better was that Raymonde's mother—worried that Noor wasn't eating well—was making healthy meals for her, lunches and sometimes dinners. As thanks, Noor gave the Prenats two fresh eggs—treasures in France's wartime diet. Three years into the occupation, eggs were luxuries for city dwellers. A friend of Noor's with a house in the country had given them to her. The Prenats took advantage of every opportunity to help Noor. When she left their house one evening during a light drizzle, Raymonde offered her a waterproof cape. Noor declined her gesture, explaining that if she was followed, she would have to throw the cape off so she could run faster. She accepted Raymonde's next offer: a navy-blue scarf. (Raymonde knew that blue was Noor's favorite color.) As Noor wrapped the scarf around her head like a turban, Raymonde realized, almost for the first time, how prominent were Noor's Indian features, and how different she was from the rest of them.

The personal messages Noor sent to England—sometimes transmitted on her radio, sometimes carried by a Lysander—were invariably full of cheer: one handwritten note asked the SOE to send her "a white mac [a waterproof rainjacket]. . . . Thanks a lot! It's grand working with you. The best moments I have had yet." In another note, Noor thanked Vera Atkins for the pin Atkins had given Noor at the cottage at Tangmere as she was about to board the Lysander to France. The brooch had

> *brought me luck. I remember you so often. You cheered me up so sweetly*
> *before I left—lots of things have happened, and I haven't been able to set-*
> *tle down properly. Still my contacts have started to be regular, and I am*
> *awfully happy. The news is marvelous, and I hope we shall soon be celebrat-*
> *ing. In fact, I owe you a date. Lots of love, Yours Nora."*

The "marvelous" news was that the Allies had landed in Sicily.

Yet Atkins could detect that Noor was under a strain, sometimes sending messages far from her scheduled time, even late into the night instead of during her normal mid- and late-afternoon slots. And Noor always seemed to be on the move, often staying at her apartment on Boulevard Richard Wallace though sometimes with friends in the SOE or the Resistance to throw the Gestapo off her trail. It's been estimated that Noor rarely spent more than four consecutive nights in the same place. No agent, Atkins knew, could keep that up for long. Even the best of them needed to briefly forget the war and the Germans and their missions. They also needed a good night's rest. Otherwise, their minds clouded, and they turned neglectful and careless, inaccurate with codes, and too trusting with strangers. Atkins also worried about Noor's increasing disregard for security. In an unciphered, handwritten note that Noor sent to London on a Lysander, she asked for new crystals for her radio and that the time of her radio operations be shifted: "Please arrange everyday scheds also using 3407—if sched is missed possible recontact at 1800 GMT same day—Please send another 3408 crystal." Noor should have coded such information. If the Germans had intercepted her letter—double agents and informers were everywhere—they would have known the exact time and frequencies of her transmissions.

Despite Noor's occasional sloppiness, there was a logic to much of her behavior. The Germans' signal-detecting equipment was good, but not good enough to keep pace with Noor's constant moving around. Compared to the Germans, Noor was a dervish, radioing from the countryside when someone had driven her there; or from friends' apartments in the suburbs, usually Bondy and Neuilly, or from Suresnes where she was surrounded by the Gestapo, or, once, from her flat at 3 Boulevard Wallace, when the SS trooper improbably helped her string up her antenna. Noor was on the run so much that on some nights she could barely keep her eyes open over dinner with Madame Peineau, in whose apartment in Bondy she occasionally stayed. And sometimes she forgot about the security she was supposed to maintain around the clock. When Noor came down for breakfast one morning, Madame Peineau scolded her. Noor had left her notebook on the kitchen table. All her messages, coded and uncoded, were there for anyone to see.

"I didn't think anybody went into the kitchen," Noor explained. "That's why I didn't trouble [to put her messages away]."

"What do you mean," Madame Peineau exploded. "You didn't think anybody went into the kitchen? I go into it."

"*You!*"

"Yes. What reason do you have to suppose that I am to be trusted?"

Noor stammered that a mutual friend, Monsieur Vaudevire, had introduced her to Madame Peineau. "*Ma petite,*" Madame Peineau replied, "you are very wrong. How do you know that Monsieur Vaudevire is not mistaken about me? That I am not a German agent? I might be a double agent. I might appear to Vaudevire and to others as if I am part of their network. Yet I could be a spy for the Germans. How do you know that this is not so? You do not know. And therefore you should regard me with suspicion and conduct yourself, when in my house, as though you were in a place where you might be under observation by the enemy. And in such a place you must never let any of your papers out of your sight for an instant."

Seeing how this troubled Noor, Madame Peineau softened her tone. "*Petite,* there are some things I must tell you. You must never trust *anybody.* It does not matter how good someone's credentials are. Sometimes, it is the person who is closest to you, and whom you least suspect in the entire world, who is the traitor. Even with those with whom you are working intimately, you must never disclose any information beyond the minimum needed to conduct an operation. We have to learn this discipline. Let it be so between us. Believe me, it is better."

. . .

Running around from one end of Paris to the other was the only way Noor could radio London about the precise coordinates for parachuting weapons to the Resistance, and how rebuilding Prosper was going, and which downed Allied pilots were waiting to escape to Spain, and where they could be found: "two American airmen who jumped by parachute on the 16th are to be found at the following address: Henri Kleroux, rue de Pontoise, Bagnolles."

While Noor was letting London know what was happening in France, France's own resistance against the Germans was splintering. Communists, socialists, centrists, Gaullists, trade unionists, and *résistants* were arguing, sometimes literally fighting with each other instead of against the Germans, succumbing to egos and ideologies and contrary visions of the France they hoped they'd lead after the war. On May 27, 1943, sixteen representatives of various groups met in an apartment in the sixth arrondissement of Paris to try to paper over their differences. At the end of the day, they formed the National Council of the Resistance to coordinate everyone's efforts against the Germans. Jean Moulin, a respected socialist, was elected chairman. The Germans arrested him a few weeks later. He committed suicide on July 8.

The council met again in late August, this time in a flat overlooking the Place de l'Alma. Many of the limestone apartment buildings bordering the plaza had long, wrought-iron balconies with clear views of the Eiffel Tower, barely a kilometer away. If there were no war, Place de l'Alma would have been full of happy, relaxed Parisians and tourists with cameras and money. Noor sat in the kitchen of the apartment where the council was meeting, waiting for the results of the discussions in the next room. When she got the word, she radioed de Gaulle's headquarters in London that Georges Bidault had been elected the council's chairman. De Gaulle was pleased: likeable, pragmatic Bidault posed no threat to him. De Gaulle should also have been pleased with Noor. Without her fist on the radio, it could have been days, maybe weeks before he learned of Moulin's successor.

. . .

Despite Vera Atkins's worries about Noor, she couldn't call her back from France. The SOE had already tried. Noor refused. And by now, Maurice Buckmaster, the head of SOE's F Section and Atkins's superior, realized how much he needed Noor where she was. As the SOE's only radio operator in almost half of France, she was indispensable. She was one of the SOE's few good hopes of rebuilding its circuits in France. So on August 15, while other agents were flying back to England, Buckmaster told his staff that if Noor did not "take Message No. 6" at 5:30 that afternoon, "please ensure that it is sent on the first possible occasion as it is extremely urgent. . . . The message is so important that I particularly want it to get to her <u>before</u> 15:00 hours tomorrow August 16th."

Message No. 6 ordered Noor to meet two Canadians in the basement of a café—Le Colisée—at 11 Champs-Elysées. She received the message on time. The Canadians—Frank Pickersgill and John Macalister—had parachuted out of a Halifax bomber into the Loire Valley two months earlier. They may have been one of the best-educated, and best-skilled, teams in the SOE. After earning a master's degree in classics from the University of Toronto and gaining fluency in French, German, Latin, and Greek (his hobby was languages), Pickersgill had traveled through Europe before the war. His three weeks in Germany, he wrote home, were "the most depressing as any I've ever spent. Honestly, this nation is possessed by the devil." He was in Paris when the Nazis invaded France. Arrested as an Allied sympathizer, he was sent to a labor camp in Saint-Denis, a suburb of Paris. Eighteen months later, he sawed his way through the bars of his cell, found his way to the unoccupied zone and then to Lisbon, and finally flew to London, where the SOE recruited him for his command of French and extensive knowledge of the French countryside. Pickersgill's wit, guts, and relaxed manner impressed everyone during training. His only problem was talking in his sleep at night. In English. Not a good habit for a Canadian who would soon be trying to pass as a Frenchman. Pickersgill's nocturnal monologues stopped by the time he finished his training.

Macalister, Pickersgill's radio operator, had studied at Oxford as a

Rhodes Scholar before earning a degree at the Institute of Comparative Law in Paris. Though three armies—the French, British, and Canadian—rejected Macalister (his eyesight was too weak for combat), the SOE snapped him up: his "easy going urbanity" and "logical, uncompromising" mind were ideal for the SOE. On top of that, concluded an internal SOE report, Macalister was "loyal, truthful, honest, good tempered and modest" and saw "the German menace as a canker which calls for drastic surgery." But Macalister's French had deteriorated after moving to England. Anyone talking with him would know he was a foreigner. And though he had studied in France, apparently that's all he did while he was there. "His ignorance of France is complete," warned one of his SOE trainers. Macalister, he said, "expressed surprise to hear that . . . [the French drink] coffee out of a glass in a café! This is only one example of what he does not know. With some people, this would not be an insuperable difficulty. But in his case, it may prove fatal . . ."

None of this mattered: the SOE needed men in France. After parachuting from a Hudson plane in June, Pickersgill and Macalister holed up on an estate near Romorantin for a few days, killing time discussing art, science, literature, philosophy—and disregarding the orders that had presumably been drummed into their heads during training: don't write down anything.

Before leaving England, an officer had briefly shown Pickersgill the instructions for his mission. Pickersgill read them quickly, then handed them back to the officer. At Romorantin, Pickersgill scribbled down what he remembered. Macalister, also worried about his memory, jotted down the security checks and transmission schedules for his radio on the back of his code pad. Pickersgill tucked his notes into a pocket. Macalister crammed his code pad into one of his boots.

Three days after they landed, two SOE agents took Pickersgill and Macalister in their Citroen to a station for a train to Paris. Along the way, soldiers stopped them for a routine security check. Frisking Pickersgill, the Germans found the notes about his mission in his jacket pocket. In Macalister's boots they found his notes about his codes, security checks, and transmission schedules. In the trunk of the Citroen were two of the SOE's latest radios and the crystals for them. As Pickersgill and Macalister were marched toward the Gestapo's headquarters in Dhoizan, only a few blocks away from where the Germans had halted the Citroen, Pierre Culioli, the driver, and Yvonne Rudelatt, his passenger, tried to run for it in their car. Racing down narrow streets at eighty miles an hour, Germans in more powerful Fords caught up with them. Bullets ripped into the Citroen, shredding tires and shattering windows. A bullet tore through Culioli's hat. Another hit Rudelatt in the head and shoulder. Feeling her slump against him, Culioli figured she was dead and that he should kill himself. Speeding up, he rammed the Citroen into the brick wall of an inn. Bouncing off the wall, the car landed in a field. The Gestapo dragged Rudelatt out of the Citroen and took her to a hospital in Blois. They had more fun with Culioli, kicking him with their steel-capped boots and beating him with their revolver butts before hauling him back to headquarters, where he "confessed": the Lysander landing site he described hadn't been used for months, the landing signals he sketched were obsolete, and, while being driven to a prison in Paris a few days later, he pointed to a field the British had never used.

Culioli's bravado lasted until he got to Gestapo headquarters in Paris. A prisoner there convinced him to cooperate with the Germans: "You can tell them everything. They're stronger than we are." Handed paper and pencil, Culioli wrote down the names of the heads of the four circuits that operated under him and where eighty-four containers of arms he'd received from the SOE were hidden. He had the good sense not to believe Josef Goetz, one of the Gestapo's lead interrogators, who told him he'd witnessed "Madeleine" arrive by Lysander the previous June. Goetz liked to make prisoners think he knew more than he actually did, and that they had nothing to lose by confiding in him. It didn't work with Culioli.

Meanwhile, back in London, Buckmaster had no idea the Germans had intercepted on Macalister's radio his message ordering Noor to meet the Canadians at Le Colisée. This was part of the Gestapo's *Funkspiel,* the "radio game" in which the Germans took over a radio without London's knowledge, sometimes forcing radio operators it had caught to send messages to England. If the agents wouldn't cooperate—most didn't—a German would impersonate the agent's fist on the radio's telegraph key. The "game" gave the Gestapo an inside look at what the SOE was up to: arms drops, agent drops, money drops, addresses and phone numbers of safe houses, the code names of agents, fellow travelers, and fellow schemers. It began in 1942 when an SOE agent in Holland, Herbert Lauwers, was caught along with his radio, ciphers, and his coded messages. For eighteen months, London—sure it was getting messages from Lauwers—sent him orders, plans, and secrets. By the time the Gestapo folded its *Funkspiel* in Holland in early 1944, it would arrest five dozen SOE agents and fifty members of the Royal Air Force, and stockpile tens of thousands of pounds of explosives, rifles, pistols, and hand grenades plus seventy-five radio transmitters, 500,000 bullets, ten raincoats, and ten pairs of boots. All that was missing was the ultimate prize of the war: the date and place of D-Day.

While they were *funkspiel*ing in Holland, the Germans acquired their first SOE radio in France, mostly because its operator knew little about codes and less about the radio he'd been given. England realized almost immediately that the Germans controlled their man and this particular "game" quickly fizzled. But by the middle of 1943—when Noor arrived on the scene—the Germans were sending messages on radios attached to at least nine circuits in France. Over the next year, seventeen agents would parachute straight into German hands. One radio alone was a gold mine. Hearing that Lysanders were en route from England, the Gestapo sent "reception committees" to greet the planes, sometimes arresting agents on the spot or following them until the Germans were ready to swoop in and destroy an entire circuit. They also learned about fifteen different parachute drops, each with a massive load of weapons. The Gestapo took real *résistants* with them to the fields where the parachutes landed. The *résistants* loaded the weapons into waiting trucks. They had no idea the drivers were actually Germans wearing civilian clothing.

The purpose of Noor's meeting with the Canadians was to tell them how to contact Maurice Despret, the head of a small group of anti-German industrialists in the town of Hirson who needed help setting up a radio post. The Germans had been trying to nab Despret for weeks and they were especially eager to see what the elusive Madeleine looked like. But now they had to come up with two men to meet Noor at Le Colisée. They chose two SS officers: Karl Horst Holdorf, who had been a steward on a United States shipping line and spoke fluent English with an American accent, and Josef Placke, who would pose as a member of the Resistance.

Le Colisée on the Champs-Elysées: almost-normal life outside—and a trap for Noor inside laid by the two "Canadians."

'When the Germans got to the café, they ignored the mothers who were pushing babies in strollers on the sidewalk, desperate to get out of their hot, cramped apartments, and they walked past the rows of tables and chairs that were arranged on its front terrace. Opening the front door, they stepped under "Le Colisée" etched in tiny lights above the entrance. They had no time for such distractions. They were there for Madeleine. They wanted to know what she looked like, how she dressed, the SOE's condition in France after the Germans had wrecked the Prosper circuit. Pickersgill and Macalister had been told to ask the coatroom attendant for "Mademoiselle Madeleine." Holdorf and Placke did that. When Noor—"Mademoiselle Madeleine" herself—arrived, she asked for "Bertrand," Pickersgill's code name. Talking with Noor in the basement of Le Colisée, the Germans memorized her face and gestures and voice. They didn't want to arrest her. Yet.

After that meeting at Le Colisée, "Madeleine" was no longer a vague, gauzy apparition—a rumor to the Nazis. She was about to become one of the most hunted British agents in France.

.   .   .

No one followed Noor after she met Placke and Holdorf at Le Colisée—an omission that seems bizarre, a failure of basic spycraft in which a prime asset of the enemy would be brought in for questioning or tailed as a lead to other "terrorists," be they *rèsistants* or SOE agents. Precisely why no one followed Noor has been debated for decades. The most likely answer is that, with so much dependent on convincing Noor that the "Canadians" were, indeed, Canadian, the Gestapo didn't want the operation blown before it reaped greater benefits. The Germans were probably confident they could arrest Noor at a more opportune moment.

Having gained Noor's trust, the "Canadians" met Noor the next day at another café—L'Etoile, a ten-block walk for Placke and Holdorf from the Gestapo's headquarters at 84 Avenue Foch. Almost in the shadow of the Arc de Triomphe, L'Etoile was a tribute to a glorious past, with bright red awnings outside, and brass fittings throughout the interior offset by floral patterns etched on fluted glass lampshades.

From L'Etoile, Noor took Placke and Holdorf to a foundry a mile east of the café. And there, at 6 Rue Cambacérès, they met Maurice Despret. Relieved that he finally had a radio at his disposal (not knowing, of course, that the Germans had found it in the trunk of Macalister's Citroen a week before), Despret and the "Canadians" began arranging drops in northern France. In the next ten months, the Gestapo arrested six SOE agents as they parachuted onto fields the Germans had actually selected. The Gestapo also deposited into German banks more than two million francs the SOE had intended for the Resistance, and shipped to Berlin over three hundred containers of weapons and explosives that England had sent over to blow up Nazis. France was becoming quicksand for the SOE.

The Germans should have moved faster against Noor. She kept sending messages to London. One of her transmissions contained what she called "very complete information" about Orly. The airport near Paris was now a Luftwaffe base, with two 1,400-foot-long runways, sixteen hangers, fifteen flak guns, and more than 3,400 workers. Orly was close enough to the coast that planes based there could easily attack the Allies whenever they came ashore on D-Day, which the Germans knew was eventually coming though they knew not where. Using Noor's report, the Allies bombed Orly as D-Day got closer, cratering its runways so badly they were barely usable.

On September 9, a Lysander took a typed memo from Noor to London: a list of factories that were helping the Germans—an airplane factory in northern France, a BMW plant in Lorraine, a Renault plant in Le Mans. Commenting that such collusion violated France's armistice with Germany, Noor asked the SOE to sabotage the factories or have the RAF bomb them. Within weeks, according to a secret SOE report, air raids and sabotage caused factory production to plummet, and the Germans armed factory guards with sporting rifles as additional protection against further sabotage. Meanwhile, the Nazis' transportation system was getting "desperate," and threats from *résistants* were "multiplying" against executives of French firms who were helping Germany.

Noor sent more than military messages to England. In mid-September, a Lysander delivered letters from Noor to her mother and brother. Upbeat and optimistic, Noor was sure the war would end soon, sure her family would be together in a few months, and sure her job was to keep everyone healthy and merry, telling Vilayat that she missed him "terribly," though she realized

now and then that there is a war on. Is your glass of sherry ready? Mine is! Skoll for Italy. [The Allies were fighting their way up the Italian boot]. Fancy not even being able to chat about all the events with you. Brother dear, it sometimes breaks my enthusiasm!

Til we meet again, old boy, and good luck and all the love in the world.

In another letter to Ora, Noor fibbed that "the leave I was hoping for has not come," then reasoned that "maybe if I don't expect it, some day it might come and I just can't imagine a sweeter dream than to be able to pop home and give you a grand surprise!" Falling into her prewar nagging, Noor inquired if Ora had seen her doctor or dentist:

Couldn't you really make a noble effort? Busy as I am, Mother dear, I manage to go to the dentist. Please don't neglect a day longer. You do keep me

*worried. Had I been sooner, Mother, I could have saved two wisdom teeth—
just had to be pulled out. Sheer neglect.*

With that, Noor reverted to her habitual assurances that no one should
fret about her:

> *. . . do be good and not worry about me because I'm fine, Mother dear, and
> looking quite bonnie! And soon I will be right there with you and there will
> be such a lot to talk about, such a lot to celebrate! Isn't the news [about
> Italy] simply grand! It won't take long [to beat the Germans], will it! Do
> send me a wire again soon. A big kiss and just tonnes of love . . .*
>
>   *From little Babu*
>
>   *PS a big goodnight kiss goes over to you every night! Mother dear! It's
> when I miss you most!*

Lysanders also flew Ora's letters to Noor though, of course, Ora had no
idea where they went after she mailed them to a dropbox in London that
the SOE used as a front. Noor memorized parts of these letters, clutching
one so tightly that it seemed to be the next best thing to having her mother
there: an epistolary substitute for home and hearth and England. Receiving
a letter from her mother, she told a friend, was "incredible" and seeing her
handwriting was "wonderful." Also wonderful was the tin of sardines that
came with one of Ora's letters. Noor delayed opening the tin as long as she
could, cherishing the silvery metal link with her mother.

One Sunday in early fall Noor ran into an old friend—Alexis Danan, a
journalist who had worked at *Paris-Soir* before the war. Distraught that inad-
equate medical care had led to the death of his five-year-old son, Danan
made his reputation writing exposés about the mistreatment of children
all over France: in slums, labor camps, and reform schools. "Houses of torture," Danan called them, where children were "morally abandoned" and
spiritually malnourished. In the late 1930s, Danan met Noor, whose poetry
was appearing in *Paris-Soir*. Poetry, Danan perceived, was Noor's "being and
her substance." In addition, her sketches that illustrated her stories were

"dazzling" and her handwriting "danced." Yet Noor was so quiet she was "nearly mute" and "so beautiful that she would have been audacious to stray from the first appearance that she made on everyone."

Noor was then in her mid-twenties. Danan mistook her for a sixteen-year-old—people often assumed she was younger than she was. He was bewildered that she essentially ran her family's household, ensuring that it was clean and orderly, and her mother was happy and well cared for, and her brothers and sister did what they were supposed to. Noor's special devotion to one of her father's lessons—"Above all, respect life"—also impressed the journalist. This, Danan would realize, stirred Noor to "defend life against all who threaten and oppress it"; to read the Bhagavad Gita several times, underlining such passages as "Do good deeds. Action is greater than inaction;" and to rescue Sufism from the pitfalls, common to many spiritualities, of being aloof from the messiness of life. Instead, Noor like her father, wanted to ensure that Sufis remained engaged with life's confusions and conundrums.

Before the war Noor and Danan started planning a children's magazine named *Beautiful Age*. Noor's ambitions were beyond their means: she envisioned a magazine with such high-quality design and writing that, as Danan pointed out, the kind of children who could benefit the most from the magazine couldn't afford it. Noor offered a solution: after reading each issue, rich children who could afford the magazine would give their copies to poor kids. She said no more on the matter. She knew Danan was right.

Danan wasn't writing for *Paris-Soir* now: the grandson of a rabbi, he was mostly in hiding though he helped the Resistance when he could. That Sunday in 1943 Danan spotted Noor on one of the twelve avenues that converge onto Place de l'Étoile. He was riveted by her "wonderful, astonished eyes and her mouth that never smiled." As they walked toward each other, Noor hesitated, signaling with her eyes that they should avoid each other. Pausing in front of a bookshop, Danan gave Noor an opportunity to approach him if she wished. Twice, she came closer. Twice, she retreated. That was the last time he saw her.

After the war, Danan recalled "the little black suitcase" he had seen Noor carry on Avenue Victor Hugo. He was struck by how her radio had transformed her—the "most detached [person] from the world"—into "the secret voice from London to Paris." For Danan on that Sunday near Place de L'Etoile, there were no "Canadians," no "Madeleine," and no Gestapo agents on Noor's tail. There was simply the "softest" person he knew, a soldier of the Gita and the daughter of a mystic.

Psychologically, 1943 was the most exhausting year of the occupation. Paris, on the cusp of hope, remained wrapped in dread and fear. After four years, the Germans' control of the city seemed to be slipping, and everyone knew D-Day was coming. Yet the Nazis were still executing "terrorists" and sending thousands of Jews to "the east," and cramming into three warehouses in Paris the furniture, paintings, stoves, and ashtrays—yes, ashtrays—they'd looted from forty thousand apartments around the city. Allied air raids were routine—sometimes twice a day, sometimes more. Half of the five hundred bombs intended for a factory missed their target, killing three hundred civilians and injuring four hundred. A bomb smashed into a train in the Pont-de-Sèvres Métro station, killing eighty. A Frenchman called the pilot who dropped the bomb that killed seven people at Longchamps race track an "imbecilic criminal." (He failed to mention that, after the bodies of the victims were laid out on the track for an hour and a half, the races resumed and people happily bet for the rest of the afternoon.) In September, bombs fell on the Left Bank, the Gare Montparnasse railway station, the fifteenth and sixteenth arrondissements, and a Renault factory, killing nearly two hundred civilians and seriously injuring another two hundred.

Noor heard the bombs. Everyone did. Quite possibly she saw the damage. Many people did. But Noor had worries beyond the bombs: every second she had to be alert, aware, awake. She was getting less rest than before: running around for drops and messages, not knowing whom to trust and worried that someone might be following her. Plus there was the physical strain of carrying her radio around and setting it up in a different place every other day or so. At any minute, someone might ask her about the contents of her suitcase. That had already happened to her on the Métro when she'd convinced two soldiers it was a film projector. She'd been lucky that day. Her luck might not hold out.

It was not uncommon for Germans to stop anyone on any pretense anywhere and ask where they were going or what they were carrying. If they had a wireless radio, they had to produce a convincing answer fast. Roadblocks had been set up across the country so the Germans could know about almost everything that was moving—cars, trucks, carts, bikes. One *résistant* was stopped in western France. His radio was in a bicycle pannier. If he turned around, he'd arouse suspicion; if he remained in line, he risked arrest. When he got to the front of the line, a German policeman tapped the panniers over the rear wheel.

"What have you got there?" the German asked.

"Milk for my children," the *résistant* said.

"Okay," barked the German. "Move on."

He was lucky; Noor might not be. When one was tired and frazzled and scared, it was harder to think fast. To one friend, Noor looked disheveled—her hair, which she had dyed too often into too many colors, was sometimes red, sometimes black, sometimes her version of blonde though the kindest adjective for it these days was that it was an unflattering yellow. To another friend, Noor looked "hunted." There was a tightening of her face, a loss of weight, a restlessness in her eyes. So she wouldn't have to travel to Suresnes every day to set up her radio antenna, Noor acquired a second flat at 98 Rue de la Faisanderie in the fashionable sixteenth arrondissement. Unlike 3 Boulevard Richard Wallace, her new apartment was large enough to spread out her antenna inside it. And there were no Nazis in the building.

To Pierre Viennot, an electronics company executive who had been working closely with Noor for about a month and a half, she seemed "dead tired." Meeting her one morning in the Saint-Lazare neighborhood, Viennot suggested they go to a café for breakfast. Realizing she was so tired she could barely sit up, he proposed they go to a hotel. Taking her by the arm, "like lovers," he recalled later, "we ask for a room. Behind the locked door, she collapses on the bed while I sit in a chair, reading. Two hours later, she wakes up, splashes water on her face, and we get ready to get on with our work." As they closed the door, Noor suggested he "mess up the bedding to make it seem real. We leave arm in arm, smartly off to do our business."

.   .   .

Viennot was an administrator at SFR. One of France's largest electronics companies, SFR had three thousand employees and several factories, and was famous for its innovative designs in radio transmission towers, radar, and early television equipment. During the war, SFR essentially became a subsidiary of its German equivalent, Telefunken, which supervised the French firm until shortly after D-Day. SFR's profits were consistently higher than similar French companies during the war, serving the Germans well with breakthroughs in radar, electronic tubes, and signal detection that advanced the Nazi cause. Below SFR's top executives were many employees who sabotaged the products that were coming out of their own factories—drilling holes with the wrong diameter, screwing nuts in the wrong way, calibrating lamps for the wrong wattage, writing manuals so whoever relied on them would damage the equipment they were using. Some SFR employees hid Jews in back rooms of the company's factories; others used the same equipment with which they printed labels and handbooks Mondays through Saturdays to create fake identity cards and passports on Sundays. Viennot hated the occupation, but he resisted it gradually and reluctantly: with a wife and three children, he didn't want to get into trouble. That changed when his eighteen-month-old son asked if the giant Nazi flag flying over France's senate was the French flag. Never, Viennot thought to himself, vowing to fight for the honor of France and the honor of his son.

Viennot's Resistance code name was "Louis Deux." He stole German seals to "authenticate" fake papers, helped a gangster kill a German officer, and, on a business trip to Berlin, hid in a double-bottomed briefcase blueprints for equipment the Nazis were using to jam radio signals. In 1943, he provided security for the August meeting of the National Council—a meeting where Noor was waiting in the kitchen to transmit the name of the council's new chairman to London. Pacing back and forth on the corner of Rue de Rennes and Rue du Four, Viennot had two hand grenades in his pocket, ready to throw them if any Gestapo agents showed up.

A friend introduced Noor to Viennot a few weeks before the council met. Her radio was broken. He returned it to her the next day: he had it repaired in his factory. (Noor had already asked London to "kindly send one more Mark II as one is u/s ["unsatisfactory" or "unserviceable"]—am trying to repair."

Viennot admired Noor's "beauty" and "coolness" and how she never let the "little suitcase" out of her sight. Only three years older than Noor, Viennot became her guardian. When Noor needed a place to send messages from the "suitcase," they sometimes used his flat while his wife was away: prudence was best during the occupation, even between spouses who trusted each other. The less Viennot's wife knew about his activities, the better. Or Viennot and Noor would meet at cafés or on benches along Avenue Foch or in the Tuileries so Viennot could tell Noor about equipment the Germans were using to jam Radio London, and about the Germans' floating radio stations in the Atlantic that guided their submarines, and the frequencies the Germans used to communicate with the subs. Noor radioed this information to London.

Occasionally, Noor and Viennot met on the small patio outside a brasserie at 119 Rue Saint-Lazare—Au Roi de la Bière ("At the King of Beer"). Anyone who looked at the exterior of the brasserie had a hard time not smiling. On the second-floor façade was a statue of Gambrinus, the king of beer himself, lifting a stein of his favorite brew. Another sculpture—a large, white stork—perched on the chimney. Underneath all this whimsy, Noor and Viennot spoke of matters serious and grim. All went well until the day Viennot saw his uncle coming their way. His uncle favored Pétain, the puppet the Germans had installed to run the "free" zone in southern France. Not wanting to give his uncle a chance to talk with Noor (whose peculiar Indian/American/French/English accent might have given her away), Viennot impulsively took her by the waist and leaned over as if he was about to kiss her. His uncle walked on as if he'd seen nothing. Stunned by Viennot's "passion," Noor laughed when he explained why he'd grabbed her. When Viennot got home an hour later, his uncle was already there, telling Viennot's wife what he'd witnessed. Elizabeth was furious, and a row ensued. The couple made up when Pierre's uncle left, and Viennot could tell his wife the truth.

In September, Noor told Viennot she was concerned about Robert Gieules, the *résistant* she had asked to introduce the two "Canadians" to the anti-German industrialist in the north who needed a radio operator. Noor hadn't heard from Gieules for a few days. Maybe he'd been arrested? Viennot suggested that Noor ring him up. A vaguely familiar voice answered, claiming he was Gieules and asking Noor to meet him at 10 a.m. the next morning on Avenue Mac-Mahon near the Arc de Triomphe. The voice *was* Gieules's. Noor and Viennot had no idea that two Gestapo agents were sitting across from him, telling him what to say. Or that Gieules was trying to subtly disguise his voice as a way to warn Noor not to fall for the trap the Germans were forcing him to set for her.

Viennot picked up Noor the next day. Dropping her off where she could get a good view of the meeting spot, Viennot drove close to where he saw Gieules sitting on a bench. Two men were standing almost directly behind him; two more were sitting on a bench across the street. Viennot didn't recognize them. He drove slowly down the street, then slowly back up. No one had moved. Sure that the men were Gestapo agents, Viennot called a friend of his—a gangster—from a phone booth. He friend promised to race over with enough men to free Gieules. Joining Noor on her bench, Viennot waited and watched, and finally saw a large Citroen pull up in front of Gieules. It was 10:30 a.m. The men Viennot hadn't recognized threw Gieules into the Citroen, then piled in themselves. Viennot's gangster friends pulled up five minutes too late.

Noor was pale. Viennot led her to a café. Sitting over a cup of coffee, she couldn't accept what she'd seen. "I can't believe he would do it," she kept mumbling. "I never would have believed it was possible." Gieules had been one of Noor's favorites—brave, reliable, trustworthy. "No, no, no," she repeated. "I didn't think he would do it. Not him."

Viennot told Noor he would warn his friends in the Resistance about what happened to Gieules. They needed to tighten their security. But that wouldn't help Noor. If Gieules gave the Gestapo the phone number of Noor's apartment on Avenue Richard Wallace, they could get her address from the phone company. "I have to leave that place in case there's a raid," she insisted. You have to do more than that, Viennot said. Change your entire appearance. Stop wearing your mackintosh. You've been seen in it all over Paris. And dye your hair a different color. And get away from that blue you wear every day.

Noor didn't have money for all of this. Viennot said he'd pay for it.

Viennot also told Noor to stop carrying around her radio and, especially, her notebook. The notebook, he said, was "dangerous." It contained every message between Noor and London since she landed in France in June. "Anyone," said Viennot, "who finds it can work out your codes." Noor argued that she kept it with her in case someone broke into her apartment when she wasn't there. Look, said Viennot, losing his patience, if the Germans catch you, even while you're walking around, they'll catch your notebook. Either burn it, he told her, or give it to him. He'd burn it. She refused. Viennot almost grabbed it from her. He restrained himself.

That afternoon, a friend of Viennot's took Noor shopping and to a hair-dresser. "My hair has been so many different colors since I came to France," Noor told Viennot's friend, "that it's become brittle and looks horrible." No one disagreed with her.

By the time they were done, Viennot almost didn't recognize her. A pleated skirt, broad-brimmed hat, and tailored coat made her fashionable and chic. Her hair, now a light brown, complemented her eyes and her olive skin, and it flowed and rippled after the hair stylist had expertly applied lotions and shampoos. Viennot was pleased Noor had been transmuted into "a real miss of Paris." But he had one problem with Noor's new look. As before, everything she wore was blue.

A day or two later, Noor went back to 3 Boulevard Wallace for the last time. She wanted to pay the balance of her rent. "Madame," she told the concierge, "I won't see you again. I'm going away and I won't come back."

The concierge was sad. She'd grown fond of Noor. Surely Noor would come back for tea from time to time? "No," said Noor, "this place isn't safe for me anymore. I'm afraid the Gestapo will raid my place in a day or two. But don't worry about me. We have twelve other apartments like this one. That makes it difficult for the Gestapo to trace us." As cocky as Noor tried to sound, she knew her time was running out. Noor gave the concierge cash toward her rent, squeezed her hands warmly, and walked away. Twenty-four hours later, the Gestapo raided the apartment.

Noor also visited the Jourdans. Her only regret about abandoning her apartment, Noor told them, was leaving behind a jar of gooseberry jam Madame Jourdan had made for her. The doctor's wife laughed: "I gave it to you a month ago. Why didn't you eat it?" Because, said Noor, when she looked at it, she felt close to her friends. "I know it's still on the windowsill, but I can't get it because the Gestapo will be there."

As kind as Madame Jourdan was toward Noor—she'd always thought of her as a daughter—she was furious with Gieules. She'd liked and trusted him. Now she could never forgive him. He had betrayed his friends and his country. The man was "shameful," "revolting." Noor protested that the Gestapo had probably threatened Gieules's wife or maybe his son. Gieules, Noor guessed, hadn't acted *against* her. He had acted *for* his son. "If we meet after the war," Noor persisted, "I won't hold it against him."

Madame Jourdan lashed out at Gieules again. Noor stopped her: "No! We must not say that. We don't know all that happened. We must not judge." Whenever Gieules came up after that, Noor insisted: "We must not judge."

After all that had happened, Noor remained her father's daughter. A Sufi, Inayat had taught, only judges himself. Never others. "We cannot judge the action of another until we ourselves are selfless. Only then will justice come to us." We can only say, "*I* must not do this." When we judge another person, "we may easily be wrong."

Even as the Germans were bearing down on her, Noor did not want to be wrong. A few years before, she had written that one of the paths to joy required us not to judge others and to always forgive them. One person's "strife may be his blessing and the easy life of the other may be his punishment . . . The life of giving," Noor concluded, and the life of forgiving "is certainly the life most void of pain."

Noor would soon put that conviction to the test.

CHAPTER 13

"WHEN I SEE YOU AGAIN, IT WILL BE AFTER THE WAR"

Occasionally, Noor went back to Suresnes to visit Madame Prenat and her daughter Raymonde. Before, these visits had almost been relaxing—a respite from the frenzy of Paris and Noor's constant running around. Noor now brought Paris with her, especially her fear that Robert Gieules would tell the Germans everything he knew about her. Noor knew it would be futile for him to try to bargain with the Gestapo. "It's so silly, and quite useless," she told Madame Prenat. "In the end, they will shoot you just the same." Bursting into tears, Noor murmured, "I wish I were with my mother."

Madame Prenat asked Noor to stay with her until things calmed down. Noor refused. She had work to do and she was certain that one member of the Resistance—Pierre Viennot—would do everything he could to help keep her safe. "I know I can rely on him in any circumstance," Noor declared. "I would trust him with my life."

She might need to. A few days later, in the Trocadéro, Noor was sure that one, maybe two men were following her. Walking slowly, then fast, then in circles, then straight ahead, Noor shook off possible tails. London must have known the danger Noor was facing. A message she got from Britain ended with an adieu that she had never seen before: "May God keep you." The farewell touched Noor. "I didn't think they ever said things like that," she told a friend. "I thought I was just a cipher in London. We have to be quite impersonal in our work. We can't let our feelings interfere. It wouldn't do."

Pierre Viennot wanted Noor to leave Paris. Remaining there endangered not only her, but others as well. "You must go," Viennot insisted. "The Gestapo knows you and will follow you to all the people you meet until they have every one of us." Anyway, the SOE in France was still so disorganized and so weak that there wasn't enough work to warrant Noor staying there.

Viennot arranged for Noor to find shelter on a farm in Normandy. At least that would keep her out of Paris. Escorting her to the Gare Saint-Lazare, Viennot bought a ticket for her, made sure she had a seat on a carriage, and waited for her train to leave the station. He wasn't pleased to see her back in Paris two days later. Noor had felt useless on the farm. She hadn't come to France to sit around. She and Viennot agreed it might be best if she returned to England. Maybe the SOE would give her another assignment someplace else.

Noor didn't argue with Viennot about this and she appeared content when telling friends in Paris she was leaving. For four months, she had passed valuable information between Paris and London and had outlived almost every radio operator in France. She had done her job, and done it well, and had little reason to balk or carp or ask for more time.

Noor could get to England several ways. On a Lysander: they were still flying over the channel when there was a full moon. Over the Pyrenees: agents were constantly smuggled across the mountains into Spain. On a boat: almost every week, small craft were ferrying agents to submarines or larger boats that were waiting offshore. With a friend who was in the Resistance, Noor went to a café near Porte Maillot to arrange getting back to England. Approaching the café, they felt queasy. Afraid they were walking into a trap, they split up to confuse anyone who might be following them. Using different Métro stations, they each got home safely.

Noor was reluctant to use her radio to arrange a flight to Britain. Given how determined the Germans were to catch her, several of their tracking devices were probably ready to detect any transmissions she might send. But taking the risk—she had little choice—Noor used her set to "book" a seat on a Lysander. On her final visit to Suresnes, she told the Prenats, "I am going to England. When I see you again, it will be after the war." Noor and Raymonde warmly embraced. Noor gave her a gold compact case as a farewell present.

. . .

Noor's last days in Paris were a whirlwind. She telephoned Pierre Viennot in his office on October 9, arranging to meet him at the Pont de Levallois-Bécon Métro station. The station wasn't far from Viennot's office. He walked there. He didn't see Noor. The next day, a Sunday, Noor did not appear at Madame Peineau's flat in Bondy for a radio transmission that Noor had scheduled. Madame Peineau stayed up late, waiting for a phone call from Noor that never came. Noor called on Monday, mostly to inquire if one of her friends in the Resistance, Charles Vaudevire, was "well"—code for asking if he'd been arrested. As far as she knew, Madame Peineau replied, Vaudevire was "healthy." Relieved, Noor hung up.

On Tuesday, Noor visited the Jourdans, telling them she'd be back in two days "if I have not been arrested by then"—and that she would stay in their apartment until a friend drove her to the country for her flight to England. Seeing how ragged and nervous Noor was, Madame Jourdan didn't want her to leave. "There's a job I have to do first," Noor insisted. "I can't come back before Thursday."

The next day, Noor called Pierre Viennot's secretary. Twenty-five years old, Simone Truffit had been a *résistante* for three years. She'd sabotaged several German facilities, printed almost 150 fake ID cards for *résistants* and escaped prisoners, and smuggled phony medical certificates to *résistants* who were in prison. These asserted that certain prisoners had to be transferred to a hospital—it was easier to escape from a hospital than a prison. Truffit and Noor agreed to meet later that day to blow up a shed full of Metoxes—small gadgets that warned Nazi subs if Allied radar was fixed on them. Noor never showed up.

Heavy haze and cloud cover turned back two Lysander flights that month—one on the night of October 8/9, another a week later. Of the next twelve flights—October 15/16 through 18/19—three failed because of weather or poor radio reception. The other nine flights took twenty-seven SOE agents, Resistance leaders, or high-level politicians into France and forty-three to Britain. Noor was on none of them. That didn't worry the

SOE or Noor's friends in France. Plans changed. Transportation to the fields where Lysanders landed was erratic. And running from the Gestapo turned every day into a deadly game of hide-and-seek. Noor was good at hiding. She didn't know she had to be just as good at ferreting out a traitor in her own ranks, someone she'd known since June and whom she'd always trusted.

Around October 7 or 8, as Noor was saying her farewells and planning her last-minute sabotage with Simone Truffit, the Gestapo got a call from a woman named Renée Garry. The sister of Noor's first contact in France, Emile Garry, Renée was a bit of a hanger-on with the Resistance: aware of its activities—she and her brother shared a flat briefly with Noor—but never significantly active in the Resistance herself. Renée offered to make a deal with the Gestapo: Madeleine's address for one hundred thousand francs, half payable when she gave the Germans Noor's address, half when they arrested Noor. The description of Madeleine that she gave the Gestapo on the phone tallied with what the Nazis already knew about her. The Germans told Renée to wait at the Trocadéro near the Eiffel Tower, holding a flower. If a man with a magazine under his arm introduced himself to her as "André," she should give him her name and the details of her offer.

Renée and André found each other in the park. About thirty years old, five and a half feet tall, and plump ("corpulent" in the words of a Gestapo agent), Renée didn't know that André was carrying a pistol and that another armed Gestapo agent was nearby. If they got suspicious of Renée, they'd been ordered to kill her. Renée's offer was too good for murder, but she hadn't done her homework. She didn't know that the woman she was handing over was near the top of the Gestapo's most-wanted list, and that she was asking a tenth of what the Gestapo usually paid for an SOE agent.

The address Renée gave the Gestapo for Noor was 3 Boulevard Richard Wallace—the apartment Noor had vacated when she was afraid Robert Gieules might tell the Germans where she lived. Gestapo agents went there and found nothing, and the concierge (truthfully) told the Gestapo she hadn't seen Noor for a while. Furious, André met Renée at a café. This time, she took him to Noor's other flat, at 98 Rue de la Faisanderie. Renée knew where Noor hid the key to her apartment. Removing the key from where Noor had concealed it, Renée and André entered so Renée could prove Noor kept a radio in the kitchen. In the bedroom, she opened a drawer full of composition books in which Noor had written every message that had passed between her and London since the middle of June. Renée opened another drawer in a desk in the sitting room. It contained Noor's instructions from Emile Garry, her first handler in France. The instructions were in Garry's handwriting. André looked carefully at all these papers, made some notes, and left everything as he found it.

A few days later, on the morning of October 13, Renée telephoned the Gestapo: she was sure Noor was in her apartment. This was the day Noor and Simone Truffit planned to blow up the warehouse full of radar detectors. The Gestapo sent two agents to Noor's apartment. They arrived just in time to see a young woman stroll out of a patisserie that was on the street level of Noor's apartment building. Wearing a dark hat and a blue tailored dress trimmed with white, she matched the description the agents had been given of Noor: slender, with a dark complexion and about five feet, four inches tall. (The agents were also told Noor was twenty-four years old. Everyone thought she was younger than she actually was.) Turning suddenly and spotting the Germans, Noor slipped around the corner. For hours, the Gestapo combed nearby streets for her. Noor had vanished.

Soon afterward, a Frenchman—Pierre Cartaud—let himself into Noor's apartment using the key Renée Garry had shown André. Cartaud would wait there until she returned. Early in the war, Cartaud had been the chief liaison officer in Paris for one of France's original Resistance groups—the Confrérie Notre-Dame. In 1942, the Nazis began cracking down on the CND in earnest, sending many *résistants* to concentration camps and executing others. Most *résistants* didn't talk. Cartaud did, after a short stay in prison and possibly some suicide attempts. He betrayed a photographer who microfilmed captured documents for the Resistance, and a blind woman whose home was used by radio operators, and he provided addresses where radio operators had sent messages while Cartaud stood guard outside. Cartaud even joined Gestapo agents as they interrogated *résistants,* guiding the questioning, filling in holes, suggesting new lines of inquiry. Overall, he may have turned as many as sixty *résistants* over to the Germans—so many that one afternoon at Mauthausen, a member of the CND looked around and saw at least sixteen of his comrades who were "victims of the treachery of the wretch Capri," the code name by which members of the Resistance knew him.

Not even the Germans liked Cartaud. From the time he signed up with them, Cartaud had been determined to be more German than the Germans, insisting they call him Peter in the German manner, and not Pierre, and that his service with the Gestapo count toward his German naturalization after the war. His hasty zeal for the German cause was so perplexing, and so naked, that the Gestapo's chief interrogator in Paris scowled when Cartaud's name was brought up. "A bit of a swine," the interrogator scorned.

The Resistance could have gotten rid of Cartaud years before. Gilbert Renault, who ran an intelligence network in France, was alarmed when he learned that Cartaud's father led French anti-Communists who were serving with the German army. While Cartaud's father was home on leave, he had called his son a coward for not joining the anti-Bolsheviks. He threatened to report him to the Germans if he joined the Resistance.

"Wouldn't it be best if you send him to the Unoccupied Zone?" Renault asked the head of the Resistance group in which Cartaud was fighting.

Jean Fleuret, Cartaud's commander, brushed off Renault. He had known Cartaud for years. "I have every confidence in Capri. Everything will be all right."

On October 13, Cartaud waited in Noor's flat for six hours, trying not to make any sounds that Noor could hear through the door of her apartment when she returned, barely moving or humming or flushing the toilet and not going near the window, so Noor wouldn't see him as she approached the building when she came back. For three hundred and sixty minutes, Cartaud was a ghost in a stranger's flat.

When Noor returned around 4 p.m., Cartaud nabbed her. Noor fought back, pulling Cartaud's hair and biting his hands until they bled. Throwing Noor onto a couch, Cartaud tried to put handcuffs on her. Noor kept struggling, shouting so loudly that Cartaud put his hand over her mouth to muffle her. She bit him again, drawing more blood. Pulling out his revolver, Cartaud threatened to shoot Noor if she moved. Backing away to a small table where a phone sat, Cartaud called Gestapo headquarters, asking for reinforcements. A few minutes later, Gestapo agents arrived—their headquarters was less than half a mile away. They were amused at what they saw:

Cartaud stood in one corner of the flat, as far as he could get from Noor. His gun was leveled on her. Noor sat on the couch, bolt upright. Furious. She couldn't believe her timing. "This would happen at the last minute," she rued. "In a few days, I would have been in England."

The Germans convinced Noor to walk to their car without putting up a fight, which was waiting outside. Before leaving her flat, they packed up her radio and the notebook she kept in a drawer in the small table next to her bed. In it, Noor had written her codes and, in full, every message she had received or sent since arriving in France. Each left-hand page had a message in code; the opposite page had that message deciphered: clear and lucid and now available to the Germans for a new round of *Funkspiel*, their radio game with London. This time they'd pretend they were Poste Madeleine, the SOE's longest-running radio in France during the entire war, and the one on which Noor sent thirty-five messages, almost more than any other agent.

A week after Noor was arrested, the SOE wrote to her mother, "We are pleased to tell you that we have received good news of your daughter and that she is very well." In truth, there was no news, good or bad (although one report, tentative and unfounded, had reached the SOE that *perhaps* Noor had been arrested). The letter to Ora, signed by Sgt. E. G. Bisset and sent from the SOE's front in the Hotel Victoria, was part of the arrangement Noor had made before going to France: not a word to Ora if Noor was caught or wounded or holed up in a safe house with the Germans after her. Only notify Ora if Noor was killed. Noor didn't want her mother to worry needlessly.

More accurate, if more grim, than Bisset's letter to Ora was an internal report that Maurice Buckmaster would make about Noor after learning she had been caught: the Gestapo's knowledge of her movements "appeared to be such that her capture seemed almost a certainty." Though ordered to return to England, she "pleaded to be allowed to remain and lie low for a month. At the end of this time, she reported that she felt her security reestablished as a result of arrangements she had made and subsequent events have fully justified her course of action." Noor stayed at her post, Buckmaster said, "often alone—and always under the threat of arrest," rebuilding the Prosper circuit while being "instrumental in facilitating the escape of thirty Allied airmen shot down in France. Her courage and devotion to duty are exemplary."

There are two stories about why Renée Garry turned in Noor: that she needed money (like many people in France during the war) or she was jealous. (These are not mutually exclusive. In fact, they could have been mutually inclusive.) Once Noor came on the scene, Renée's brother and a *résistant* on whom Renée had a crush ignored her. Renée wanted revenge. More baffling is *why* Noor kept in writing every message, ciphered and clear, that was sent between her and London. Her final orders from the SOE were to *file* her messages: "you must be extremely careful with the *filing* of your messages [italics added]." More likely, though still unknowable, is that the SOE used "file" in the same sense that a journalist would: when reporters submit stories, they *file* them. Noor was probably more familiar with the parlance of secretaries who *file* papers, memos, letters, transcripts, to keep them orderly and neat and easily accessible. Noor did the same with her messages, though that contradicted the training she had received at Beaulieu: agents there were told to keep written copies of messages only "if absolutely necessary." The nuances of "file"—submit a story like a reporter versus retain every copy of that story like a secretary—may have been lost on Noor.

Noor *did* break an SOE rule—she asked friends and neighbors she had known before the war to help her. But none of them betrayed her, and without their help Noor's messages might have ceased as early as July. Noor wasn't the only agent who committed certain infractions of SOE rules. Pickersgill and Macalister committed equal or greater sins. When Odette Sampson had mistakenly tried to purchase a ticket for a movie theater in Cannes that was reserved for German soldiers, she had broken a fundamental rule of the SOE: don't make yourself conspicuous. Always be unobtrusive and adjust your behavior to the prevailing norm. When agent Hans Zomer was arrested in Holland, the Germans reconstructed his codes from the messages they found *next* to him. Also in Holland, Herbert Lauwers was about to send messages to England when four black cars pulled up to the apartment building he was in. Lauwers threw his radio out the window and ran down the steps, straight into German soldiers. In Lauwers's pockets were the ciphered texts of the messages he was about to send, and the Gestapo found his radio tangled in a clothesline behind the apartment building. Almost immediately the Germans used it for their *Funkspiel*. Soon they knew the name of every British agent in the Netherlands, the schools they'd attended, their preferred brand of cigarettes or pipe tobacco, and who was married, single, or divorced.

If both sides, German and British, agreed on anything, it was that radio operators were indispensable for secret work. Communication, reflected Colin Gubbins, the head of the SOE, was the "prerequisite" for everything the agency did. Hans Kiefer, the commander of the Gestapo in Paris agreed, admitting after the war that he had let "plenty" of the "colleagues" of radio operators go free: "They were of no interest to me." Radio operators were his utmost concern. And no radio operator gained Kieffer's attention more than "Madeleine." "She was of the greatest interest to us," Kieffer acknowledged. "We were pursuing her for months." The Gestapo would discover that keeping Noor was as difficult as catching her.

PART FOUR

IN THE WORLD

OF NO WORLD

Let courage be thy sword
& patience be thy shield.

—HAZRAT INAYAT KHAN

CHAPTER 14

"MADELEINE, DON'T BE SILLY. YOU WILL KILL YOURSELF"

he Gestapo took Noor to 84 Avenue Foch, one of several buildings it had confiscated along that wide and famous boulevard. By 1943, Avenue Foch was so Germanized that Parisians called it "Avenue Boche"—short for *alleboche*. *Alleboche* was probably a conflation of *allemand*, French for "German," and *caboche*, slang for "skull" or "hardheaded." The origin of the terms are lost to history. What is certain is that no French citizen wanted to see the inside of any of the mansions along Avenue Foch, where the Gestapo did its dirty work.

Once through the black iron fence that surrounded no. 84, prisoners were marched (or dragged, depending on what the Gestapo had already done to them) through double doors, then down a long, narrow lobby and through another set of doors into a small foyer. A marble staircase led to the second floor, which was devoted to Section IV, the Gestapo's wireless unit. Section IV sent bogus messages to London on the SOE's own wireless sets that the Gestapo had seized while arresting radio operators or as the sets were parachuted into France. Around the middle of 1943, as the Resistance and the SOE really began to threaten the Germans, the Gestapo started torturing prisoners in earnest on the second floor of no. 84, often by waterboarding, electric shock, or pulling out prisoners' fingernails with pliers.

Helmut Knochen, the Gestapo's senior commander of security in Paris, had his offices and several conference rooms on the third floor. A large map of France hung on the wall of one of these rooms. At the top of the map was a diagram of everything the Gestapo knew about the SOE's French section—the names of the officers who ran it from England and some of its agents who were already in France. Hans Kieffer, the head of the Gestapo in Paris, turned the fourth floor of no. 84 into his personal apartment along with a small working space for his secretary who, according to rumor, was his mistress. On the fifth floor were seven cells—formerly maids' bedrooms. Each cell had a chair and a narrow iron bed with a green blanket. The cells' only natural light came through shafts leading to the roof. Also on the fifth floor were a guardroom, a lavatory, and a separate room with a tub. A small library for prisoners was stocked mostly with detective novels.

Eighty-four Avenue Foch was the Ritz of the entire prison system in the Greater Reich, a mansion in the most beautiful city in the world where prisoners could wash and shave and wear a shirt and tie, not prison garb, and enjoy what, by wartime standards, were rare delicacies: meat, vegetables, butter, eggs, desserts, and real coffee, not the barely swallowable substitute most of France was brewing from acorns, chickpeas, chicory, or grass. (Most of the fine food came from parachute drops that the Germans intercepted.) On Sunday mornings, the head of 84 personally distributed chocolates, pastries, and cigarettes to prisoners while making small talk with them. Friendly persuasion was the preferred motif on the fifth floor. It was also where Ernest Vogt, no. 84's chief translator and interrogator, had his office.

Vogt—tall, thin, brown-haired, and bespectacled—was an anomaly on Avenue Foch: more cosmopolitan and better traveled than most of the Gestapo's agents, and slightly less German than they were. With a German father and a Swiss mother, Vogt had been raised in a village along the Rhine where the river was so narrow you could shout to relatives and friends on the Swiss side, and so calm Vogt could swim across it as a boy (though he was so tired when he reached the Swiss side that he had to be ferried back to Germany).

When Vogt was twenty-one, he left for Paris, working as a clerk first in a bank, then for a patent attorney. At one point, he took three weeks off for a vacation in England. The French jailed Vogt as an enemy alien shortly after war broke out in 1939. When Hitler's troops arrived, the German military ruled that he wasn't army material—he was too color-blind and nearsighted. Instead, he was sent to 84 Avenue Foch to interpret for Kieffer. Commissioned as a second lieutenant, Vogt never joined the Nazi Party, and never wore a uniform. He was given a pistol, yet never taught how to use it. But he respected the English notion of "honor," and used that to his advantage when convincing prisoners to cooperate or, at minimum, to promise not to escape. Those vows relieved the guards at 84 Avenue Foch of much effort, time, and anxiety: an escaped prisoner could cost them a severe dressing down by their superiors or transfer to a less enviable post. Even during a war, Paris was a desirable place to be.

The weeks Vogt had spent in England taught him the premium the British placed on manners. Polite and almost solicitous, he greeted new prisoners wearing his civilian clothes, assuring them, especially if they came from a prison where they'd been roughly treated, "Here, things are different. Here, if you cooperate, you will be treated as an officer, as a prisoner of war." Opening the thick files on his desk, Vogt bluffed and lied, attempting gingerly to persuade the prisoner sitting in front of him that resisting the Nazis made no sense. Germans were too smart, too clever, too shrewd, and too sly. "We already know a great deal about you and your operations," Vogt would assert, no matter how little he actually knew. As he casually referred to the prisoner's cover name or to the name of his circuit or radio operator—information he wasn't supposed to know—Vogt would ask where arms or radios were being hidden. If the prisoner was silent, and most were, Vogt would say, "You are doing your duty as an officer. We understand this. It speaks well of your sense of honor. But these weapons or radios will be dispersed to unsound elements, to terrorists who will use them for their own criminal purposes. Unlike you, they do not have the best interests of their country at heart. They will not bring *gloire* to France [or to England, depending on who Vogt was talking to]. Think about this, I implore you."

Vogt also knew the value the British placed on tea. After enjoying his lunch in the early afternoon, Vogt read the files of one or two prisoners, then opened the doors to their cells around 3 or 4 p.m., and asked, "Will you take tea with me?" Invariably, they did. With their tongues and minds loosened by Vogt's etiquette, his innocent looks, and his fond reminiscences of his youth in a village next to the Rhine, a few prisoners let slip more than they should have. One *résistante* who spent time at 84 Avenue Foch said Vogt treated her as an "enemy of his country, but correctly and even with humanity."

. . .

Noor was taken to Vogt's office as soon as she arrived at no. 84. Vogt was indispensable to much of what went on in the prison: His boss, Hans Kieffer, barely spoke French and relied on Vogt to get information out of prisoners. But after interrogating *résistants* and SOE agents for almost three years, Vogt realized that Noor was one of the more stubborn prisoners he'd encountered. Before he could ask a single question, she blurted out, "You know who I am and you know what I've been doing. You have my radio. I will tell you nothing. I have only one thing to ask of you: Shoot me as quickly as possible."

Assuring Noor that he had no plans to kill her, Vogt began peppering her with questions gently, trying to appear reasonable and rational, not like the Neanderthals SOE agents had been told to expect. After an hour, he gave up. Noor had told him nothing, not even her real name. Maybe Noor should cool off in her cell for a while? Fine with her, but first she'd like a bath—an odd request, especially in the early afternoon. Vogt agreed. Anything to calm her down.

Ordinarily, a small brick kept the bathroom door ajar. That way, a guard stationed down the hallway could keep an eye on its window that faced the street: the Nazis didn't want prisoners jumping to their deaths. Noor refused to bathe unless the door was completely closed. Vogt removed the brick, but, uneasy about it being shut, he went to the room adjacent to the washroom. Looking out the window,. he panicked: Noor had climbed through the window in the washroom and was balancing on the rain gutter that ran beneath all the windows on the fifth floor. Already it was wobbling underneath her. The rain gutter—barely five inches wide and inherently unstable—could buckle. Noor risked tumbling five floors down as she was edging her way toward a ledge that led to the roof. Once there, she could escape, rooftop to rooftop. As she got closer to the window that Vogt was leaning out of, he said to her, almost in a whisper, "Madeleine, don't be silly. You will kill yourself." Vogt stretched his hand toward her. Noor grasped it.

Guiding her inside, Vogt led Noor to her cell. There, she slumped on her bed, crying and calling herself a coward. An hour before, she'd demanded to be shot. Now she couldn't follow through with an escape. After the war, Vogt told British investigators that Noor told him, "When I looked out on

Eighty-four Avenue Foch: as Noor balanced on a rain gutter five
floors up, a Gestapo officer talked her inside.

that gutter, I said to myself, 'It's death or escape. One or the other.' I don't
know why I took your hand. Maybe just because you held it out."

Noor was inconsolable. Vogt remembered that an SOE agent who Noor
knew was in another cell. Maybe Jean-Paul Archambault could console her.
Vogt let him spend five minutes with her. By the time Archambault left,
Noor had quieted. Slightly.

That afternoon, a guard brought lunch to Noor's cell. She didn't touch it.
At eight that night, Noor was taken to Vogt's office. He'd asked that dinner
for two, including English tea and biscuits and cigarettes, be brought to him.
Noor didn't touch the dinner, the tea, or the biscuits. She did smoke the
cigarettes. Vogt showed her photos of a letter she had sent her mother and a
handwritten message she'd sent the SOE in London. Both had been flown to
England on an outgoing Lysander. Noor cried softly when she saw the letter

to her mother. (Most likely, a double agent had photographed the message and letter, then stuffed them in mailbags intended for London.) Vogt told Noor some of what he knew about the SOE: Its offices were on Baker Street. Maurice Buckmaster ran the F Section. Noor had been trained in Scotland and at Beaulieu. After Vogt rattled off the names of some of Buckmaster's assistants, Noor sighed, "You know everything. You must have an agent in London." "Perhaps," Vogt said, shrugging with a vague smile. For the next few hours that they were together, Noor barely spoke. Vogt did most of the talking. Around midnight, he took Noor to her cell, wished her a good night, and suggested she reflect about everything he had told her.

Outside, Paris was quieter than before the war. It was almost as still as Suresnes—Noor's cocoon when she'd been a child and after her father died, and while writing poems and stories and essays about themes large and small: birthdays and fairies and butterflies, and the joy of sacrifice, and the realness of life coming forth when the heart was broken. Since 1940, Paris had had less traffic than when Noor had lived across the river. Now that it was past the curfew the Nazis had imposed, even that traffic had diminished to a fraction of what it had been earlier in the day. The barest sounds penetrated Noor's cell: almost sixty feet above the grandest street in Europe and insulated by thick plaster walls. If sleep eventually came. Noor would need it. She would spend most of the next day with Vogt, enduring his interlocutions, and his reasonable and calculated manner, and his ostensible concern for Noor's well-being and the clarity of her conscience and her heart, neither of which had ever been challenged in this manner before or with such high stakes.

Over the next few weeks, Vogt saw Noor every day, sometimes for a few hours, sometimes for as little as twenty minutes. He admired her, and—if there wasn't a war—would have liked to have been her friend. In his office, Noor held her ground, and held her tongue, her fists clenched more tightly than her mouth. Leo Marks, the SOE's code maven, had worried that Noor's Sufi taboo against lying would collapse if the Germans caught her. Her strategy for how she'd handle the Nazis—"Suppose that I refuse to tell them anything at all, no matter how often they ask?"——had sounded simple and naive. Marks should have believed her. She never lied to the Germans or told a half-truth or the smallest, barely consequential fib. Bound to her promise to Marks, and to herself, Noor did not break it.

In his office, Vogt often referred to names that appeared in Noor's messages that the Gestapo had obtained. Maybe some of them, he asked, were minor players in all of this—neither SOE agents nor *résistants,* but innocents who had given Noor a night's lodging or let her use their home for some purpose about which they knew nothing. If Noor told the Gestapo which of them had nothing to do with sabotage or with gathering intelligence, they wouldn't be arrested. If Noor didn't help the Gestapo with these names, *everyone* would be arrested.

Noor began to speak. Maybe, Vogt thought, Noor was abandoning her exasperating silence? Maybe she'd come to her senses, accepting that the Nazi juggernaut was too powerful, too omnipotent to resist? Vogt was mistaken. Noor did speak, but she was so cleverly evasive that she was more frustrating than helpful. Vogt was wasting his time with her.

One day, Josef Goetz, whose unit three floors down sent fake messages to England on the SOE's own radios, came for Noor. Goetz hoped she would explain certain aspects of the technical side of her work. He returned two hours later. Noor had told him nothing. "She's impossible and won't trust me," he told Vogt. "She has a certain confidence in you. If you try, maybe you'll get something. I've never met a woman like her."

During another of Noor's interrogations, Hans Kieffer, the officer who ran no. 84, poked his head into Vogt's office. "How far did you get?" he asked.

"Nowhere."

Kieffer sat down in Vogt's office. Kieffer had a certain presence—one prisoner at no. 84 described him as "square-headed, not tall, hair cut short, strongly built, energetic, about 40, rather dark. . . ." He demanded that Noor explain an SOE message that the Gestapo had just intercepted. She stared coldly at Kieffer. "To you, I will tell nothing—even less than to him," nodding toward Vogt. "I don't trust you. You are false, and you are trying to set a trap for me. I can read it in your eyes."

Furious, Kieffer turned to Vogt. "Why don't you give her a slap?"

"Because afterward, she would tell me nothing at all."

Turning to Noor, Vogt said almost plaintively, "Madeleine, you should not be rough with the chief. It does not matter that you are rough with me. But you should not be rough with the chief. For your own sake, it is foolish to make him angry with you."

"It's all one to me," Noor answered. "I don't care."

Most of the time, Vogt met alone with Noor, talking about the war and about Noor's work with the SOE and of many things that had nothing to do with either of these, trying to help Noor relax and trust him and see how helpless she was: 84 Avenue Foch was not for amateurs or picture-book heroines. The Gestapo was playing a deadly game. Vogt wanted Noor alive at the end of it. He liked her.

On a few nights Vogt and Noor had dinner in his office, sometimes late into the night. Once Noor raised what was probably most on her mind: torture. The SOE had told her the Germans would torture her. Every time she was taken from her cell, especially during her first week at 84, she expected horror and pain. So far, the Germans had been gentle, almost respectful toward her. Though there's no evidence that Noor was tortured at no. 84 Avenue Foch, other SOE agents, like Odette Sansom, were. In a small room on the third floor, several of Sansom's toenails were pried out with pliers. The handsome young Frenchman who administered the torture—the Germans enjoyed collaborators torturing their own countrymen—calmly deposited the nails, one by one, in a small steel pan he had placed on the floor. To survive, Sansom told herself she was "born to endure this. If I can survive another minute, then that is another minute of life." If the Germans killed her, "they will have a dead body, useless to them. They will have a body, but they will not have me."

Sansom learned that if she treated the Germans "like they were your servants, then they had a certain respect for you." Though a prisoner, she looked at the Germans as if to say, "Well, you are here, but what does it matter? You do not exist."

Noor knew the Germans existed. She did not treat them like servants. Neither contemptuous nor condescending, she quite possibly remembered an aphorism from her father: "Make the snake your friend rather than your enemy." Noor didn't intend to make friends at Avenue Foch though she had never set out to make enemies, not with her Sufi creed grounded in love.

With her fear of torture abating, Noor was relaxing slightly, sitting more comfortably in Vogt's office and bringing up matters that were distinct from the war (like the arts—Bach and Beethoven, she told Vogt, were her favorite composers), and requesting fresh clothing and cologne and face powder from the apartment where she'd been arrested, and for paper for writing poems and stories in her cell, mostly for children and usually full of animals. She wouldn't show these to Vogt. "I don't like people to read my stories before they are finished," she told him. Otherwise, the two of them had quiet, civilized conversations about the life of the imagination and a life without war, a sensible exchange between people straining to recall the good that prevailed before the bombs fell and before the death counts grew.

Amid all this, Vogt believed that Noor "understood that I was her friend, as far as the circumstances would allow." And yet, while laughing together one night over dinner, Vogt looked up. Noor was crying. Had he said anything that hurt her? "No. It's not you. Its just everything. I was thinking of my mother."

Noor had not seen Ora for almost half a year. She was afraid she would never see her again.

Vogt got up and stood beside Noor. As she leaned her head against him, he stroked her hair. Suddenly, Vogt got afraid. For Noor. "Don't forget," he said, "I am your enemy, Madeleine. Never forget I am your enemy."

"Thank you," Noor replied.

Walking Noor back to her cell, Vogt placed one kiss on her forehead before locking her door. Vogt knew that the kiss and reminding Noor that he was her enemy would not have pleased Hans Kieffer.

About the only use Vogt had made of Noor so far was learning that a prisoner could possibly escape through the window in a lavatory on the fifth floor. No one had tried that before. Other than that, the Gestapo gleaned no benefits from having Noor at 84 Avenue Foch. About all she told Vogt was that she was a lieutenant in the RAF and her "real" name was "Nora Baker." Vogt accepted that Noor's last name was "Baker": the copy of Noor's letter to her mother that he had seen was addressed to Mrs. Ora Baker. But he didn't care about Noor's rank or her name aside from "Madeleine."

Those were useless for his investigation. Who, he kept probing, were Noor's friends, accomplices, allies? How had she survived in Paris since the middle of June? What did the SOE know? What was it planning? When would it do it? Where were other SOE radios hidden? Vogt never found out.

Noor's silence gradually thawed, though not in the way Vogt hoped it would. He knew Noor was studying him, maybe more than he was studying her. She focused on his eyes and movements and gestures until, one day, she asked from frustration and annoyance and probably more than a little fear: "What are you trying to know with all these questions? You talk 'round and 'round. It infuriates me. I don't know what you're trying to get at. Please tell me what you want to know. Since I won't tell you in any case, it won't make any difference."

By the time Vogt concluded that he'd never get anything from Noor—all his tricks had failed—he'd come to respect her. She was talented and smart and could have offered the world so much more than coming to France for the SOE. "Don't you feel it's a pity you came on this mission, Madeleine?" he asked. "It seems to be such a waste. You're exceptionally intelligent and gifted. If you had not accepted this terrible mission, you could have done so many interesting and valuable things."

"If I had to make the choice again," Noor answered, "I would make it the same way."

"Even though you've seen how things are here? You realize we've mopped up three-quarters of the [SOE's] French Section and that your sacrifice won't end up counting for much."

"It doesn't matter," said Noor. "I've served my country. That's my reward."

After the war, Kieffer told the British, "Noor showed great courage. We got no information whatsoever out of her." Noor had practiced what Sufis call *taqiya,* literally "prudence," though in its more severe form *taqiya* lets Muslims dissimulate (usually about their faith) if that protects lives, their own or others'. The practice dated back to the early days of Islam when Muslims were persecuted for following whom others deemed to be an upstart of a prophet. Another form of *taqiya* lets Muslims shield their faith and their beliefs with silence. No dissembling, deceiving, or deception. Just silence, the void that let Noor protect her mission, and herself. Noor's reticence frustrated the Germans as much as it preserved her devotion to truth and to honor.

The Gestapo in Paris: Hans Kieffer, who ran 84 Avenue Foch, fourth from right, front row; Ernest Vogt, Noor's interrogator, third from right, second row.

And yet the Gestapo already had Noor's biggest secret: all her radio traffic, written in plain, uncoded English *and* ciphered in her notebook. This made the job of Josef Goetz on no. 84's second floor much easier. After learning Noor's code, Goetz began sending phony messages to London on her radio, telling the SOE where to drop new agents or crates of weapons. The Germans plucked off agents as soon as they landed and sent most of the weapons to Berlin—gifts, as it were, from London.

Goetz's first message on Noor's set went out on October 17, a few days after she was caught. By then, Buckmaster was concerned about Noor: no handwritten letters had come from her since September. That was not like her. Her latest message requested a new letterbox. It relieved Buckmaster's anxieties:

MY CACHETTE UNSAFE. NEW ADDRESS BEILLIARD RPT BEL-
LIARD 157 RUE VERCINGETORIX RPT VERCINGETORIX PARIS
PASSWORD DE PART DE MONSIEUR DE RUAL RPT DE RUAL
STOP THIS PERFECTLY SAFE TRUE CHECK PRESENT BLUFF
CHECK OMITTED GOODBYE.

Three floors up from where Goetz sent this message, Noor had no idea anyone was playing *Funkspiel* on her wireless. Or that, thanks to the game, the Gestapo would eventually catch seven SOE agents with her set alone. Some of these agents, like France Antelme, were good friends of hers. Nor did she (or anyone at SOE in England) know that the Germans were employing *Funkspiel* on radios they'd seized from thirty-three other SOE agents in France. This would lead to the capture of at least fifteen SOE agents and to London filling the Gestapo's *Funkspiel* requests for almost 5.5 million francs and over 1,900 containers of weapons and explosives.

By now, Noor didn't tear up when Vogt questioned her. She knew what he would ask, and he knew that she wouldn't answer. They went through their paces, aware of what was expected of them and what they expected of themselves: an almost-friendly match of two foes going through familiar motions, day after day, on the top floor of one of the more notorious buildings in Paris. At night, Noor was different. There were no distractions then, barely the sound of the few cars whizzing by below to remind her that she was in one of her favorite cities in Europe. Noor had only herself in these hours, and her memories, and her tears. She cried often.

Two prisoners, Léon Faye and John Starr, tried to console Noor, each in his own way, each with an entirely different background, and each with a different sense of duty. Starr was so close to the Germans that charges of collaboration would hound him for the rest of his life. Faye was one of the most celebrated heroes of the Resistance, a man who had been fiercely opposed to the Nazis before the war and who had devoted his life to fighting them since it started. The partnership between these two men was purely of convenience, with some distrust on both sides and Noor serving as the reliable tissue linking them.

Léon Faye had been at 84 Avenue Foch about a month longer than Noor. He had been questioned relentlessly though never tortured, and his cell was next to hers. Not long after she arrived, they began tapping messages on the wall separating them. Both wanted to escape. Neither knew if that was possible. Their cells were constantly guarded and all possible exits were blocked. But if anyone could break out of 84 Avenue Foch, it was Léon Faye.

The escape artist of the Resistance, he had already slipped out of two other German prisons.

Faye was the very image of a Frenchman fighting for his country: charming, dapper, and so dashing that when Marie-Madeleine Fourcade, the head of the Resistance group in which Faye served, first met him, she was enchanted: "His whole manner, his drive, and the boldness of his plans left me gasping," Fourcade wrote in her memoir, *Noah's Ark.* Soon they were lovers matched in courage and in beauty: Faye tall and lean, with gray-green eyes and thick black hair; Fourcade—chic, and born into wealth and privilege—so striking that one *résistant* later confessed that he, "like so many other young men in Vichy, was madly in love with the fabulously beautiful Marie-Madeleine."

Faye had been in the military since he was seventeen, first in the army, then the air force. He joined Alliance, one of France's first Resistance groups, soon after France fell. After a five-month jail sentence in 1941 for plotting a coup in Algeria that would have kept the Germans out of North Africa, he was appointed Alliance's chief of staff. A former officer in France's air force introduced him to other *résistants* as "completely fearless." And when Alliance suffered its first casualty, Faye told his new friends, "Since 1917, I've seen many comrades disappear. I know only too well that men like that are few and far between."

"We will avenge him," said a *résistant.*

"I don't think he would like that word," Faye advised. "We shall carry on. That was his great wish."

Faye shuttled between England and France so often that, through sheer osmosis and powers of observation, he could have piloted Lysanders by himself. After strategy sessions in London in August and September 1942 Faye returned to France in October, determined to convince General Pétain, the Germans' puppet in Vichy, to rise up against the Nazis: the Allies were now in North Africa and there were constant rumors that the Germans were on the verge of occupying Pétain's "free zone." The general's days were numbered. Pétain disagreed and sent Faye to a prison in Val-les-Bains, a former spa town. The Resistance smuggled a rope and hacksaw to Faye. On the night of November 23, he sawed through the bars of a window in a fourth-floor lavatory, threw the eighty-foot rope to *résistants* waiting below, and launched himself toward the ground. By the time Faye hit the ground, his hands were raw. He had been in prison for only seventeen days.

After more meetings in London, August through early September 1943, British intelligence urged Faye to stay in England. He'd survived three arrests, two escapes, and three two-way Lysander flights. MI6 was sure the law of averages was against him. Marie-Madeleine Fourcade, the head of Alliance, agreed. Faye didn't. "Never, do you understand," he shouted when Fourcade ordered him to remain in Britain. "I'll never agree to fall down on my job. Damn their law of averages. . . . Tell them I've also got fifty bombing missions to my credit, that I was a volunteer at the age of seventeen . . . in the trenches. According to their calculations, I should have been dead long ago. I *am* dead. This ghost's going."

Fourcade warned Faye that "the Nazi vise is getting tighter every day." She'd let him go to France if he promised to "slip away from the reception committee, go to Paris under your own steam, and thoroughly investigate what has been happening while you've been away before you make the slightest move."

On September 16, a Lysander dropped Faye in northeastern France. The Nazis knew he was coming. Four days after Faye stepped foot in France, the train he was on stopped at Aulnay-sous-Bois, the last station before Paris. Gestapo agents rushed the carriage Faye was in so fast that he had no time to pull out his revolver.

Aware of Faye's escape record, the Germans bound him hand and foot and took him to the fifth floor of the most secure building in Paris. When Faye arrived, he was questioned for so long that the interrogator was exhausted. Faye told the Germans nothing.

Faye enjoyed escaping from German prisons, but he was stumped about how to get out of Avenue Foch. Guards were everywhere, the building seemed airtight, and he wasn't sure where to go if he did slip away: the layout of the nearby streets was a bit of a mystery to him. In code messages that Noor tapped to Faye on their cells' adjoining wall, she mentioned that she was already communicating with an SOE agent whose cell was directly opposite hers. Noor and John Starr had been leaving written messages in a crack in the wall under the sink in the lavatory on their floor. A prisoner at no. 84 since July, Starr had almost free rein in the building. An artist before the war, he was kept busy painting portraits of the Germans, copying maps, making greeting cards to send to their families back home, and fixing the English grammar in the messages they were sending London on the SOE's own radios. Maybe Starr knew the weak spots in no. 84? Faye asked Noor to sound him out through the messages they were exchanging in the lavatory.

Starr was a conundrum. The Gestapo took only one SOE prisoner out for dinner—Starr. And not once. Three times. No other prisoner was as frank about his fondness for the comfortable, opulent mansion in the middle of Paris, telling other prisoners he preferred "living in Avenue Foch to breaking stones in Germany." Nor did any other prisoner encourage others to cooperate with the Gestapo as Starr did. "Don't lead them up the garden [path]," he told newcomers to 84 Avenue Foch. "It's quite useless. They know everything." The other prisoners didn't know what to make of Starr. What they did know, they didn't like.

Thirty-five years old, short, and with a mustache and a moon-shaped face, Starr ran his first mission for the SOE in 1942. Sent to ensure that *résistants* around Marseille and Antibes had enough food, he purchased large amounts of chocolate, wheat, dried bananas, and a flock of sheep that were butchered as needed. Starr got bored. He hadn't signed up to run a grocery store for freedom fighters. Back in England three months later, he got the action he wanted on his next mission. Parachuting into the Jura region in May 1943 with hundreds of thousands of francs and new codes and sets for radio operators, Starr rode trains throughout eastern and central France, arranging plans and security with members of his circuit. When police at a train station asked him to open his attaché case (which was full of cash), Starr leaped onto the footboard of a moving train, clinging there until the train slowed down at the next station. A few weeks later, the SS arrested Starr when they found thirty-five thousand francs on him—a large sum for an ordinary citizen. As the van he was in passed through the gates of a prison in Fresnes, Starr jumped out. A bullet pierced his left thigh. Another dug into his left foot. The Germans threw Starr into a cell and tortured him for days. The beatings stopped briefly so a doctor could open his wounds. The Gestapo hit Starr's swollen thigh until, as he said after the war, "it was a huge mass of pus and bruises." The next day, the doctor pushed a steel rod into Starr's wound. It came out the other side of his thigh. Starr still didn't talk. Twenty days later, Starr was sent to 84 Avenue Foch. Maybe Hans Kieffer's kinder, gentler ways would work with the Englishman. Kieffer and his staff grew fond of Starr. Reasonably affable, they figured the torture he'd received in Fresnes had broken his will.

Starr saw Noor when she first came to Avenue Foch. With her light-brown hair, navy-blue slacks, and a light-gray jumper topped with a rolled-up turtleneck, she looked French. But once Noor settled into a routine at no. 84, it was apparent she was as English as she was French, and she and Starr exchanged the briefest of pleasantries when she came to the guardroom to borrow books from the small library the Germans had set up there. This was where Starr worked as a draftsman. It was too dangerous for him and Noor to say more than a few words to each other. A guard was always present.

Moved by Noor's crying, which he heard every night, Starr was determined to somehow communicate with her. With a wife and child back in England, he knew what it was like to miss your family and to be alone. With some of the drawing supplies the Germans had given him, Starr wrote a note to Noor: "Cheer up. You're not alone. Perhaps we'll find a way to get out of here"; then he described the crevice under the sink in the lavatory where they could swap messages. To get this note to Noor, Starr dropped a pencil while walking in the hallway between their cells. Stooping to pick it up, he slipped the note under the door of Noor's cell. The guard at the end of the corridor never noticed.

At first, Starr wanted no part of the escape Faye and Noor were proposing. Avenue Foch was almost impregnable, the jewel in the crown of the Gestapo's prison system in Paris. There were only four ways out:

Overpower the guards. Frank Pickersgill, one of the two real Canadians, had tried that the previous June. Using a bottle as a weapon, he knocked down a guard on the fifth floor, shoved guards out of his way on the fourth floor, then leaped from a second-floor window to the street. After weeks of inactivity, Pickersgill couldn't run fast. Gestapo agents sprayed him with submachine guns, hitting him four times. Pickersgill fell, tried to run again, collapsed, and lost consciousness.

Jump. Jumping was too dangerous and not advisable. Pierre Brossolette, a leader in the Resistance, would try that the following March. He died of injuries in a hospital a few hours later. Almost every bone in his body was broken from his five-floor fall.

Go down. Maybe, Faye asked Starr via Noor's tapping, they could go down the stairs at night? The guards would be sleeping. The place would be dark. Starr's answer: "Impossible."

Go up. The only thing above the fifth floor was the roof. Skylights in each prisoner's cell led there through an air shaft several feet long. After a prisoner escaped through a skylight early in the occupation, the Germans had installed bars at the bottom of each airshaft. Theoretically, Noor, Faye, and Starr could remove the bars, climb to the roof, and work their way to the ground via fire escapes or "ropes" they made from strips of their blankets that they had tied together in their cells.

In the notes Noor left in the crack in the wall in the lavatory, she kept badgering Faye, asking about possibilities and strategies and the potential for success if the three of them worked together, especially with Faye, who had escaped from other prisons and knew how to outsmart the Germans. Noor also held out the hope of a Lysander evacuating them to England, since she knew of cafés in Paris where such flights could be arranged.

Encouraged by Faye's previous escapes and by the possibility of a Lysander to Britain, Starr agreed to join them. Their only chance, the three conspirators agreed, was scrambling through the skylights to the roof.

CHAPTER 15

SACRED HONOR

An escape required meticulous planning, precise timing, and fastidious coordination of three getaways from three cells, all communicated through notes left in the lavatory or tapping on the wall between Faye's and Noor's cells and without a single face-to-face conversation between any of the conspirators. Starr wanted to delay the escape until Christmas, when the guards would be distracted and less vigilant. Noor and Faye wanted to escape as soon as possible. By Christmas, the Germans could send them far from Paris. Starr gave in.

The question was: how would they remove the bars in their cells that led to the skylights? One day, Rose-Marie, the cleaning woman at 84 Avenue Foch, poked her head into the guardroom: her vacuum cleaner wasn't working. Could someone fix it for her? The guards didn't move. Claiming he was familiar with vacuum cleaners, Starr turned it upside down, shook it vigorously and tried to take it apart. Dust flew everywhere, annoying the guards, who asked how long the repair would take. It would go faster, Starr said, if he had the proper tools. The guards told Rose-Marie to fetch her toolbox. Now that he had a screwdriver, Starr began tinkering with the vacuum cleaner in earnest. He had an ulterior motive: the screwdriver could help him, Faye, and Noor remove the bars in their cells. Maybe he could pocket it when no one was looking. But suddenly the guards were curious about Starr's appliance repair. He deliberately fixed the vacuum cleaner so it would break down in a few days. Maybe the guards would pay less attention to him then.

The second time, the guards ignored Starr. He fixed the vacuum cleaner properly, then hid the screwdriver in a fireplace grate. When no one reported the missing screwdriver, a few days later Starr retrieved it and began loosening the screws on the bars in his cell—a few more turns on the night of their escape and the bars in his cell would be removed. Noor and Faye had a harder job than Starr: thick plaster, not screws, held theirs in place. And chipping away at plaster made more noise than rotating screws. Still, when Starr passed them the screwdriver through the "dropbox" in the lavatory, they tapped away gingerly at the plaster, covering with kneaded bread the holes they made. But the bread was a slightly different shade than the plaster. By blending it with facial cream and cosmetic powder that the Germans let Noor keep, she concocted a compound that matched the plaster and passed some of this to Faye through the crack under the sink. (Along with the makeup and clothes that Noor had requested the Gestapo bring from her apartment on Rue de la Faisanderie, in a coat pocket Noor had found tickets for the Paris Métro. She planned to use them when they escaped so she, Faye, and Starr wouldn't waste time buying tickets.)

The shortest of the three conspirators, Noor had to stand on her bed to reach the plaster that was caked around the bars on her ceiling. Late one night, she fell. Guards raced to her cell. Noor told them she had attempted to hang herself.

On November 19, Starr got an unexpected cellmate—John Young, an SOE radio operator. Starr and Young had parachuted into France together the previous May. Arrested the day before he was brought to 84 Avenue Foch, Young had been beaten and whipped in a Nazi prison in Lons-le-Saunier, a small village in eastern France. Lifting his shirt, he showed Starr his scars and bruises. Despite the pain, he never told the Germans where he'd hidden his radio. Young spent his first night on Avenue Foch in Starr's cell. They hardly spoke to each other, knowing that the Germans would not have placed two men in the same cell who knew each other unless the room was bugged. The next day, Young was given a cell next to Starr's. After a few nights, they assumed the Germans were no longer surveilling them and began tapping messages on the wall conjoining their cells. Starr invited Young to join the escape, offering to pass him the screwdriver so he could loosen the bars on his skylight. Young declined: he had given Vogt his word of honor that he would not escape, and he would not go back on his word.

On November 24 they were ready to move. The plan was that Noor and Faye would climb up their airshafts around 10:30 p.m. Starr would follow a few hours later when he returned from his late-night shift at his drafting table in the guardroom. Tonight he was working on a portrait of Hans Kieffer—Kieffer planned to send it to his wife back home in Karlsruhe. While Noor and Faye finished scraping away at the remaining plaster in their cells, sometimes with their fingers, Starr's job was to mask any noise they made. He talked loudly with the guards, turned up the radio that they enjoyed listening to, and fussed distractingly with his paints and supplies. Mostly, he made a pest of himself.

Faye easily reached the roof by pressing against the sides of his air shaft: he'd been exercising for weeks in his cell. He was thrilled to be outside. The weather was clear, the stars were bright, he had a perfect view of the Arc de Triomphe only a few blocks away, and he could faintly hear the nightlife of Paris, however soft it might be this late at night. But he was annoyed that Noor was still in her cell, noisily scraping away at the plaster that was keeping the last bar in her skylight in place. Faye whispered to her to be quiet and lie down while he scouted the roof. He'd already glanced around. Nothing squared with what Starr had told them about the layout of the roof and the nearby buildings.

Heading toward the rear of no. 84, Faye caught himself from sliding down a steep portion of the roof. If he hadn't, he would have plunged six floors into a small courtyard enclosed by no. 84 and a few other buildings. From a more secure portion of the roof, he looked down. Balconies on an adjoining building might prove useful, but Rue Pergolese, which Starr said would lead them away from Avenue Foch, was nowhere in sight. Starr's information was worthless.

Scrambling back to Noor's skylight, Faye found that she still had one more bar to remove. She'd ignored his admonition to be quiet. It was 11 p.m. Faye knew that if he got to the street, any street, he could find his way to friends whom he had kept out of the Resistance for their own safety. Now was their chance to help him. They could smuggle him to the Free Zone.

But first he had to get off this roof, and Noor, who was making a racket in her cell, wasn't helping. Faye begged her to work more discreetly.

At 1:30 in the morning, a guard escorted Starr to his cell. This was the moment he was waiting for. By ingratiating himself with the Germans, he'd learned what they knew about SOE agents who were already in France, which fields they knew were being used as landing strips for Lysanders, where weapons from England were being stored, and which agents' radios the Germans were using for their *Funkspiel*. If Starr got to London with this information, he'd be a hero.

Starr grabbed his notes, which contained all this information. Before climbing through his skylight, he left a note for Kieffer:

As you will have realized when you get this, we are trying to escape. Now that I hope we shall not be meeting again, I should like to thank you for the good treatment we have received here, and to say we shall not forget it.

Wishing you the best of luck in the chase that will follow, but much better luck to ourselves.

As Faye helped Starr through the skylight in the Englishman's cell, he assumed that the parcel Starr was carrying had everything he said he would provide for the escape: a rope tied together from strips from his blanket, some tools, a flashlight, and a master key for any locks they encountered. Faye was pleased Starr had joined him, but it was apparent that the Englishman was in a funk. To boost his spirits, Faye pointed out the balconies they could use as escape routes. That didn't help. Starr responded with a battery of questions: Was anyone living in that building? Had the Gestapo taken it over? Were the streets below clear? Were they guarded by Germans? Any resolve Starr once had was rapidly fraying.

Faye and Starr walked back to Noor's skylight. She needed help. The two men—mostly Faye: his arms were longer—reached in to help her remove her last bar. They finished around 3:30 a.m. and Faye helped her up to the roof. He was jubilant. Kissing Noor, he exclaimed, "We've done it! We're free!"

Tying their shoes around their necks so they'd make no noise, the three prisoners headed toward a building that would take them to a street behind 84 Avenue Foch. Suddenly, air-raid sirens began blasting. Noor, Faye, and

Starr froze: at that moment, they knew, guards were checking each cell in no. 84: they did this during every air raid to ensure that prisoners weren't somehow signaling to the planes flying overhead. Finding three empty cells, Germans poured into the streets and onto the roof. Noor, Faye, and Starr flattened themselves against the roof as flashlights scanned the air over them. As soon as the Germans left, they ran to the edge of the roof. Along the way, Starr, who was now sure they'd never get away, hid the notes he was carrying in a flowerpot that he passed. The Germans would badly punish him if they found the notes on him. Tying Faye's "rope" to an iron post on the roof, the three shimmied to a balcony on the fourth floor of a building next door. The door from the balcony into the adjacent apartment was locked. They then thought about climbing to the ground on the rope that was supposed to be in Starr's parcel.

The one rope they had—sixty feet of tied strips from Faye's blanket— was still dangling from the post on the roof. Reluctantly, Starr admitted that his parcel contained his intact blanket —he'd never torn it into strips to knot together. He also admitted he didn't have the flashlight and tools he'd promised. But even if Starr had brought a rope, it wouldn't help them reach the street. A solider patrolling the courtyard directly underneath them would have seen three prisoners lowering themselves to the ground. So Noor, Faye, and Starr jumped to the third-floor balcony of an adjacent building, smashed the glass on the door leading into the apartment, and stumbled inside. Feeling their way through the apartment in the dark, they reached the main staircase and climbed three flights down to the front door. They opened it a crack. The apartment building they were in was at the end of a cul de sac. Soldiers were patrolling the end that opened into a street. Noor, Faye, and Starr could wait inside the apartment building, hoping the Germans didn't find them. Or they could make a run for it. Faye talked the other two into running. Pressing themselves into the shadows opposite the building, they tiptoed single file toward the street. Faye ran out first. A German fired in his direction. Faye threw himself to the ground, got up and was about to run again when several SS men converged on him, clubbing him with their revolvers before dragging him back to 84.

Watching all this from where they were hiding, Noor whispered to Starr, "What do we do now?" "Go back," he motioned. Finding an unlocked door for an apartment in the building they'd come from, Noor and Starr let themselves in. Sitting on the couch, Noor burst into tears, sure she had lost her one chance for freedom. Hearing the racket, the woman who lived there came out of her bedroom, demanding to know what these strangers wanted. German troopers barged in as Noor was explaining that they had escaped from 84 Avenue Foch. Noor and Starr were marched right back where they had come from.

On the first floor of no. 84, two guards were holding Faye. Kieffer paced in front of him, barely in control of himself. When he saw Noor and Starr, Kieffer yelled that all of them would be shot: "Stand them up against the wall."

As the Gestapo lined the prisoners up, Faye protested that he had only been doing his duty by trying to escape. A guard slugged him. Meanwhile, other guards were telling Kieffer what they'd found in the prisoners' cells. Noor had drawn a "V" on the walls of her cell, and Starr had left a letter for Kieffer. Kieffer softened as he read Starr's comments about how well he'd been treated at no. 84. He softened more when a German found in Starr's pocket the photo of Kieffer that Starr was using as the basis of his unfinished portrait of the Gestapo chief.

"Why are you taking my photograph with you?" Kieffer asked.

"A little souvenir," Starr answered with a small smile.

Kieffer needed Starr for more than the portrait. Starr hadn't finished a map of the area that was controlled by one of the stronger Resistance groups. Kieffer told Starr that he wouldn't be sent to a prison in Germany if he gave his word of honor not to escape again. Twelve SOE agents would be shot if Starr reneged on his word. Starr promised, adding that the escape had been Noor's idea. Starr had gone along with it, he said, perhaps puckishly, because if a woman had the courage to escape, and he didn't, he would have been mocked if he ever got back to England. He later explained to the British that he vowed not to escape from 84 Avenue Foch so, if another prisoner had a reasonable chance of escaping, Starr could give him what he had learned about the German penetration of the SOE. Starr was sure that if he was transferred to a prison or a concentration camp in Germany, he could never convey any information to London.

Separately, Kieffer made the same offer to Noor and Faye: your word of honor that you will not escape again. If not, you will be sent to a prison in Germany. Both refused. To each, honor was inviolable, unbreachable. To Noor, it was also sacred. Her father had taught, "Break not your word of honor whatever may befall." If we couldn't build "our hope" on truth, he asked, then "on what shall we build" it? Noor clung to that hope.

Less than twenty-four hours after they were on the roof of 84 Avenue Foch, Noor and Faye were in a second-class compartment on a train. Several SS guards were watching them. The train had left the Gare de l'Est in Paris, then passed through suburbs and the countryside and rubble from recent bombings and orchards and fields, and finally over the Rhine into Germany. Faye was being taken to Bruchsal, about 336 miles east of Paris. Marie-Madeleine Fourcade, the head of the Alliance group, had intuited that Faye would not return from this mission he had insisted on joining. Aside from Faye's importance to the Resistance, Fourcade had another reason for him to survive: three months before Faye flew into France, Fourcade had given birth to their son. Fourcade had told only one *résistant* that she and Faye were engaged. Only one or two knew about their child. The boy would never meet his father.

Faye remained at Bruchsal for eight months. In June 1944, a military court sentenced him to death, and he was transferred to a concentration camp in south-central Germany. Himmler initially hoped to trade Faye to the Allies for Angelo Chiappe, a French official whom the Allies had sentenced to death for collaborating. On January 3, 1945, Faye was moved to Sonnenburg Prison in West Prussia. Twenty-seven days later, SS guards killed him and 318 other prisoners.

Noor's ultimate destination was Pforzheim, eleven miles deeper into Germany than where Faye was taken. The jailers who received each of them were given special orders: "*Ein wichtiger Terrorist, ein Spezialist des Entfliehens*" ("An important terrorist, an expert escapist").

Noor was the first British agent imprisoned in Germany, and one of the few locked up during the entire war under Hitler's *Nacht und Nebel*—Night and Fog—decree. Johann Wolfgang von Goethe, Germany's most acclaimed poet and playwright, coined the term in the nineteenth century, intending it to describe clandestine acts concealed by fog and the darkness of night. An enlightened liberal, Goethe would have been appalled by Hitler's appropriation of his eloquent locution. He would have been more bothered if he had known what happened to Night and Fog prisoners like the Dutch lawyer, Floris Bakels, who spent four years in solitary as a Night and Fog prisoner in six different concentration camps. Bakels learned about cold and rats and torture, and experienced how the Nazis created, in Bakels's words, "absolute uncertainty, from A to Z." Somehow, Bakels didn't break. Deeply religious, his survival rested on his faith: "When everything and everyone has been lost, you grasp instinctively for the one primary certainty: God's presence." Even so, Bakels longed to be with other people. He especially missed the curiosity and hope of children. In 1942, while shuffling through a village to another concentration camp, Bakels saw "a strange phenomenon." Behind the windows of the homes he passed, shadowy figures became visible— children. When he looked carefully, he could see they were wearing pajamas or nightdresses. "Mostly," Bakels wrote in his memoir published in 1977, "the shadowy figures stood motionless . . . Occasionally, someone waved, secretly. Waving children were rapidly pulled away. We were parting with civilization. We were now in the realm of ghosts."

In 1941, Hitler ordered his military to end "all chivalry" toward their enemies and disregard "every traditional restraint on warfare." "Efficient and enduring intimidation" in countries the Germans were occupying required killing prisoners within eight days after they were caught or clandestinely taking them to Germany. Shorn of their names, confined in cold cells, almost starved, Night and Fog prisoners were, in the Nazis' argot, "*vernebelt*"— transformed into mist. In the fog and the night, they would vanish without a trace. In a German prison, Noor would vanish.

CHAPTER 16

THE REALM OF GHOSTS

Before arriving at Pforzheim, Noor spent two nights—November 25 and 26—in a prison in Karlsruhe. Another SOE agent who was taken by railway from Paris to Karlsruhe around the same time described the people on the train platform in the German city as "plump and richly dressed." Though the women carried on their bodies the sartorial harvest of Europe, they succeeded in grafting onto their plunder "a native bad taste which had to be seen to be believed. A hat stolen from the Rue de la Paix was perched on a tight bun of tow-coloured hair; sheer silk stockings from the Place Vendome vanished into brown, flat-heeled boots; a mink cape from Rostov covered a knitted artificial silk jumper; rings from the ghetto of Warsaw were worn over deerskin gloves from Brussels. Among men, uniforms abounded but everywhere there was a sense of heaviness. Faces were drawn and anxious and there was many a glance at the sky."

The prison in Karlsruhe was the opposite of what Noor had been accustomed to at 84 Avenue Foch: not an elegant mansion, but dank and gray. Avenue Foch had seven cells on one floor. Karlsruhe had forty-one cells on four floors. All the prisoners at no. 84 had fought for the same cause: freedom. Karlsruhe's hundred prisoners were a shabby lot: crooks, rapists, a murderer or two. Avenue Foch was quiet, almost posh. Karlsruhe was noisy, scary.

In Karlsruhe, Noor was placed in chains: chains between her hands, chains between her feet. A chain joined the chains.

After forty-eight hours in Karlsruhe, Noor was transferred to a prison in Pforzheim, seventeen miles to the west. Prison authorities registered her

Angaben zur Person (Personal Information) as "Nora Baker," the only name by which the Germans knew her other than "Madeleine." Her *Geboren am* (birth date) was listed as January 1, 1920—the correct month and date, but off by four years. Her *Annahmetag und Tageszeif* (acceptance Day and Day Time) was 2:30 p.m., November 27. Her *Nummer des Gefangenbuches* (number in the Prisoner Book) was 461.

The prison in Pforzheim was surrounded by a high wall, and its four floors were topped by a steeply raked, red-tiled roof. New prisoners passed over a small bridge, then through a stone gatehouse that extended from one side of the massive building. It was like entering a medieval fortress. Pforzheim had originally been intended as an ordinary prison for ordinary prisoners. This changed. During the Great War, captured Allied officers were quartered here; during the current war, about one hundred political prisoners, *résistants,* and SOE agents were locked up here. At least eleven were women.

Noor was given the uniform worn by all *Nacht und Nebel* prisoners—a shirt with yellow horizontal stripes on the back along with the letters "NN." Yellow stripes were painted on her trouser legs. She remained in the leg irons that were chained to the handcuffs in which she'd been outfitted at Karlsruhe. "Bracelets of steel," one prisoner called them. The guards disliked the handcuffs: they were a nuisance to unlock. They had to do this sometimes so Noor could feed herself. The women who worked in the prison balked at cleaning the cells of prisoners who were shackled and in solitary. These cells were dirtier and messier than those of other prisoners.

Noor's cell—Cell no. 1—on the ground floor was essentially a square, roughly eight feet wide, eight feet high. Its one window was too high— almost six feet from the floor—for Noor to look out. Looking upward at a severe angle, she could see the sky, and nothing else. A black curtain was drawn over the window at night to prevent light from seeping out in case of an air raid. The walls of the cell were gray, the wooden floor was infested with bugs, and the narrow iron bed was attached to the wall. During the day, the bed could be swung up and folded against the wall. Some cells had washbasins and a toilet: Noor's had neither. To wash herself, a guard slid a bucket of water into her cell. To relieve herself, another bucket served as a toilet. The door to her cell was always locked. Prisoners walking by on their way to the courtyard wondered who was in there: no one emerged from Cell no. 1 and no sound came from it. This was not surprising: the walls were one and a half feet thick.

In this aloneness and this darkness—the lights in each cell went out at 7 p.m.—Noor spent her birthday on January 1, 1944. She turned thirty years old.

The women in Cell no. 12 couldn't restrain their curiosity about the prisoner in Cell no. 1. With a knitting needle, they scratched a message on the bottom of a mess tin, "Here are three French women." The tins were taken away every day to be cleaned. After a few rounds of washings, the women received a reply. On the bottom of a tin, Noor had scratched, "You are not alone. You have a friend. Cell no. 1." "That was the beginning of our correspondence," one of the women in Cell no. 12, Yolande Legrave, later recalled.

Over the years, historians have advanced many ideas about how Noor was able to scratch her messages to the women in Cell 12. Maybe she used the edge of a broken spoon, a knitting needle, a sewing needle, a pin, nail clippers, a nail file? Ernest Vogt, who had interrogated Noor at 84 Avenue Foch, rejected all of these. "To a prisoner under 'strictest conditions,'" Vogt said, "nothing is brought." Vogt was sure Noor used a sharp point that was on her handcuffs or chains. If so, the irony did not escape him: "She could subvert anything. The very chains that were used to keep her secure she used to send messages to London." This was Vogt's way of saying Noor hoped the women with whom she communicated at Pforzheim returned to England and conveyed her messages to the parties for whom she intended them. At least one woman did.

Noor had no idea that the women in Cell no. 12 belonged to Alliance, the group led by Léon Faye—Noor's rooftop companion at 84 Avenue Foch. In her "correspondence" with the women in Cell no. 12, Noor said she was "unhappy, very unhappy," and that she was manacled except at mealtime. The French women asked her name. At first, Noor replied, "I cannot give it." Later, she told them it was "Nora." On another tin, Noor asked the women not to tell her mother she was in prison. Ora should only learn about Noor's fate through a good friend of her mother's who worked at a school in the Porte de Lilas neighborhood of Paris. Noor gave them the name of this woman. On another tin, Noor wrote, "Think of me."

The days crawled by. Through the barred window that was too high for Noor to reach, she knew when a new day had broken, a day barely different than the one that preceded it. Every day would have been as identically dull and enervating as all the others had the prison guards not been so capriciously unpredictable. Their violence and their tempers distinguished Monday from Tuesday and Tuesday from Wednesday. And yet, through Noor's interior clockwork and through sotto voce "newscasts" that Noor heard from other prisoners, Noor kept track of calendrical milestones and of history, especially history: the past was keeping Noor alive more than the present.

On the day that marked the independence of the United States, Noor scratched, "Here's to the Fourth of July." On Bastille Day—July 14—she wrote, "Long live free France for that keeps us together." Next to that Noor scratched two flags: one British, one French. That year—1944— those days came a few weeks after D-Day. Noor had scratched to her friends in Cell no. 12, "Give me some news if you hear of any." Soon after D-Day, they did. Walking past Noor's cell on their way to the prison courtyard, they sang loudly in French about the invasion. Their voices carried through the barred grill above the door to Noor's cell. The news must have thrilled Noor although she never learned further details that would have buoyed her more: the groundwork she had helped lay down before her capture had contributed to D-Day being less of a bloodbath than it could have been. The day before the invasion, the SOE and the Resistance sabotaged 950 trains throughout France and dynamited hundreds of petrol dumps. On D-Day itself, about 100,000 *résistants* ambushed thousands of German troops. Much of this could not have occurred without Noor's help in rebuilding the SOE in France, ensuring that arms and money kept flowing to the Resistance as information about German targets flowed to England. One plan had been in the works since the previous July, when

Noor asked London to send a plane to pick up two French agents from a field near Auxerre. The agents had precious cargo: what Noor called a "basket of cherries"—a map of German defenses near Morbihan in Brittany. Two weeks before D-Day, Free French paratroopers jumped into Morbihan, teamed up with three thousand *résistants,* and shredded most of the Nazis' communication network in the region, slowing down a hundred thousand German troops who were desperately trying to get to Normandy on June 6 to stop the Allied forces flooding into France. The pilot who had flown the "cherries" to England in 1943 was Frank Rymills. A few weeks before Rymills picked up the "cherries," he had flown Noor to France in his Lysander. He carried the "cherries" to London on his last flight for the SOE.

Wilhelm Krauss, the warden of the prison in Pforzheim, was elderly and, by Nazi standards, kind and paternal. His orders had been that cells on either side of Noor's, and above hers and below hers, would be empty to ensure that she could not communicate with other prisoners.

The Gestapo had also ordered that no one—not even the prison staff—talk with Noor. One day, though, Krauss went into Noor's cell. He had never seen a prisoner in chains, and never imagined a woman would be treated this way. On further visits, they talked about music and literature and Indian philosophy, and about Noor's father and Sufism, and why she had come back to France. Noor was too decent to be in manacles and chains, Krauss decided. He removed them. "I felt sorry for the English girl," he told the Allies in 1946. Removing the chains relieved Noor of more than their weight. A prisoner elsewhere whose chains were removed after he spent two years in them experienced the "weird sensation to be able to move my hands individually, to be able to hold two things at once. . . ." His arms felt long, almost not quite part of him, "like uncaged birds, simultaneously happy and perplexed what to do with themselves. For a little moment, I am disposed to wonder if all this freedom may not become a menace. . . . The more man has, the more he wants."

Noor could hold things and stretch her arms and wiggle her feet and indulge in a captive's peculiar facsimile of freedom and liberty. Quite likely, the kindness Krauss had shown her by removing her chains required her to recalibrate whatever equilibrium she had established. As another inmate who had also received a human gesture from the Nazis observed, "a little indication of chivalry from an enemy" is like "a stab in the back of one's equanimity."

Krauss's gesture let Noor return, briefly, from the realm of ghosts. He even let her take walks in the prison's courtyard. Through the window in their cell that overlooked the courtyard, the women who had scratched "letters" to Noor on mess tins could see her, and she could see them. One day, Noor smiled at them. They saw Noor only three times.

The Gestapo, furious when it learned Krauss had removed Noor's chains, ordered him to put them on her and keep them on. If Krauss didn't do this, he could "expect a violent escape attempt from the English prisoner." The Gestapo also reminded Krauss that two guards had to be present whenever the door to Noor's cell was opened. Krauss did as he was told. Unknowingly, he behaved as if he was familiar with what Noor's father had once said: "The warden of the prison is in a worse position than the prisoner himself; while the body of the prisoner is in captivity, the mind of the warden is in prison."

Other prisoners tried to lift Noor's spirits, especially the women in one cell, who sang so loudly that their voices carried to Noor. Hearing this, a guard raced to Noor's cell, dragged her to the basement and beat her. "Poor Nora," the women said.

Half a year after Noor came to Pforzheim, a guard noted that her "state of mind has worsened considerably. . . . She is not able to read German books. There is nothing for her to do. She is left alone and left to herself." The guard heard Noor murmur, "My loneliness is unbearable." The rest of Noor's murmuring was jumbled and incoherent.

Some prisoners locked in solitary found freedom in a few ways:

Silence: The silence of the prison gave inmates access to thoughts they would have ignored if they were anyplace else. These ramblings of their mind were a relief. They confirmed they were alive and sentient, and they frustrated the Gestapo's efforts to reduce prisoners to a lesser and cruder species.

Dreams: On the wings of their visions and their imaginings, prisoners could float through time and space, meeting other people or themselves on high peaks or busy cities or faraway places. In any place but Pforzheim.

Introspection: A recluse, a male prisoner reflected after surviving years in solitary in Nazi prisons, educates himself in "the beauty of simple things, things that would pass unnoticed, or, at best, be considered a nuisance in the world outside." This prisoner gave names to flies and attributed nationalities to them. He let them alight on his nose or his forehead, and was entranced by one, "a delicate little person . . . profoundly conscious of the seductive contours of her own loveliness." "Incomparable pleasure" was extracted from "the meanest of acquisitions—a nail, an inch of pencil lead, a scrap of paper, a splinter of glass, an empty toothpaste tube, a string, a twig with a leaf upon it. . . . For the recluse, deprived of human, animal or material contact, there is perhaps a fragment of nature to gaze upon—a cushion of moss high up in the arch of the window; the anatomy of a tree clothed in summer, naked in winter. What else is there for the man to do but escape inside himself?" Quite likely Noor also retreated into herself. Before the war she had written that solitude was a way to know what she called her "true self." Everyone, she believed, descends into a darkness "before realization shall come." In the darkness of Pforzheim, she would have tested that conviction. The darkness would worsen as the city of Pforzheim received some of its worst bombing of the war.

For most of the war, Pforzheim was spared. In September 1939, there was one air raid though no planes appeared. In 1940, there were thirty-five air raids. The only damage occurred on August 19 when bombs destroyed two buildings and harmed no one. After that, Pforzheim was virtually ignored until early 1944. Then, the city was pounded relentlessly. The Nazis knew the attacks were imminent: in December, police warned Pforzheim's officials that local utilities and factories were tempting targets for the Allies. The city had to build more air-raid shelters. Fast. A few months later, at 11 a.m. on April 1, ninety-eight American bombers swept in from the southeast, dropping 269 tons of bombs. Ninety-five people were killed and 127 homes were destroyed. Raids continued throughout the spring and summer. The worst bombing was near the train station. Noor's prison was a few blocks away. It shook with every explosion.

\   .   .   .

Back in London, a few people in the SOE were worrying about Noor. In early October, a radio operator in France had sent a message to London that Noor had been arrested—"had serious accident and in hospital," in the SOE's standard euphemism. The SOE ignored the message. Noor's radio then went off the air for ten days. When it returned, its messages lacked Noor's security checks. (Though the Gestapo had obtained Noor's codes and messages when it arrested her, it didn't have her security checks. Those were in her head, not her notebooks.) Leo Marks, the SOE's codemaster, warned Maurice Buckmaster about the omissions. Buckmaster brushed Marks off—London would keep listening to Noor's radio. She was reliable and she hadn't failed yet. As Marks walked away, he prayed "that Noor was not having one of her lapses" even as he knew he was "having one of my own [lapses] not to accept the truth."

Around Christmas, the SOE was sufficiently concerned that it tried to determine exactly who was using Noor's radio. Gerry Morel, a highly respected officer, worried that recent messages lacked Noor's "fist." London radioed Noor to send personal information about her family. Kieffer, the Gestapo officer who ran 84 Avenue Foch, didn't know some of the answers. An aide he sent to Pforzheim came back empty-handed: Noor wouldn't help him. Kieffer cobbled together what he'd gleaned from Noor's letters to her mother, hoping that would satisfy London. Also helpful was what Noor had let slip about her life to the one Gestapo agent she'd semi-trusted at 84 Avenue Foch. Kieffer's answers were enough for the SOE.

For almost two years, London had been ignoring the absence of security codes from some agents' messages. Up to fifteen percent of transmissions from Europe were so garbled that London was content deciphering what it could while ignoring the frequent dearth of security codes. London even ignored a warning that was typed at the top of some messages after they had been decoded: "Identity Check Omitted." An "identity check" was the same as an agent's security code. The SOE's eagerness to "set Europe ablaze," to borrow Churchill's phrase, blinded it to the failure of its own precautions.

Fooled, the SOE continued to send agents to France that "Madeleine" requested. On the night of February 8/9, four agents parachuted near Poitiers—R. E. J. Alexandre, Robert Byerley, Fred Deniset, and Jacques Ledoux. On

February 28/29, three more agents parachuted into a field near the village of Saintville—Madeleine Damerment, Lionel Lee, and France Antelme. The Gestapo was waiting for all of them. The Gestapo, as "Madeleine," radioed London that six of these seven agents were safe. Antelme, the Germans transmitted, "severely damaged his head" while landing and was in "critical condition" in a hospital. On April 21, "Madeleine" radioed that Antelme had died. In truth, the Gestapo was torturing him, first at 84 Avenue Foch, then in its more notorious cellars devoted to pain and misery at 11 Rue des Saussaies.

Meanwhile, Maurice Buckmaster was recommending Noor for a George Cross, a medal for exceptional heroism that King George VI had created soon after the war began. Buckmaster extolled Noor's "cool initiative" and "truly remarkable courage." She had survived "several narrow escapes" and possessed a preternatural knack to "always save her . . . [radio when her "safe" house] became unsafe and re-establish it elsewhere." Despite "all personal danger," Noor had refused to go home. "As a result," said Buckmaster, the Prosper circuit "today is in perfect order. . . . It is unique in the annals of this organization for a circuit to be so completely disintegrated and yet to be rebuilt," all while Noor never broke her radio contact with England and the Gestapo was constantly pursuing her. "Inayat Khan's work and example has been beyond praise," Buckmaster concluded. "Had she been a man she would have been recommended without hesitation for the Military Cross," a more prestigious award that was not awarded to a woman until 2007.

The medal was an honor, and a well-deserved one. Yet a few weeks later, Buckmaster accepted what Leo Marks had been saying for months: the Gestapo had Noor. The fist on her radio had changed, and security codes had been missing from all her recent messages. And then there were those seven agents the Gestapo was waiting for in February. Details about their arrival had been sent to only one radio in France: Noor's.

Leo Marks was training a new agent when he received a phone call from a signal master who was convinced the Germans were operating Noor's set. Marks looked away from the agent, pretending to be absorbed in a coding problem. When he had a few moments to collect himself, Marks prayed silently: "Please God . . . can anything be done to help Noor, who knows you by another name? I can feel her pain from here, and I know how much worse it must be for you."

. . .

Throughout, the SOE kept assuring Noor's mother that Noor was fine. In January 1944, Col. E. G. Bisset wrote to Ora, "We have just received the following message for you from your daughter: 'Happy New Year to all at home and love. A big kiss and thanks a million for the birthday greetings'"—Bisset's letter was dated four days after Noor's birthday. "Could you please," Bisset asked of Ora, "send me a letter by return, which I could pass on to her. I should be glad if you would write it on thin paper." The next letter Ora received came from Major L. K. Mackenzie, who was "pleased" to tell her that "news of your daughter continues to be good. She is very well and working hard. She sends you the following message: 'All my love to mother, Claire and Vic.'" Mackenzie's letter was dated May 29, 1944—four months after the SOE concluded the Germans had caught Noor and were using her radio.

Ora's letters to Noor were steady and regular, addressed to her "dearest little daughter" and "sweetest little daughter" and full of news about Vilayat ("Vic has been over here several times. He longs for a letter from you") and about Claire ("She is doing well and visits once or twice a week") and assuring Noor that, "when we are together, we miss little Babsy, and just imagine her coming in the door. What a glorious day it will be when she does come!"

```
                              War Office,
                              Room 238,
                              Hotel Victoria,
                              Northumberland Avenue,
                              London, S.W.1.

                              29th May, 1944.

        Dear Mrs. Baker-Inayat,

                    We are pleased to tell
        you that our news of your daughter
        continues to be good.

                    She is very well and
        working hard.  She sends you the
        following message:  "All my love
        to mother, Claire and Vic."

                              Yours sincerely,

                              (I. K. Mackenzie  Major)

        Mrs. O. R. Baker-Inayat,
        4 Taviton Street,
        London, W.C.1.
```

The SOE's letter to Ora, May 1944: Noor was "well." In truth, she had been in German prisons for ten months.

CHAPTER 17

GETHSEMANE AND GOLGOTHA

Nineteen forty-four was not a good year for Hitler. Nineteen forty-three hadn't gone too well, either. This wasn't the war he'd imagined: England was supposed to surrender, Russia collapse, and the United States stay away from these messy European eruptions. Only France, which crumbled in six weeks, did as Hitler expected. But after 650,000 Russian troops surrendered in 1941 at the Battle of Kiev, winter came, and the temperature dropped to sixty below, and the next spring, Russia came roaring back to life. Half of Germany's Sixth Army were dead or dying and 91,000 were in POW camps. An internal report by the SS spelled out what everyone knew, and what no one was saying: "Stalingrad means a turning point in the war . . . Stalingrad is the beginning of the end."

Then came D-Day, and ten days later over one million British, Canadian, and American troops were in France and Hitler began retreating—first to his bunker, then from all reason. At a meeting with Hitler on July 20, General Claus von Stauffenberg slid his briefcase underneath the table, then quietly left the room for a prearranged phone call. Seeing a cloud of debris behind him and members of the high command hurled through doors and windows, Stauffenberg assumed the bomb in his briefcase had killed Hitler. He was mistaken: the Fuehrer was barely scratched. By the time Stauffenberg joined his fellow conspirators in Berlin, Hitler was shrieking about revenge. In the witch hunt that he unleashed, seven thousand people were arrested and almost five thousand were killed. Most were innocent of any crimes against the state. The executions continued to the last days of the war. And somehow, even as the Russians were closing in from the east and the Americans, British, and Canadians from the west, Hitler made time for the SOE, ordering that "all terror and sabotage troops of the British and their accomplices, who do not act like soldiers but rather like bandits, will be ruthlessly eliminated."

The Gestapo had kept most SOE agents alive. That gave the Germans a chance to extract secrets or personal information from them to convince London that *Funkspiel* messages were genuine. But the games from Paris were over now: on D-Day, the Germans sent their last message to London from 84 Avenue Foch, thanking the British for "large deliveries of arms and ammunition" and gleefully anticipating their "visit for which we have prepared everything nicely." London responded just as puckishly: "Sorry to see your patience is exhausted and your nerves not so good as ours. . . . Give us ground near Berlin for reception . . . but be sure you do not clash with our Russian friends."

As the Allies neared Paris, the Germans who had been *Funkspiel*ing from Avenue Foch took one radio with them, continuing to fool Britain with transmissions first from Nancy in France, then in Germany from Offenberg, Freiberg, and lastly near Lake Constance as late as April 1945. The game worked as well as ever: in January, several Allied agents dropped straight into German hands.

With the radio games over from Paris, the Germans had no need for the 136 SOE agents they were holding. In the spring of 1944, the Gestapo began transferring all of the agents it had caught to Germany, a few to prisons, most to concentration camps where they were usually killed. In June, ten agents were shot at Gross Rosen. On July 6, four female SOE agents were given lethal injections in Natzweiler. The killing accelerated in the fall. Between September 4 and 11, seventy-seven agents were shot or hanged at Gross Rosen, Mauthausen, and Buchenwald. Also on September 11, Noor scratched her last message to the three women in Cell no. 12 in Pforzheim: "I am going." The three women in Cell no. 12 were bereft; one of them, Yolande Lagrave, told investigators after the war: "She was no longer with us." With the Allies advancing, the women thought maybe Noor had been sent to a prison or a camp farther from the front lines. If all went well, they would be reunited in London after the war, celebrating their victory.

. . .

At 6:15 on the night of September 11, the Gestapo drove Noor to the prison in Karlsruhe, where she had spent two nights the previous November. Noor wasn't told why she was being taken to another prison. She spent part of the night of September 11/12 in a cell in Karlsruhe. Around 1:30 a.m., an elderly prison orderly—described by one prisoner as "small, shrunken and gray-looking"—woke Noor up and took her to the warden's office on the ground floor. Three other women—Yolande Beekman, Madeleine Damerment, and Eliane Plewman, all SOE agents and all French citizens—soon joined her.

Noor and Yolande Beekman had trained together at Wanborough Manor in 1943. A corporal there had dismissed Beekman as someone who "would make an excellent wife for an unimaginative man, but not much more than that." He was wrong. Once she got to France, Beekman—a thirty-two-year-old native of Paris—operated a radio in northern France for four months. Her transmissions helped the Royal Air Force accelerate the rate of its arms drops. Within months, there were twenty large deliveries of Sten guns, bazookas, and explosives. Beekman served in the reception committees for most of these drops, then distributed the munitions to Resistance groups. Also, ten locomotives were destroyed, and numerous signal boxes, storage sheds, and more than a hundred miles of tracks were in shreds.

Like Noor, Beekman had been told to destroy all the messages she received or sent on her radio. She kept them. Also contrary to her orders, she contacted friends she had known before the war. Unlike Noor, Beekman rarely changed the location that she used for her radio, transmitting for months from the attic of the same house in Saint-Quentin. In late December, the Gestapo arrested her. She said nothing. They tortured her. She revealed nothing. When she was moved to 84 Avenue Foch and refused to help the Gestapo's *Funkspiel*, Beekman was transferred to the prison in Karlsruhe. To kill time, Beekman drew on toilet paper: prison authorities refused to give her paper. For ink, she pricked herself with a needle and used her blood to paint imaginary feasts of plates heaped with grapes and meat and bread. Somehow that assuaged her hunger.

Also brought to the warden's office that night was Madeleine Damerment. She had helped seventy-five Allied aviators escape over the Pyrenees.

When it was obvious in late 1942 that a *résistant* had betrayed her, she was flown to England, volunteered for the SOE, and flew back to France on the night of February 28/29, 1944, parachuting near Chartres. The Gestapo was waiting for her. They'd heard about her arrival on Noor's radio.

Finally, there was Eliane Plewman. Asked during her SOE training why she wanted to fight the Germans, she blurted out, "Because I hate them." Plewman parachuted into France on August 13/14, 1943, to join a cell in the Marseilles area where 240,000 Germans were waiting for the Allies to invade. For six months, Plewman coordinated sabotage and intelligence-gathering groups in southern France, often loading onto trucks explosives and arms the RAF had just dropped. On some of these trips, her driver gave lifts to hitchhiking Germans soldiers who were unaware they were sitting on top of boxes of arms and dynamite. Arrested in March 1944, Plewman was tortured with electric shock. The Germans got nothing out of her and locked her up in solitary in Cell no. 16 in Karlsruhe.

In the warden's office, the four women expressed surprise to each other about how well they looked, especially Noor who had been in solitary for almost a year. A Gestapo agent, Christian Ott, then handcuffed the women in pairs—"the usual manner" to restrain prisoners, he later told British authorities. "I had been warned to exercise every care." Around 2:30 a.m., Ott drove the women to Bruchsal, about sixteen miles away. Max Wassmer, the Gestapo agent who was in charge of the transport, joined them at the train station. Wassmer had left Karlsruhe the day before to visit his family in Bruchsal. The six of them boarded a train for Stuttgart.

In Stuttgart, the group waited almost an hour at the station for the train to Munich. The temperature was in the mid-fifties, the skies were clear, and the women were happy to stand outside on the platform and talk among themselves. For the first time since her arrest, Noor could talk freely with other SOE agents without worrying about Germans overhearing her. The two Gestapo agents were far enough from the women that they couldn't eavesdrop and, anyway, they didn't understand English. Though train service was as regular as five years of war allowed, the station was surrounded by devastation. Stuttgart had suffered twenty-six bombing raids since 1940. The twenty-seventh raid would begin nineteen hours after the train carrying Noor left the station—211 planes from the Royal Air Force would drop over 184,000 incendiary sticks, 4,300 explosion bombs, and 74 blockbuster bombs. The firestorm would spread over two square miles, killing almost one thousand people and injuring another sixteen hundred. People died in cellars, tunnels, churches, in the street, in a slaughterhouse. "We thought the end had come," said a priest. "Gethsemane, Golgotha—it seemed so near." By then, the four women who had been waiting at the train station early in the morning were long gone.

Christian Ott knew from the start that they were going to Dachau. He'd volunteered so he could visit his family in Stuttgart on the return trip. But he was confused: since 1933, when Dachau was built, only men had been sent there. Ott kept asking Wassmer if Dachau was now taking women. Annoyed at Ott's badgering, Wassmer handed him a telegram from Gestapo headquarters in Berlin: "The four prisoners will be transferred from . . . KARLSRUHE to the KZ DACHAU and will then be immediately executed." Realizing, as he put it, "the seriousness of this transport," Ott was sorry he had volunteered: "If I had known this. I would have foregone the pleasure of a visit to my family in Stuttgart." Besides, the prisoners had "made a good impression" on him and he "regretted their fate."

On the 150-mile train ride to Munich, the two Germans who were escorting the women thought the prisoners were enjoying themselves though they had no idea what their charges were saying. They were certainly pleased when Wassmer told the one woman who spoke German—Yolande Beekman—that they were going to a camp in the south where they would farm and get lots of sun and never be locked up in a dark cell. In Munich, they changed to a train for the fifteen-mile ride to Dachau. During the Great War, the economy of the town of Dachau had largely depended on a new munitions factory. When that closed, there was talk of the factory's grounds being used for a gynecological clinic. The Nazis soon made other use of the factory's five acres.

For the Nazis, Dachau was a "model" concentration camp. Weeks after coming to power in 1933, they began housing political opponents in the workers' barracks that were still standing from the abandoned munitions factory. The first prisoners—two hundred—arrived on March 22. By the time Noor arrived, over thirty thousand prisoners were crammed into thirty-four barracks—the camp had been built for six thousand men— and the death rate was roughly four hundred a month.

Germans came to Dachau—the Nazis called it their "Academy of Violence"—to learn how to run death factories. Once they mastered this monstrous craft, they were "promoted" to other camps in Hitler's efficient gulag. Dachau invented the architecture and the mechanics of Hitler's slaughterhouses: The three-story gatehouse—the *Jourhaus*—that contained most of the camp's administrative offices. The towers along the perimeter of the camp manned by SS troopers with machine guns. "*Arbeit Macht Frei*"—"Work sets you free"—arced in metal letters above the entryway. The guards who shot dead any prisoner who ventured into the ten-foot-wide no-man's land that fanned out along the entire border of the camp. Beyond no-man's land was an electric fence. Beyond that was barbed wire. Prisoners at Dachau were tortured, starved, gassed, shot, pummeled, and forced to be guinea pigs for medical experiments. Many killed themselves. Dachau, said one inmate—a Catholic priest, Father Sales Hess—was "*Eine Welt ohne Gott,*" a world without God.

This was Dachau. The model camp.

Around 10 or 11 p.m. on September 12, the women from Karlsruhe walked the three kilometers from the train station in the city of Dachau to the concentration camp. They reached the camp about forty-five minutes later. More than twenty hours had elapsed since they had left their prison cells. Walking under the *Arbeit Macht Frei* sign, the women disappeared into the camp. Christian Ott spent the night sleeping on the second floor of the gatehouse. He never saw Noor or the other women again.

Ott later claimed that Max Wassmer, with whom he had accompanied the women to Dachau, went into the camp early on the morning of September 13—the day after all of them left Karlsruhe prison. Returning about 8:30 a.m., Wassmer told Ott that the commander of the camp had informed him the women would be executed at 9 a.m. Wassmer promptly left, then returned about 10:30 a.m. with a report: the women had spent the night in separate cells. Around 9 a.m., several SS troopers took them to where they would be

executed. With only the camp commander and two SS men present, Wassmer read the death sentence to the women. Yolande Beekman translated the
verdict to the other three. They "grew pale and wept," Wassmer told Ott.
Beekman asked if the sentence could be appealed. The camp commander said
no appeal was possible. He also declined Beekman's request for a priest: there
were no priests, he said, at Dachau. (That was a lie. Since the camp opened
in 1933, more than 2,500 priests had been interned there. By September 1944,
when Noor and the three other women were taken to Dachau, about half of
the priests had died or been killed. and roughly 1,200 were confined to barracks
26, 28, and 30, barely five hundred yards from where the women were standing.)

The women were ordered to face a small mound of earth and kneel.
Lowering themselves to their knees, two of the women held hands. The
other two did, also. The SS troopers then shot each of them in the back of
the neck. Three of the women died instantly. Beekman showed some signs
of life. She was shot again.

The "small mound of earth" was a ditch about 130 feet to the right of the
crematorium and parallel to the seven-foot-high wall that surrounded the
camp. The wall was topped by three rows of barbed wire. Many prisoners were executed here. Yolande Beekman's husband later speculated that,
"upon arriving at this spot, they must have seen the bloodstains from the
previous victims."

After the killings, Christian Ott said Wassmer told him, four prisoners
loaded the bodies of the women onto handcarts. Wassmer wasn't certain
what happened to them. He assumed the bodies were cremated. Ashes from
cremations were usually buried in holes in the ground to the side and the
rear of the crematorium, which had been constructed by imprisoned priests
after they received a crash course in bricklaying. Hidden from outside view
by a tall hedge, immediately in front of the crematorium was a small formal garden, neatly cut grass, a water fountain, and several birdhouses from
which turtledoves came and went.

Wassmer's version of Noor's death was more selective than Ott's. In 1950,
a friend of Noor's wrote to Wassmer. She tried to put him to ease with
assurances that she had no intention of prosecuting him: she was simply
seeing Noor's story through to its end. Surprised when Wassmer responded,
she might have been more surprised by how much Wassmer's story differed
from Ott's. (In those years, the British government embargoed almost all

official documents related to the SOE. Ott's deposition would have been among them.) In Wassmer's telling, the women traveled in a reserved compartment on the train from Stuttgart. He let them have the window seats, treated them to bread and sausages, and shared his cigarettes with them. The women talked in a "lively fashion" in English. When the train stopped briefly between Stuttgart and Augsburg during an air raid, all the passengers stayed aboard. The women continued talking and did not seem afraid. At Dachau, he handed the women over to camp authorities and didn't learn until returning to Karlsruhe that they had been killed.

In a face-to-face interview three years earlier with Vera Atkins, the F Section officer who had seen Noor off to France from Tangmere air base in 1943, Wassmer gave essentially the same story that he would later provide Noor's friend—except then he said he knew the four women had been murdered before he left Dachau: the SS had given him a "receipt" for their bodies. And rather than simply *omit* the details of being at Noor's execution, he explicitly denied to Atkins that he had been anywhere near it.

A third account of Noor's murder came from H. C. Wickey, who served in Canadian intelligence during the war and participated in the War Crimes Commission afterward. A "minor official" from Dachau told him soon after the war that Beekman, Damerment, and Plewman had been taken to a spot near the crematorium a few hours after arriving at Dachau. There, most of their clothes were ripped off them—"they were in rags, anyhow"—and they were kicked and slapped, then shot. Meanwhile, Noor was chained outside the crematorium, "almost naked." A man "who was fond of this type of sport" beat Noor before she was thrown into a cell in "the bunker," a long, low building at the other end of the camp that had 136 cells for prisoners who were defiant and uncooperative. Noor spent the night on the floor of her cell. In another cell a few doors down from Noor's was Martin Niemöller, the Lutheran pastor who had vigorously fought the Nazis' takeover of churches in Germany. After the war, Niemöller gained fame for his confession about the timidity that had contaminated Germans during Hitler's reign:

> First they came for the communists, and I did not speak out—
> Because I was not a communist.
> Then they came for the trade unionists, and I did not speak out—

Because I was not a trade unionist.
Then they came for the Jews, and I did not speak out—
Because I was not a Jew.
Then they came for me—and there was no one left to speak for me.

At Dachau, no one spoke for Noor.

The morning after Noor was beaten near the crematorium, the German who had struck her the previous night beat her again, this time in her cell. Then he shot her and ordered several inmates to carry her body almost one-third of a mile to the crematorium. There, the inmates tossed her body into the oven. At that point, the "minor" German official told Wickey, the Canadian, Noor was either "dead or half dead."

A fourth account of Noor's hours at Dachau came from Dirk Johannes Christiaan Peters, a Dutch policeman the Nazis arrested in 1942 for allegedly being in the Resistance. According to Peters, one night Wilhelm Ruppert, who supervised executions at Dachau, ordered Peters to find a kapo named Joop and bring him to the crematorium. There, Joop and Peters found Ruppert and two SS men. With them was a "beautiful, dark girl." Twice she

The crematoriums at Dachau where Noor's body was burned.

At a trial in 1945, a former prisoner at Dachau charged Wilhelm Ruppert (standing, right) with war crimes. Ruppert was not accused for another twelve years with executing Noor with a bullet in her head.

looked at Peters who "could not say anything. She knew that her time was coming to die, but she did not suffer." Peters returned to his barracks. Joop later told him that after the SS men stripped Noor of all her clothes, Ruppert beat her "all over her body. . . . She did not cry or say anything. When Ruppert got tired and the girl was a bloody mess, he said he would shoot her. She kneeled. Ruppert shot her from behind and through the head. Her only word before the execution was "Liberté!" Noor's body, according to Joop, was burned in the crematorium that same night.

Four stories. Each a slight variant of the others. None came from anyone who admitted he had killed Noor or that he had witnessed her murder. Or from a prisoner who had thrown Noor's body into the crematorium. Rather, there were accusations—Max Wassmer's and Christian Ott's against unnamed SS men, and Dirk Peters's against Wilhelm Ruppert. And though Ott said Wassmer was present at Noor's murder, Wassmer claimed at one point that he didn't know *until* he returned to Karlsruhe that Noor had been executed and, at another point, that he had received a "receipt" for Noor's body *before* leaving Dachau. Even if Wassmer didn't pull the trigger, he had figuratively pulled it: he had known Noor's doom from the start of their journey from Karlsruhe, and he had shown Ott a telegram to that effect while the two men were waiting for the train in Stuttgart as the four women stood only a few feet from them. And though Peters said Ruppert shot Noor in the back of the head, Ruppert could never respond to that accusation: he was hanged on May 28, 1946 after a military tribunal convicted him for executing Soviet prisoners and for beating and whipping other prisoners, often until they lost consciousness. Survivors of Dachau said Ruppert was like a blacksmith striking cold iron when he beat prisoners: he never changed his expression.

Unraveling war crimes is not a precise science, and executioners rarely come forward to clear their conscience (especially if they were committed Nazis, for whom the idea of conscience was alien and discordant). Whether Wassmer or Ruppert pulled the trigger, whether Noor was beaten all night or "only" a few hours, whether she was killed soon after arriving at Dachau or the next morning or in a cell or in a ditch near the crematorium, whether she was silent or stoic or defiant—all that, in the greater scheme of things, doesn't matter. All the accounts have certain commonalities: Noor was taken by train to Dachau. She was beaten. She was murdered. All the rest, as they say, is commentary.

Still, perhaps, one comment is warranted. More than seven decades after Noor was killed, a German woman showed an American through Dachau. Both the German and the American were driven by the unknowability of Noor's death and by the collision of "details" about it that could have been myth or legend or the self-exculpation of culprits and their accomplices. The German and the American also didn't understand the Nazis' compulsion to kill Noor, especially as mighty armies were advancing on Germany. Those were the enemies on whom the Nazis should have been concentrating, not this woman who was murdered in a cell or in a ditch, depending on which of the versions of her death carries the scent of truth.

"What makes sense?" the German woman asked, struggling for comprehension. "Did it make sense to kill four young women? Were they that dangerous? Was Noor dangerous? Who did she threaten? What makes sense? I do not know. I don't think we will ever know."

The SOE continued to send Noor's mother positive reports about her daughter. Eight days after Noor was killed at Dachau, Ora responded to a "letter" from her daughter:

> We are so happy to know you are well. . . . How we long to see you again, little Babs! You are always and always in our thoughts. When shall we be given the happiness of having you again in our midst, bringing sunshine into the home? Each day closes with disappointment . . . .
>
> It is a real sacrifice to live through these months without receiving your sweet little letters. I am sure it is terribly difficult for you, also, to be silent to your family, knowing you as I do. I suppose though that we must have still more patience, hoping for a final reunion.
>
> Love always and always from Mother

On September 29, 1944, another letter from the SOE reiterated its optimism about Noor: "I am glad to tell you that we have good news of your daughter." This was now sixteen days after Noor's murder, and the SOE knew little more about Noor's circumstances than her mother did.

After D-Day, some of the SOE's top officers went to Paris to learn more about what had transpired at 84 Avenue Foch. By then, some SOE agents operating in France had come forward, relieved that they no longer had to hide in the shadows. Noor was not among them. No one knew where she was. On October 15, 1944, the SOE sent Ora an entirely different letter than those she had recently received:

> Dear Mrs. Baker Inayat:
>
> I am extremely sorry to have to inform you that we have recently been out of touch with your daughter. Due to the confused state of affairs in France, we were not unduly worried. But I am afraid now that your daughter must be

considered as missing although there is every reason to believe that she will eventually be notified as a prisoner of war. . . ."

We depart from earth, Noor's father had said, when we have "fulfilled the purpose" for which we had come. With "nothing more"—Inayat's words—holding us here, our soul journeys elsewhere, attending to the work that lies ahead. While older souls that have departed from earth ascend toward God, newer ones descend toward earth. The older souls impart knowledge and talent to those who are descending, helping them "determine the path they tread in the future." This collaboration between souls is not reincarnation. Inayat did not believe in that. Rather, certain souls may come to earth already endowed with specific talents—say, a flair for poetry or music or a heightened acumen or military prowess—not because they had honed these in previous lifetimes, but because they received these qualities from souls who were ascending toward God and who had nurtured these skills on earth. By transferring talents in this manner, Inayat wrote, "the attributes of the past souls are manifested again. A soul may receive the impressions of one soul or of a few souls or of many souls." Thus, giving is as essential in the next world as in this one. Here, it enriches others; in the next world, it enriches others also, as it lightens an ascending soul of "all its properties" until it loses the memories of its various manifestations, and of its individuality, so it can ultimately "merge in the infinite, divine Consciousness."

Noor agreed with her father about the synergy between old and new souls. But she was more emphatic about certain matters than he was, returning again and again to the principle that only by *not* judging others and by *always* forgiving them can we proceed to the "highest and most inconceivable" joy of all—"the experience of non-existence and the experience of God." Forgiving and being nonjudgmental relieve us of the ballast that weigh us down, freeing us to ascend to increasingly more rarefied planes and dimensions.

At Dachau, Noor became powder: ashes floating with the wind, darkening the clouds that hung over an already dark Germany. If we accept what Noor believed and what her father taught, her spirit was already mingling with new souls, offering them her skills and her talents, her optimism and her hope. What happened to her beyond that is not for any of us to say.

Though the afterlife is a hope and a conundrum, a condition beyond us and a condition that may always be with us, the renowned Sufi poet Rumi had a fairly specific idea about it. "Through love," wrote Rumi, whom Noor's father had greatly admired,

> bitter things become sweet,
> Through love bits of copper are turned to gold.
> Through love dregs become purest wine;
> Through love pain becomes a healing balm.
> Through love the dead become alive . . .

"I PRAY *WITH* NOOR"

Concentration and contemplation are great
things; but no contemplation is greater than the
life we have about us every day.

—HAZRAT INAYAT KHAN

K illed three months after D-Day, Noor had no way of knowing Vilayat's role in the invasion for which she had been so essential, and he, of course, had no way of knowing hers. Two nights before June 6, Vilayat's minesweeper helped clear the Channel so ships could land Allied troops. The sailors on his command were as terrified as he was when a mine had to be defused: the Channel was saturated with explosives, each powerful, formidable, frightening. Often, Vilayat had to defuse them himself. On the second night, he fell into the water. If not for his shouts and his life preserver—he had never learned to swim—he would have been swept away.

Between June 6 and 19, Vilayat and his crew docked four times on the beaches in Normandy, bringing men, weapons, and equipment as the battles raged farther and farther inland.

With the Germans on the run, Vilayat had an opportunity to visit his family's home in Suresnes in the spring of 1945. "Crowds gathered to welcome him most enthusiastically," his mother wrote to Noor, still believing she was alive. Initially disturbed that "every piece of furniture" in Fazal Manzil "had been removed," Vilayat soon located most of it in neighbors' homes. He badgered soldiers, officers, officials in the SOE and the Red Cross—*anyone*—about Noor. Trying to remain optimistic, he wrote to his mother, "Camp after camp are being rescued and prisoners retrieved. So it is now just a question of time [before the war is over] and this, judging from the general situation is going to be short. . . . Another month or two should see Germany in full retreat and overrun. . . . The names of people released [from camps] are not given for obvious reasons & there is always quite some delay in their coming back. For all we know, it is not impossible that Babuli should even be making her way back just now." Three months later, in July 1945, Vilayat was more glum. Waiting for news about Noor, he wrote to his mother, was "terribly worrying. Surely there can be some information by now! I can never keep my mind off the subject & it is becoming unbearable. . . . The absence of news is enough to make one go mad." He did his best to shelter Ora from the news, any news, asking the War Office to "be so kind as to communicate with me, not my mother, who becomes hysterical at the mention of my sister's name. She has been so deeply grieved."

With no official word coming about Noor, Vilayat dreamed one night that she was walking toward him, wearing her uniform and enveloped by a bright, blue light. With a radiant face, she said, "I'm free." He described the dream to a close friend of Noor's, who interpreted it differently. The friend was certain it meant Noor had been liberated from a POW camp and was on her way home. "No," said Vilayat. "It means she is dead."

In early 1946, the British government wrote Noor's family that, with the passage of time and the absence of hard facts, it had concluded that Noor *was* dead. Noor's siblings didn't tell their mother—she was too fragile. A month later, the War Office erroneously reported that Noor had been given a lethal injection at Natzweiler, then cremated. "I hope," the War Office wrote to Vilayat, "that the knowledge of the invaluable contribution that your sister made toward final victory in preparing the ground for the invasion of France will comfort you in your great loss. All who came into contact with her during the time of her imprisonment have spoken most highly of her courage and morale." Not until 1948 was a more accurate account of Noor's death pieced together. When the War Office informed Vilayat that British newspapers would soon publish reports about Noor, he and his sister, Claire, were alarmed: their mother bought newspapers almost every day, searching for news of Noor. To prevent Ora from reading about Noor, Claire took her to their family home in Suresnes. As always, Fazal Manzil was their refuge. Ora and Claire stayed at Fazal Manzil off and on for almost a year, sometimes visiting friends in The Hague who provided them with their own apartment, but always returning home to Suresnes. Ora died there on May 1, 1949, still not knowing of Noor's death.

For a few nights after Óra's death, Claire slept in her mother's bed at Fazal Manzil, "attempting," said Claire, "to fill the void she had left." One night, Claire dreamed that she opened the front door of Fazal Manzil. Noor was standing on the top step, wearing a heavy jacket, a Russian fur hat, and high leather boots and asking, "Where is Mother?"

"She is no longer here," Claire answered.

In Claire's dream, Noor ran down the steps of Fazal Manzil, then through the gate to the street, as if searching for Ora—whose fifty-seventh birthday would have been the next day.

Vilayat's father, mother, and beloved sister were gone. Then, in the late 1940s, his fiancée was killed in an accident on the motorcycle he was driving. For months, Vilayat sought solace in the Mass in B Minor, the masterpiece Bach wrote to glorify God and refresh the human spirit. Vilayat worked as a journalist in Pakistan, as an assistant to Pakistan's first prime minister, and as an attaché to Pakistan's delegation to the United Nations. In 1949, Vilayat attended the trial of Renée Garry, the woman accused of betraying Noor to the Nazis. Vilayat realized that he could not forgive her—it was easier to forgive the Nazi who had kicked and beaten Noor nearly to death at Dachau, knowing that, as Vilayat wrote, "the Nazis used psychopaths as jailers. When I consider the fact that the man might have been brought up by a stepfather who was a drunk, or who beat him or kicked him out of the house, my resentment is not as easy to sustain." More difficult was forgiving a woman who had betrayed Noor for money.

Vilayat accepted, finally, the mission his father had bestowed upon him to lead the Sufi order in the West. Inayat had done that a few days before leaving for India in 1926. Vilayat taught Sufism in Europe and the United States; meditated for long periods in India, Jerusalem, America, and a cave in the French Alps where neighbors called him *le vieux de la montagne*, "the old man of the mountains." He often talked with his students about Noor's spirit and her willingness to sacrifice herself. And sometimes while alone he could not enjoy food without thinking of the tasteless soup Noor ate for the ten months she was chained and in solitary in Pforzheim. And still, after all these years, he could not forgive the woman who had betrayed Noor. And if he could not forgive, how could he teach his students about forgiveness? The lesson, Vilayat ultimately understood, was not to forgive, but to confront the corrosiveness of *not* forgiving. Though absolution, Vilayat said, "requires much of us," not forgiving entrenches us more deeply in our own suffering "and stands in the way of our progress. Sometimes we have to open up these wounds and cleanse them."

For several months after the end of the war, Vera Atkins sought throughout Europe for the women from F Section who hadn't returned. As a top SOE officer, Atkins felt responsible for each agent, especially for Noor, whom Atkins had been uncertain about from the start: not only was Noor "otherworldly," but her almost devout attachment to her mother could have interfered with her duties.

Atkins was keen to interview Hans Kieffer, the SS commandant who had transferred Noor from 84 Avenue Foch to a prison in Germany. She found him in a British prison in Wuppertal, charged with ordering his men to kill at least thirty British airmen and one downed American pilot. After their murders near a small village in southern France, Kieffer instructed his troops to replace the Allied soldiers' uniforms with civilian clothes and bury them in a mass grave with Sten guns to make it look as though they had died in an accidental shootout with local *résistants*. Tall and good looking, Kieffer carried himself with a confidence that belied his circumstances: if convicted, he could be executed. (He was.) Open and voluble, he was proud of how he had run the most notorious prison in Paris and asserted that, under the circumstances, he had always intended the best for Noor. Her courage and stubbornness particularly impressed him: he could never rely on anything she said and if she had successfully escaped from 84 Avenue Foch, "all the radio plays"—the Gestapo's *Funkspiel*—"would have been finished."

Kieffer admitted that though he had ordered that Noor be placed in some kind of restraint after leaving no. 84—she was "dangerous"—though chains and manacles were never on his mind. His plan had been for Noor to remain in the prison in Karlsruhe for the balance of the war. Karlsruhe was "well run," he told Atkins. He knew that from firsthand experience:

he had worked in the prison before the war and was sure that Noor and the other prisoners he sent there from Avenue Foch might have their movements restricted, but not their spirits impaired. Still, Kieffer continued, Karlsruhe was "overfull" when Noor arrived and Pforzheim—not far away—was an acceptable alternative.

"It was nice for you to select Karlsruhe for your convenience," Atkins retorted, "since you happened to live there. It was nice for you to have an excuse to return home from Paris whenever you felt like it."

Atkins then told Kieffer that Noor had been killed at Dachau. Not expecting this, Kieffer began to cry. "Kieffer," Atkins chided, "if one of us is going to cry, it is going to be me. You will please stop this comedy."

Though Atkins and Vilayat were each unaware of the other's quest for Noor, some Sufis say Noor had intuited that they would search for her. They were sure Noor had written about this in "Snow Drop," a story she scribbled in a notebook during her training with the SOE. In these few pages, Great Sun dearly loves his selfless and beautiful daughter. As she looks through the clouds one day, tears roll down her cheeks: the world below is gloomy and sad. Wanting to restore its happiness, she flies down from the sky. Skipping and dancing through the world, Little Daughter brings life wherever she goes: flowers bloom, birds chirp, rabbits come "bouncing out from every hole." Everyone loves Little Daughter except Queen Winter, who summons her guards. "If you wish that the kingdom of cold abide," she orders, "Great Sun's little daughter must die. . . . Seize her and hide her under the earth so . . . no soul can find her again!"

The queen's guards creep up to Little Daughter. Frost-Bite freezes her until she is stiff and Fog-Gloom makes her invisible. The North Wind carries her far away and, together, they hide Little Daughter underground. No one sees them do this except two robins.

Soon, Queen Winter is ruling again. The two robins fly to where Little Daughter is buried. Tapping on the ground with their beaks, they call, "Are you there, Little Daughter?"

"Yes, robins. I am here."

"Do come back, Little Daughter. The big world is so sad without you."

"I cannot, little robins. For if I did, Queen Winter and her guards would kill me."

"Do come back," the robins persist, telling Little Daughter that the birds aren't singing, and the flowers aren't blooming, and her father, Great Sun is so upset that he is rarely shining his bright rays upon the earth. "If you don't return, Little Daughter," the robins plead, "he may never come again."

Little Daughter agrees to return. She will appear as "a flower as tiny as a drop, and as white as the snow" so Queen Winter will not see her. As the snowdrop flower sprouts through the snow, color returns to the world, and Great Sun smiles "as never before for his little daughter was found and all the big world was happy again."

In certain Sufis' interpretation of Noor's "Snow Drop," Hazrat Inayat Khan is Great Sun, Noor is Little Daughter, Hitler is Winter, the Nazis' *Nacht und Nebel*—Fog and Night—is Fog-Gloom, and Vera Atkins and Vilayat are the two birds who search for Noor. To these Sufis, Noor is not a storyteller. She is an oracle who knew her fate, and accepted it.

Two other people tried to determine what happened to Noor. One was a young woman in London who lived down the street from Ora and became exceptionally close to Noor. Confronting Frank Spooner, the SOE officer who had written a damning report of Noor—"not overburdened with brains"—Noor's friend inquired about his motive. Spooner explained that he hadn't judged Noor as a human being or been commenting on her faith or philosophy. He simply didn't think she had the grit, the toughness, for the job. She was too impulsive, too nervous. Spooner preferred someone with a "more phlegmatic kind of courage"—less sentimental, more stoical and sophisticated. When Maurice Buckmaster angrily overruled him—"We don't want them with brains. Makes me cross"—Spooner fruitlessly appealed to an officer higher in the chain of command. A few years after the war, Spooner still regretted the outcome. "If I had had my way," he told Noor's chum, "your little friend would be alive today."

And in 1947, Elie (Azeem) Goldenberg asked an international service that was finding people displaced by the war to help him locate Noor. Giving his address as 57 Grande Rue Saint-Maurice in Paris, he identified himself as Noor's fiancé and stated that the last he knew of Noor was that she had been "arrested in Paris." Azeem was eventually told Noor had been killed at Dachau. "*Umgekommen*" was the word used. "Perished."

Azeem's whereabouts during the war are not known, though almost certainly he did not remain in Suresnes. Germans occupied dozens of buildings in the town, including three close to where Azeem had lived before France fell. In 1971, he recorded his only album, "Music for New Forms of Modern Dance." Along with works by Debussy, Chopin, Brahms, and Gershwin, he included one by himself: *Recherches d'équilibre*—"Research for equilibrium."

Meanwhile, in The Hague, Henriette Willebeek Le Mair, the illustrator with whom Noor had collaborated on *Twenty Jataka Tales*, grieved for Noor. Henriette and Noor had grown tremendously close while working on the book. So had Henriette's husband, Baron H. P. van Tuyll van Serooskerken. His family motto could have been Noor's: *Virtus vim vincit*, "Virtue defeats force."

After the war, Ernest Vogt, the German who had dined with and interrogated Noor at 84 Avenue Foch, and once kissed her on the forehead, hid for a year, afraid that the current occupiers of Germany—the victors of the war—would kill anyone who had served Hitler. Eventually, Americans found Vogt and sent him to a concentration camp that was now being used for deserters from the Russian army and for almost eighteen thousand former members of the SS—Dachau. "If I had known Madeleine died in Dachau," Vogt told a friend of Noor's, "I should have felt it poetic fate."

No charges were pressed against Vogt. He was simply a dubious character, as was anyone who had served at 84 Avenue Foch as long as he had. After a year at Dachau, the Americans sent him to the British, who kept him in a prison in Staumuhler for three months, then returned him to the Americans. Having no use for him, the Americans passed Vogt to the Germans who put him back in Dachau. The camp had recently been returned to German jurisdiction. Twelve months later, the Germans transferred Vogt back to the British. He spent a year in Staumuhler as a semi-prisoner—his cell wasn't locked and he was free to walk around the town. But lacking money so he could eat in restaurants and without the credentials he needed to get a job, Vogt had to return to his cell for his meals. Finally, the British closed the prison, and Vogt returned to his home, which was in the French zone of occupied Germany—"a town out of fairyland, a toy town" according to Noor's friend who found Vogt while she was trying to determine Noor's fate. "A painted town, the houses jade and rose," and "windows with ornaments in quartz," and "very slowly moving little white trams."

Since the war, Vogt had thought of Noor as a constant in his life—a "warm, friendly ghost." "I don't fear to be haunted by Madeleine," he told Noor's friend. "I hope she is really here." Vogt maintained that he was always "soft" with Noor. "I let her have everything she asked for—baths, cream, eau de cologne [from her apartment on Rue de la Faisanderie]. She thought I was kind. I did try to do things in a kind way."

"By being kind," Noor's friend murmured, "you were more her enemy than if you had been hard."

Vogt flinched. "What do you want?" he asked, almost inaudibly. "What do you want I should have done?"

Noor's friend didn't answer.

Vogt was certain Hans Kieffer, the head of 84 Avenue Foch, didn't want Noor to be killed. She gave him no choice but to transfer her when she refused to give him her word of honor not to escape again from no. 84. "There was nothing Kieffer could do," Vogt said. "He could not keep her longer at Avenue Foch. It was not a strong house"—a penitentiary, a stockade. "It was where Kieffer lived."

One day, Vogt and Noor's friend took a cable car to the top of a mountain. It was clear and cloudless and they could make out the striations of the rocks on other peaks, and the rich green of the valleys below, all blooming with bright flowers and some with streams coursing through them. This was the Germany that had withstood kings and putsches and fuehrers; that stood for more than conquest and struggle, blood and soil. This Germany was beyond time, and beyond the fresh miseries and the recent conflagration.

"I should have liked to show Noor this country," Vogt mused about the woman he had questioned for weeks in a Gestapo prison in Paris. "I cannot believe she is no more. She was so alive. Because of her, I believe in immortality. . . . If we survive, do we meet again all those who died in our concentration camps? There are some people to whom I want to explain something. Some people to whom we promised they would not be shot." Continuing, Vogt said he had never made such promises to Noor because "she never did anything for us. She knew she would be shot. When I brought her to Avenue Foch, she said, 'Shoot me at once.' I would not be ashamed to meet Madeleine again. She does not reproach me.

"Truth," Vogt ruminated, "is the most powerful thing in the whole world. That is why it is used only in small doses."

After 1945, there were claims that the SOE had sacrificed some of its agents to distract the Germans from more promising operations. And that it knew an SOE operative in Paris, Henri Déricourt, was probably betraying agents to the Germans. Noor was possibly among them. None of this was proven. The only SOE officer who testified at Déricourt's trial was Nicolas Bodington—Maurice Buckmaster's confidant who had tried to persuade Noor to return to England in August 1943. Bodington stated that he had authorized Déricourt to engage in counterespionage and that the Frenchman had never handed any agents over to the Germans.

The charges that he was cavalier with the lives of his agents outraged Maurice Buckmaster. "Monstrous and intolerable accusations," he fumed. "I challenge anyone to substantiate them." No one did. Further infuriating Buckmaster were assertions that the SOE was an ineffective vanity project. Though the Germans' penetration of the SOE in France in 1943 was a "serious setback," the SOE "undoubtedly" outwitted the Nazis, hounding their military, killing officers and soldiers, derailing trains, blowing up bridges, and loosening their stranglehold on the French economy. How else to explain the three hundred parachute drops of arms that *résistants* used to stop a Panzer division from reaching Normandy on June 6? (The Panzer's twelve thousand men, two hundred tanks, and numerous halftracks, mortars, howitzers, and heavy machine guns could well have turned the battle.) And why else would Eisenhower have said the SOE helped "shorten the war by nine months"?

Buckmaster conceded there were costs: agents were caught, and agents were killed. But the casualty rate was less than in an ordinary brigade. In the final accounting, 470 agents were sent to France. About a quarter of these—188—were killed or sent to concentration camps. Fewer than forty did not return. Thirteen were women.

In 1946, France awarded Noor Inayat Khan the Croix de Guerre with Gold Star, its highest award to a civilian. At a ceremony in Paris, the head of an organization of *résistantes* praised Noor's willingness to take up the battle: "Nothing, neither her nationality nor the traditions of her family, obliged her to take her position in the war. She chose it." Returning to France, Noor struggled "til the end against all natural prudence til her arrest. . . . For all of us, for the children of our country, what a marvelous example."

Jacqueline Fleury, who covertly distributed newspapers printed by the Resistance when she was seventeen years old, first heard of Noor from a *résis-tante* at Ravensbruck with whom she shared a bunk. Noor, Marie said, was "very brave, very bold." Most impressive was that Noor had not remained in England: "It was Noor's destiny to return to France. She could have stayed in England. She selected to fight with us, and for us."

England acknowledged Noor more slowly than France did. When Maurice Buckmaster recommended Noor for a George Medal before the war ended, the SOE was confident Noor was safe in Paris, sending messages to London and rebuilding cells the Germans had wrecked. A few weeks later, the agency decided the "fist" on Noor's radio wasn't hers. Not until after the war did it learn about Noor's imprisonment on Avenue Foch and at Pforzheim, and about her execution at Dachau. In 1947, Vera Atkins set out to elevate Noor's award to a George Cross, England's highest medal for bravery. That wasn't easy. England's Honours and Awards Office was dubious that Noor had been in chains at Pforzheim. After Atkins convinced them of this, she had to persuade the awards office that Noor had communicated with other prisoners at Pforzheim by scratching messages on the bottom of the tin plates and mugs that were issued to them. "How they exchanged mugs I cannot say," Atkins frustratingly responded, "but that they did is proved by the fact that Mlle. Lagrave [who had been a prisoner in Cell no. 12 at Pforzheim] was in possession of Madeleine's names and address and many other details concerning her." Ultimately, testimony from an SS man—Hans Kieffer, Noor's jailer at 84 Avenue Foch—carried more weight than anything Atkins said. Kieffer stated that Noor never told him anything worthwhile, and he disclosed details about her two escape attempts, adding that John Starr had insisted that escaping from 84 Avenue Foch was Noor's idea, not his.

In 1949, St. James's Palace announced that Noor would receive a George Cross; that August, Noor's brother, Vilayat, and her sister, Claire, accepted the medal at a ceremony at Buckingham Palace. Vilayat especially appreciated Vera Atkins's efforts to determine Noor's fate. The year before, he had sent Atkins a card. On the front was a particularly lovely photo of Noor. Inside, Vilayat wrote, "To Vera Atkins. With gratitude—a feeling I know Nora would have shared for your enterprise in following in her tracks in the German wilderness of the aftermath."

Vilayat and Claire accepted Noor's George Cross at Buckingham Palace, 1949.

Suddenly, Noor was the stuff of headlines ("G/C For Braver Than They Thought Girl," "Betrayed, Chained, She Did Not Flinch"), and of books (the first of these, by a friend, appeared in 1952), and of stories for children, like the one in a children's supplement to the London *Daily Express* in 1955 that added some melodrama to Noor's story while necessarily simplifying it: children can handle only so much complexity. "Secret Agent 'Madeleine,'" wrote the *Junior Express*, "carried her radio through the streets in a little black box. For four months, she bluffed the Gestapo." With hyperbolic mistruths—Noor "heard champagne corks pop" as the Gestapo celebrated her capture—Noor was given a new life not long after her old one had ended. Elsewhere, a journalist who had known Noor before the war wrote that she spoke with the "tenderest of voices" and possessed an "inner poise which never seemed to leave her." This author had "not a doubt in the world" that, in the solitude of her cell at Pforzheim, Noor "meditated upon her father and tried to get in touch with him." Possibly. Possibly not. More certain is that these gauzy tributes made Noor more otherworldly than she had been in life. We could admire her feats, but we could never emulate them. The rest of humanity fell short, and always would.

In time, the accolades became more modest. Most were in the form of memorial plaques. One at St. Paul's Cathedral in London lists Noor among the fifty-two women who died in Europe where the SOE operated. Outside the church of St. Peter in Tempsford, fifty miles north of London, a memorial bears the names of female SOE agents who were flown to Europe from secret bases in Tempsford and nearby Tangmere. Noor, who Frank Rymills flew from Tangmere in 1943, is among the seventy-five women listed. Other remembrances in England have taken different forms—a bust of Noor stands in London's Gordon Square, a few blocks from where Noor's family once lived, and in 2014 Britain issued commemorative stamps honoring ten individuals whose "extraordinary achievements helped define the past century." Among them were actor Alec Guinness, poet Dylan Thomas, theater director Joan Littlewood, the Nobel laureate and physicist Max Perutz— and Noor, whom the Royal Mail described as "one of the silent heroes of the Second World War."

At Dachau, Noor is remembered twice: on a large plaque—white marble with gold lettering—in the Room of Remembrance, and on a solitary plaque in the crematorium building that is inscribed with four names: Madeleine Damerment, Eliane Plewman, Yolande Beekman, and Noor Inayat Khan—the four SOE agents whose bodies were burned here in September 1944.

And in Suresnes, a plaque was installed on the wall in front of Fazal Manzil in 1967:

> *Here Lived Noor Inayat Khan, 1914–1944*
> *Called Madeleine in the Resistance*
> *Shot at Dachau*
> *Radio operator for the Buckmaster network*
> *Awarded the French Croix de Guerre 1939–1945, and the English George Cross*

At the dedication, Vilayat sought to make Noor more human, more like the rest of us. "In the middle of her biggest achievements," Vilayat said, "she was afraid, which made her courage even more deeply moving. This is what emboldened those who were afraid of lacking courage." Recalling his discussion with Noor about what to do as the Germans were invading France,

Noor on a 2014 British stamp.

Plaque in the crematorium building at Dachau honoring Noor and the three other female SOE agents who were killed with her.

Vilayat asked, "Was it a contradiction to kill in order to stop violence? . . . In front of the extermination of millions of Jews, how can one preach spiritual morality without participating in preventive action? Spirituality in action— this was the real teaching of our father."

Though Noor's father was Indian, and though Noor greatly favored Indian independence from Britain, the Indian government ignored her for years. Finally, in September 2006, India's defense minister visited Fazal Manzil. In the guest book near the front door, Pranab Mukherjee wrote, "Noor-un-Nisa Inayat Khan was an extraordinary heroic woman who fought and gave her life for freedom and liberty." Mukherjee retired as defense minister the next month, then served as India's president from 2012 through 2017—a time of rising Hindu nationalism and violence against Muslims. In that context, it's no surprise that, in those five years, neither Mukherjee nor any other Indian official mentioned Noor.

In 2012, Princess Anne unveiled a bust of Noor in London's Gordon Square, a few blocks from where Noor's mother had lived on Taviton Street.

The bust had been privately funded with the support of the prime minister and several members of Parliament. As the princess praised Noor's valor and ultimate sacrifice, Noor's cousin Mahmood Youskine Khan swelled with pride. "This is a beautiful place to remember Noor's story," he reflected. At eighty-four years old, Mahmood was one of the last living members of Noor's family who had known her: he had last seen her when he was twelve. "Noor made a beautiful impression on everyone who met her," Mahmood reminisced. "An intelligent, charming, dainty girl, and so beautiful." As her father's eldest child, "much was expected from her," and fighting the Germans was part of that equation: for Noor, "an absolute question of conscience and conviction. . . . She could not do otherwise with such a shadow hanging over Europe."

Six years later, there was another flurry of attention in the United Kingdom about Noor when the Bank of England announced it was seeking nominations for historical icons to place on the redesign of its fifty-pound note. Several government ministers favored Noor. Seeing her face on the note would make you pause and "think about the fantastic work Noor did and the ultimate sacrifice she made," said Nusrat Ghani, the transport minister. A petition to place Noor on the note drew several thousand signatures. The campaign fizzled out when the bank limited nominees to scientists in the United Kingdom.

Plaques and busts, currency, and speeches are the formalities we expect for the heroically departed, the tropes through which we remember and vow not to forget. Yet these are static, easy to miss on the walls where they hang, tempting to ignore as we walk by them in a park or block them out as a speaker is droning on beyond his allotted time. Concerts, the enthusiasm and creativity of children, and the animated power of place—the places where Noor's story transpired—may have greater sway to convey the memory of Noor to the future.

In 1996, Vilayat went to Dachau for the first time. He was eighty years old. Lacking the strength for one last pilgrimage to India, he conducted a concert in Noor's honor—Bach's Mass in B Minor, the same piece that had comforted him while mourning his mother, his sister, and his fiancée years before. During the Mass, the word *eleison* ("mercy") signifies the difficulty of rising from spiritual sleep before the notes turn almost dance-like, leading the spirit upward as the sopranos catch hold of the updraft and the other voice parts follow. Vilayat's concert was held in a large white tent that had been erected near the crematorium where Noor's body was thrown in 1944. On the rear wall of the tent, facing the conductor's podium, was a photo of Noor. To Vilayat, the photo seemed to have a life of its own, its expressions subtly changing as the music soared through despair, hope, resurrection, glory. It was a gray day. Rain seemed imminent. As the chorus rejoiced in Christ's resurrection, a shaft of light broke through the gloom. Vilayat, the mystic, received this as a reunion of sorts with the sister, for whom he had never ceased grieving.

Vilayat had canonized Noor in the 1990s. A Sufi saint—a *wali,* or a "friend of God"—is defined by his or her closeness to God. This differs from the Catholic notion of sainthood, which requires saints to be dead, celibate, distinguished by at least two miracles that science deems inexplicable, and confirmed by a thorough legal process authorized by the pope. A Sufi saint can be alive and married, need not necessarily produce miracles, and is recognized by popular assent rather than by institutional decree. Their canonization reflects the will of the community rather than the formality of a hierarchy and bureaucracy.

After Vilayat's concert, little attention was paid at Dachau to Noor until 2015, when Tanja Mancinelli, an Italian Sufi, organized what Sufis call an *urs*—a memorial service to a saint on the anniversary of his or her death. It was held on September 13, the date Noor was murdered. An *urs* is customarily held at the grave of a saint. Noor doesn't have a grave. Her *urs* was held as close to the probable location of her ashes as could be arranged.

Mancinelli expected that the *urs* would be held once—during a visit that year of Zia, Noor's American nephew, to Munich, only fifteen miles from Dachau. It has since become an annual event, with music, readings from writings by Noor and her father, and testimony by some of those present about what Noor's life, and death, means to them.

The *urs* is held in the chapel of the Carmelite convent adjacent to Dachau—about four hundred feet from the crematorium where Noor was incinerated. Sitting in a small office in the convent a month after the *urs* that was held in 2017, sipping tea with Sister Irmengard, the mother superior, that another nun had brought in, I gestured toward a crucifix that was on the wall above us. "I'm sure you pray to him," I said, pointing to Jesus on the cross. "Do you pray for Noor?"

"I do not pray *for* Noor," Sister Irmengard replied. "I pray *with* Noor."

Each year, Sister Irmengard welcomes up to 150 guests to the *urs* that convenes in the chapel of her convent. Once, she bowed before a photo of Noor that had been placed on the altar. Though Noor perplexes Sister Irmengard—"I don't understand how an Indian princess came here and was tortured"—she is also "totally fascinated by someone who radiated such bravery in such a time. I have learned much from Noor and from Jesus. Both force me to grapple with how human beings can be so cruel. I get strength from the suffering of Jesus, who suffered before our time. And I get strength from the suffering of Noor, who suffered in our time. Noor could only have lived as she did by embodying faith and grace. To me, Noor is a saint. I am sure she is in eternal heaven. I hope to join her."

Elsewhere, other ways to remember Noor emerged, less religious, more secular, and just as effective. In Manchester, England, a mother started an organization named after Ahmed Iqbal Ullah, a thirteen-year-old Bangla-deshi who often defended younger Asian boys when they were attacked by bullies. In 1988, Ahmed was stabbed to death outside his high school as retal-iation for protecting some boys. As part of its mission, the foundation asked sixth-graders in a local school to write and illustrate a book about Noor. In *Liberté: The Life of Noor Inayat Khan,* the students wrote letters in the voice of Noor. In one, Noor posthumously sums up her life—her happiness in Sures-nes, the death of her father, the gun pressed against her head at Dachau. She concludes her letter in this manner: "One more thing: when I was going to die, I wished that I had lived longer."

And in Suresnes, the town across the Seine from Paris which had nur-tured and sheltered and loved Noor, students from the local elementary school that was named after Noor occasionally visit Fazal Manzil, about two miles away from their *école*. Vilayat had lived there, off and on, until his death in 2004. His wife, Mary, remained there until her death in 2018. A few months before she died, she told me that Vilayat could rarely speak about Noor without crying. "Yet," she said, "for all the tears, it was in Noor's nature to do what she did."

And what, I inquired, was in Noor's nature that led her from believing in fairies to resisting the Nazis, then trying twice to escape from 84 Avenue Foch—a long journey for anyone, but maybe not so improbable for a slight young woman who had been reared in a mysticism grounded in service to others and who had embraced the world as much as she had embraced herself? Considering my question, Mary paused as the sun shone into the dining room where she and Vilayat had enjoyed many meals and hosted many visitors and helped bring Sufism back to life in the West. Looking directly into my eyes, and speaking clearly and calmly, Mary said, "Noor always believed in the unbelievable."

At the close of the day when life's toil fades away,
And all so peacefully sleep,
No rest do I find since Thou left one behind,
'Till Death around me doth creep.
Bitter nights of despair hath made fragrant the air,
Tear drops hath turned into dew,
I watch and I wait 'till Thou openeth the gate,
And Thy love leadeth one through.

—"UNTITLED," NOOR INAYAT KHAN

ACKNOWLEDGMENTS

This book is the beneficiary of the wisdom and knowledge of a corps of confidants and pals, old and new, some of whom I've never met. A convention of these far-flung, kind individuals is in order. Some day. But first . . .

In Moscow, *spasiba* to Sergey Moskalev. In Holland, *beedankt* to Aya Dürst Britt and Alexandra Nagel. In Germany, *danke* to Bridgitte and Gerhard Brandle, Angelika Eisenmann, and Sister Irmengard, mother superior of the convent at Dachau, whose deep faith doesn't have to be spoken to be known. In France, *merci* to Guy Caraes, Emmanuel de Chambost, Jean-Pierre Viennot, Raphael Crevet, Emile Trion, Patricia Baillier, Ophelie Léger, Marie-Laure Curie; also to Aurore Renaut and Bernard Payen—fine hosts and passionate conversationalists about films. In England, much gratitude to Giles Milton, Lauren von Bechman, Gary Haines, Patrick Yarnold, and to Jameela Siddiqi and Randeep Singh Soin for being warm hosts and insightful guides.

In the United States and Canada, thanks to David Ball, Jonathan Vance, Vladimir Alexandrov, Seyyed Hossein Nasr, Carl Ernst, Jeanne Kassof, Mandile Mpof, Carol Sokoloff, Howard Bryan, Nancy Hurrell, Martin Moeller, John Devaney, Rafe Martin, Marianne B. Leese, Tammy Taylor, Sean Hogan, Annabel Coleman, and to Amy Rubin, researcher extraordinaire, who never rested until all curiosities and possibilities were settled.

Steady encouragement came from Rob Kanigel, Rosie Crafton, and Aiman Khan, and much gratitude goes to Marc Steiner, Kenny Klein, and Leslie Rindoks, all of whom graciously commented on an early draft of the manuscript.

I first learned about Noor from *Enemy of the Reich*, a splendid PBS documentary about Noor produced by Rob Gardner, Michael Wolfe, and Alex Kronemer. My agent, Claire Anderson, immediately grasped the power of Noor's story. Lucky for me, Claire placed it with Alane Mason at W. W. Norton. Anyone whose manuscript passes through Alane's hands will end up with a book that exceeds the sum of its origins. Claire and Alane understand the virtues of craft, and the vagaries of today's unpredictable, still flourishing market.

Others on Norton's team were highly talented and immensely helpful: Mo Crist, Erin Sinesky Lovett, Don Rifkin, Nancy Green, Lauren Abbate, Meredith McGinnis, Rebecca Homiski, Ingsu Liu, and Chris Welch.

The Sufi community was unhesitatingly cooperative and enthusiastically comradely: Hamida Verlinden in The Hague; Anne Louise Wirgman and Martin Zamir Rohrs in Suresnes; Jennifer Alia Wittman in Richmond; and Tanja Mancinelli in Dachau, London, and Suresnes, who introduced me to Sufi chivalry and openheartedness, and Mancinelli stubbornness, refinement, and love.

All of the present principals in Noor's family have their own way of living what Noor and her father taught. In The Hague, Noor's cousin, Mahmood Youskine Khan, is a remarkable storyteller, as adept at structuring his stories as he is at extracting meaning from them. In Virginia, Pir Zia Inayat Khan—Vilayat's son and president of the Inayati Order—is sensitively attempting to meld the innovative Sufism of his father with more traditional Sufism. And in Germany, David Harper, the son of Noor's sister, Claire, appreciates good food and good wine and does a passable impersonation of a Frenchman. Noor's artifacts, which his mother entrusted to him, could not be in more respectful hands.

FOR FURTHER READING

For readers who would like to delve deeper into the many aspects of Noor's story—courage, faith, history, morality, feminism, the horrors of Hitler's dark universe, and more—below is a far-from-exhaustive set of books and resources.

Sufism, of course, was at the center of Noor's life. In *The Shambhala Guide to Sufism* (Shambhala, 1997), Carl Ernst of the University of North Carolina provides a balanced, judicious introduction to this mysticism—its roots, traditions, practices, and experiences. Wary of the ease with which Sufism can be misinterpreted—"Sufism is not a thing that one can point to; it is instead a symbol . . . used by different groups for different purposes"—Ernst concludes that the term "Sufism" must be "pretty elastic" to accommodate the many strains that fall under its tent.

Many books have been collected from the writings and lectures of Hazrat Inayat Khan. Highly recommended is *The Inner Life* (Shambhala, 1997), which includes lectures Inayat gave during his last tour of the United States in 1926. Inayat's *The Mysticism of Sound and Music* (Shambhala, 1996) has influenced such musicians as John Coltrane and John McLaughlin. And a well-organized compendium of Inayat's writing and lectures is at The Teaching of Hazrat Inayat Khan: http://hazrat-inayat-khan.org/php/views.php. For a biography of Inayat, see Elisabeth deJong-Keesing's thorough *Inayat Khan* (East-West Publications, 1974).

Jean Overton Fuller's *Noor-un-nisa Inayat Khan*, the first biography of Noor, was published in England in 1952. Overton Fuller, a friend of Noor's, labored admirably to chronicle Noor's service in the SOE when most of the agency's records were embargoed.

Noor's own two books provide a closer glimpse of her as a person and a writer. With animals galore, Noor's *Twenty Jataka Tales* (Inner Traditions International, 1985) can be mistaken for Aesop-like fantasies for children. But each story animates the Buddhist doctrine about boddhisattvas—enlightened beings who refuse to enter nirvana until *all* beings are also enlightened. *King Akbar's Daughter* (Suluk Press, 2012) collects Noor's poems and stories not published during her lifetime. Henriette Willebeek Le Mair illustrated *Twenty Jataka Tales*. Also charming are *A Children's Bedtime Book* (Frederick Warne, 2000) in which Le Mair illustrates classic bedtime rhymes and fairy tales. and *A Gallery of Children* (Philomel, 1988), her 1925 collaboration with A. A. Milne. Milne would publish *Winnie the Pooh* the next year.

Rafe Martin's *Before Buddha Was Buddha* (Wisdom, 2018) is a stellar exploration of how jatakas reveal what it means to be human. Like the Buddha, Martin says, each of us "falls down and gets back up, nothing special or fancy, just the continuing effort of spiritual practice."

Two books in particular shed fascinating light on ancillary characters in the history of Noor's family. *The Black Russian*, by Yale historian Vladimir Alexandrov, follows Frederick Bruce Thomas, the son of former slaves in Mississippi, who owned the nightclub in Moscow where Inayat Khan performed in 1913 and 1914. And in *The Great Oom* (Penguin, 2010), Robert Love exhumes the life of Pierre Bernard, the libertine huckster brother of Noor's mother, whom Ora was wise to keep at a distance from her children.

Books about the SOE have turned into a cottage industry. One of the first was M. R. D. Foot's *SOE in France*, originally published by HMSO (Her Majesty's Stationery Office) in 1966. A historian and professor at Oxford, Foot spent two years writing it, then endured four years of the government vetting his manuscript. Publication was followed by litigation from SOE agents who disliked how Foot portrayed them. Foot prevailed in court. *Between Silk and Cyanide* (Free Press, 1999) by Leo Marks, the SOE's coding czar, is a brisk account of how he created codes, trained agents, fooled the Germans, and fell in love with Noor. Jonathan Vance's *Unlikely Soldiers* (HarperCollins, 2008) tells of Frank Pickersgill and Ken Macalister, the two Canadians Noor was supposed to meet in August 1943 at a café in Paris. Lynne Olson's

Madame Fourcade's Secret War (Random House, 2019) is the definitive biography of the tough woman who ran the largest Resistance group in France. Fourcade was engaged to Léon Faye, with whom Noor tried to escape from 84 Avenue Foch in November 1943. Vera Atkins, who searched exhaustively for Noor throughout France and Germany after the war, comes alive in Sarah Helm's *A Life in Secrets* (Anchor, 2007). And Patrick Yarnold's *Wanborough Manor* (Hopfield, 2009) offers excellent descriptions of life at the manor where SOE agents, including Noor, trained.

We'll never know precisely how Noor suffered while in prison at Pforzheim, yet *The Valley of the Shadow* (Panther, 1956) provides significant hints. The author, Hugo Oloff de Wet, was a Night and Fog prisoner who survived six years in German prisons. Grim and occasionally sardonic, de Wet is a rare guide through a land where hope shriveled.

NOTES

Abbreviations

HIK	Hazrat Inayat Khan
ZIK	Pir Zia Inayat Khan
PVIK	Pir Vilayat Inayat Khan
NA	National Archives, London
IWM	Imperial War Museum, London
MUS	Museum of Urban & Social History, Suresnes
HSRC	Historical Society of Rockland County, NY
TTHIK	The Teaching of Hazrat Inayat Khan
SSM	Stichting Soefi Museum
NF	Nekbakht Foundation
DH	David Harper

In these notes, several different spellings are used for Noor's name—Noor, Noorunissa, and Noor-un-nisa. The spelling used in each case is that in the original source material. When appropriate, Noor is referred to as "NIK." Other variations occurred in how original source material referred to Vera Atkins—variously Atkins, V. M. Atkins, Vera Atkins. The notes below conform to the style used by each source.

Prelude: The Moon Goddess

2 **212 miles an hour:** Derek N. James, *Westland Aircraft since 1915* (London: Putnam, 1991), 253.

2 **1,150 miles . . . turnaround time:** Bernard O'Conner, *RAF Tempsford* (Stroud, England: Amberley Publishing, 2010), 31.

2 **"The moon was as much of a goddess":** M. R. D. Foot, *SOE in France* (HMSO, 1966), 60.

2 **solid cloud cover:** Mike Sattler, email to author, Dec. 8, 2015.

3 **"looked like a vicar's wife":** Hugh Verity, *We Landed by Moonlight* (Manchester, England: Crecy Publishing, 2005), 94.

3 **"a splendid, vague, dreamy creature":** Verity, 298.

3 **flasks he had stowed:** Verity, 97.

4 **"Now, madame":** Verity, 94.

4 **"perfect June day":** Sarah Helm, *A Life in Secrets* (New York: Anchor Books, 2007), xxii.

5 **"a little hunk of dynamite" . . . "struck flesh":** Henry M. Stebbins, Allen J. E. Shay, and Oscar R. Hammond, *Pistols: A Modern Encyclopedia* (Harrisburg, PA: Stackpole, 1961), 252.

5 **"quality and reliability":** Stebbins, Shay, and Hammond, 167–68.

5 **Atkins then went through the agents' pockets:** O'Conner, 126.

5 **every inch of their clothing . . . French-style haircuts:** Maurice Buckmaster, *Specially Employed* (London: Batchworth Press, 1952), 72.

6 **studying a *prewar* French railway timetable:** William Stevenson, *Spymistress* (New York: Arcade Publishing, 2011), 299.

6 **"You are so clever":** Helm, 21.

6 **a powder compact . . . fountain pen:** M. R. D. Foot, *SOE: The Special Operations Executive, 1940–46* (London: Pimlico, 1999), 61–62.

6 **"ultimate benediction":** Leo Marks, *Between Silk and Cyanide: A Codemaker's War, 1941–1945* (New York: Free Press, 1998), 65.

7 **"nerve the French":** Buckmaster, 65.

7 **prearranged Morse-code letter:** Verity, 11.

7 **inverted L-shape:** Foot, *SOE in France*, 86.

7 **like meditating:** Noor-un-nissa Khan, "Symbologies," unpublished essay, probably written in 1943, DH. Noor's attitude toward shooting corresponded to Zen adepts' toward martial arts. The Zen master D. T. Suzuki said such disciplines in Far Eastern countries are intended to bring our minds "into contact with the ultimate reality. . . . When this is attained, man thinks yet he does not think." Suzuki's introduction in Eugen Herrigel, *Zen in the Art of Archery* (New York: Vintage Spiritual Classics, 1999), vii, ix.

8 **"for taking an initiative":** HIK, "Gathas: Superstitions, Customs and Beliefs," TTHIK, www.hazrat-inayat-khan.org.

8 **"if it is bad":** HIK, *Education* (Claremont, CA: Hunter House, 1989), 38

8 **"We should first try to become":** HIK, *Sufi Teachings*, vol. viii (Delhi, India: Motilal Banarsidass, 2018), 236.

Chapter 1: The Air of Heaven

13 **"For every blow":** Tipu's letter, in Richard Sambasivam, "The Tiger Aids the Eaglet: How India Secured America's Independence," *Journal of the American*

Revolution, April 26, 2016, https://allthingsliberty.com/2016/04/the-tiger-aids-the -eaglet-how-india-secured-americas-independence.

14   **"The signs of God":** HIK, *A Sufi Message of Spiritual Liberty* (London: Theosophical Publishing Society, 1914), 8.

14   **he was a seeker:** Inayat's appreciation of other mysticisms was evident in San Francisco when the Zen master Nyogen Senzaki attended one of his lectures. Inayat asked Senzaki to explain Zen's significance. Senzaki was silent for a while, then he and Inayat smiled at each other. Later, Senzaki said to Inayat, "I see a Zen in you." Inayat replied, "Mr. Senzaki, I see a Sufism in you." When one of Inayat's students asked Senzaki to talk more about Zen, Inayat and Senzaki laughed, knowing that their teachings were beyond words and what had been requested was the equivalent of an unanswerable Zen koan. Murshid Wali Ali Meyer, "A Sunrise in the West: Hazrat Inayat Khan's Legacy in California," in PZIK, ed., *A Pearl in Wine* (New Lebanon, NY: Omega Publications, 2001), 400–402.

14   **"into the world":** HIK, *Sufi Message,* 15.

14   **"to admire the works of God":** "Professor Inayat Khan on Indian Music," *Mysore Herald,* Nov. 28, 1907, as cited in Aya Johanna Danielle Durst Britt, "Tuning Souls to Harmony" (master's diss., Leiden University, Aug. 26, 2013).

15   **seven-act dance:** Suzanne Shelton, *Ruth St. Denis* (Austin: University of Texas Press, 1991), 59–64.

15   **scandalous:** HIK, *The Autobiography of Hazrat Inayat Khan,* unpaginated.

15   **"in true Oriental fashion":** "Hindoo Prayers Postpone Show," *San Francisco Chronicle,* Apr. 1, 1911, 2.

15   **"alternatively blinked":** Elisabeth deJong-Keesing, *Inayat Khan* (London: East-West Publications, 1974), 96. St. Denis challenged local mores. The *Washington Herald's* critic called her show "nothing but lascivious posings," with "several big Negroes . . . naked to the waist, literally and disgustingly so. . . ." If Washingtonians "will tolerate" white women and "colored men exposing their bodies on the stage, then we are very much mistaken." "Mixed Entertainment at Columbia Theater," *Washington Herald,* Jan. 4, 1911, 4.

15   **"I have fashioned him":** *The Holy Quran* (Medinah, Saudi Arabia: The Custodian of the Two Holy Mosques, no date), 1388.

16   **"Allah is all, all, all":** Walt Whitman, "A Persian Lesson," Walt Whitman Archive, https:whitmanarchive.org/published/LG/1891/poems/390.

16   **"like sailing in the sea":** HIK, *Autobiography.*

16   **"divine wisdom is not limited":** HIK, "Is Sufism Muslim?," TTHIK.

16   **"religion of love, harmony and beauty":** HIK, "Sufism—Beyond Religion," TTHIK.

17   **"was all the religion there is":** HIK, "Nirtan: Dance, Aphorisms," TTHIK.

17   **"felt inferior":** Seyyed Hossein Nasr, interview with author, Apr. 1, 2019.

17   **"everyone would have deserted him":** Carl Ernst, email to author, July 11, 2017. During his lifetime, Inayat was known as "Murshid"—an abbreviation of his

full esoteric title, Pir-o-Murshid. "Pir" is a traditional Sufi title for an elder or guide; "Murshid" is "teacher." Inayat's brothers called him "Hazrat," an honorific in India for a highly respected person. "Hazrat," or "presence," became attached to Inayat more generally after his death. In the West, it carries the same weight as "His Holiness." PZIK, email to author, May 10, 2018.

18 **"Sufism without Islam":** Nasr interview.

18 **"polished gentleman":** "Sinuous Gent from Orient," *Los Angeles Times,* Apr. 26, 1911, page unknown.

18 **"great and illuminated intelligence":** Kambiz Ghanea Bassiri, *A History of Islam in America* (Cambridge: Cambridge University Press, 2010), 128.

18 **yoga, breathing techniques:** Inayat, letters to Ada Martin, May 4, June 19, July 23 and 29, Aug. 3, Dec. 11, 1911, DH.

19 **Women were Bernard's weakness:** Robert Love, *The Great Oom* (New York: Penguin, 2010), 9, 45, 83.

19 **"love nest":** "Girl 'Yogi Wife' of Oom Tells How Faker Lured Her," *New York Evening World*, May 6, 1910, 1.

19 **crossed state lines:** "Police Break In On Weird Hindu Rites," *New York American,* May 3, 1910, 1.

19 **"learned societies and academies":** Pierre Arnold-Bernard, ed., *A Prospectus, Sanskrit Studies* (New York: American Import Book Co., date unknown), 1–2.

19 **"seemed to get the impression":** AMA letter, Dec. 17, 1923, to Dr. Kate C. Mead, Middletown, CT, HSRC. AMA to Miss Mabel M. Reese, Dept. of Surgery, Johns Hopkins Hospital, Baltimore, July 12, 1929, HSRC.

19 **Baby, Budh, Juno, and Old Man:** Love, 230.

20 **"deserting home and husband":** "American Women Victims of Hindu Mysticism," *Washington Post,* Feb. 18, 1912, SM1.

20 **dark-skinned man:** deJong-Keesing, 107.

20 **"Your blood will never mix":** Claire Ray Harper and David Ray Harper, *We Rubies Four* (New Lebanon, NY: Omega Publications, 2011), 32.

20 **"in the presence of niggers":** Pierre Bernard's lecture notes, Oct. 3, 1920, HSRC.

20 **gun in a drawer:** Harper and Harper, 195. Two of Ora's children, Claire and Vilayat, visited Pierre Bernard in 1954. Recounting Ora's elopement with Inayat decades earlier, Bernard pulled out a pistol, shouting, "If I had found him, I was going to kill your father with this gun!"

20 **"the saddest girl"** . . . **"Oh, my soul"** . . . **"Who could"** . . . **"Where is":** Harper and Harper, 31, 32, 34–35.

21 **On March 20:** Certified copy of Ora and Inayat's marriage certificate, issued Oct. 19, 1928, General Register Office, Somerset House, London, DH.

21 **Muslim ceremony:** Harper and Harper, 36. Accustomed to subservient women in India, Inayat's brothers found Ora brash and bold, exemplified by how she threw herself at Inayat in New York. Inayat proceeded anyway, possibly surprised, said one

of his relatives decades later, that a white woman desired him while, simultaneously, pleased about a potential marriage after being widowed twice. Ora might be his last chance for marriage. Mahmood Khan, interview with author, Oct. 9, 2017. According to one legend, in addition to fleeing from Ora's brother, Ora and Inayat fled the United States to avoid laws banning marriage between whites and members of other races. But Ora lived in New York State, which *never* banned interracial marriages.

22 **"First . . . she swayed to the right":** deJong-Keesing, 114.

22 **Claude Debussy:** Preface, anonymous, in HIK, *The Mysticism of Sound* (Vancouver: Ekstasis Editions, 2003), 9.

22 **two hundred acres:** Vladimir Alexandrov, *The Black Russian* (New York: Grove Press, 2013), 1.

22 **London, Paris, Monte Carlo:** Alexandrov, 51.

22 **rich fabrics:** Alexandrov, 89.

22 **"first-class variety theater":** Alexandrov, 91. For a century, the Khan family has said Inayat performed at "Maxim's" in Moscow. The club was actually named "Maxim." In a Jan. 8, 2019, email to the author, Yale professor Vladimir Alexandrov said, "In Russian, it was always and only 'Maxim.'" Alexandrov's book *The Black Russian* is the authoritative account of Frederick Bruce Thomas, the African American who owned Maxim. All the club's ads, his email stated, "referred to 'Maxim' (Максим). Perhaps foreigners called it 'Maxim's'—there were places all over Europe with that name because the prototype in Paris was (and is) 'Maxim's de Paris.'"

23 **"air of heaven":** HIK, *The Sufi Message of Hazrat Inayat Khan* (London: Barrie and Rockliff, 1968), vol. 1, 182.

23 **"the Beethoven of India":** Carol Ann Sokoloff, Editor's Note, HIK, *Mysticism of Sound*, 11.

23 **elevation in Maula's rank:** Mahmood Khan, emails to author, Sept. 25 and 28, 2018. There is some dispute about whether Noor was a princess. Her family's history, going back several generations, confirms that she was. And comments scribbled on reports about Noor from the SOE, in which she served during World War II, strongly imply that she considered herself royalty. What was initially typed as "Noor Inayat Khan" on many SOE documents was amended, often in blue ink, as "*Princess* Noor Inayat Khan [italics added]." It is unlikely that the SOE researched Noor's genealogy and concluded by itself that she was royalty. Noor must have told the SOE of her royal roots.

23 **where in Moscow she was born:** Noor was lucky to survive beyond her first twelve months: one-third of babies born in Moscow at the time died before their first birthday. Moscow was among the deadliest cities in Europe—annually, twenty-seven percent of its residents died, double the rate of Paris, London, or Vienna. Statistics from Robert W. Thurston, *Liberal City, Conservative State* (New York: Oxford University Press, 1987), 196.

25 **the Monastery of St. Peter:** Elena Balashova, historian, Monastery of St. Peter

in the Synodal Dept. of Religious Education and Catechization, Russian Orthodox Church, emails to author, March 14 and 20, 2017.

25 **Catherine the Great's plan:** Roger Bartlett, *Russia in the Age of Enlightenment* (New York: Palgrave Macmillan, 1990), 182–83.

25 **quality of its care:** John Hayes Holmes, "An American Hospital in Moscow," *New Republic,* Nov. 1, 1922, 252.

25 **Afghan Sword Dance:** Anonymous, Preface, HIK, *Mysticism of Sound,* 9.

26 **on a British passport:** Mahmood Khan, email to author, Nov. 26, 2017.

26 **"warm people in a cold land":** HIK, *Autobiography.* The musical on which Inayat and Tolstoy were collaborating—*Sakuntala before Shiva*—was a Hindu story about a king's new bride. She loses the ring which proves she's his wife. When a fisherman finds the ring in the belly of a fish, she is reunited with the king.

26 **felt most at home:** Harper and Harper, 8.

Chapter 2: Never Be a "Naughty Girly"

27 **loaf of bread . . . meal of rice:** Claire Ray Harper and David Ray Harper, *We Rubies Four* (New Lebanon, NY: Omega Publications, 2011), 46. That hunger in wartime London was severe was not surprising given how the price of food shot up during the conflict—mutton by 224 percent, sugar 251 percent, eggs 436 percent. Amid such expensive food, it seemed *everyone* was hungry. I. F. W. Beckett, *Home Front: 1914–1918* (Kew, Richmond, England: National Archives, 2006), 111.

27 **as long as 650 feet:** Christopher Klein, "London's World War 1 Zeppelin Terror," http://www.history.com/news/londons-world-war-i-zeppelin-terror.

27 **kill 557 people . . . and H. G. Wells would say:** Ian Castle, *London, 1914–17: The Zeppelin Menace* (New York: Osprey Publishing, 2008), 7, 36, 86, 91.

27 **"that the Zeppelins may not drop":** HIK letter to NIK, Dec. 9, 1917, SSM.

27 **"musical little voice":** NIK's report cards from Notting Hill High School, Summer and Autumn, 1918, and Spring and Summer, 1919, DH.

29 **Suresnes, a largely blue-collar town:** Permanent exhibit, MUS.

29 **you could walk into:** Emile Trion, interview with author, Oct. 11, 2017.

29 **small ferries:** Karl Baedeker, *Paris and Its Environs* (London: George Allen & Co., 1937), 92.

29 **"Away to my hermitage":** James M. Gabler, *Passions: The Wines and Travels of Thomas Jefferson* (Baltimore: Bacchus Press, 1995), 133.

30 **1.4 million of their countrymen:** Vincent Cronin, *Paris: City of Light, 1919–1939* (New York: HarperCollins, 1994), 45.

30 **picking apricots:** Hamida Verlinden, email to author, May 6, 2019.

31 **invited her to move in:** Mahmood Khan, email to author, Nov. 26, 2017.

31 **almost a salon:** Harper and Harper, 66.

31 **large bedroom . . . provided allowances:** Zamir Rohrs, interview with author, Jan. 16, 2017.

32 **Ora opposed the marriage:** Mahmood Khan, email to author, Nov. 26, 2017.

32 **"Even if the whole world":** Noor, "To Our Amma," in Harper and Harper, 117.

32 **Never . . . Always . . . :** Notes from H. Ivan Gool, student in Noor's 1930s Sufi classes for children at Fazal Manzil, DH.

32 **"first and most sacred duty":** Noor, undated and untitled essay, DH.

33 **"nursed . . . with the milk":** "Brotherhood Called Nation's Foundation," *San Francisco Journal,* Apr. 23, 1923, page unavailable.

33 **"with anxious eyes" . . . "America sets the example":** "Mystic Comes to Put America 'Wise' to Orient," *New York Herald Tribune,* Aug. 12, 1925, 8.

33 **"respond more quickly":** "Sufi Mystic Says Americans Know Their Destinies," *New York Herald,* Feb. 22, 1925, page unavailable.

33 **serving tea:** Elisabeth deJong-Keesing, *Inayat Khan* (London: East-West Publications, 1974), 198.

34 **"I wanted to be bad":** Jean Overton Fuller, *Noor-un-nisa Inayat Khan* (The Hague: East-West Publications, 1988), 41.

34 **"We were brought up":** Vilayat quoted in Overton Fuller, 105.

34 **When Inayat was home:** Aya Johanna Danielle Durst Britt, "Tuning Souls to Harmony" (master's diss., Leiden University, Aug. 26, 2013), 70.

35 **"Keep burning the fire":** HIK, "Fires of Truth," http://www.pirzia.org/writings /hik-fires-of-truth.

35 **"every night and every morning":** HIK letter to NIK, undated, SSM.

35 **"sat with dignity":** HIK letter to NIK, Jan. 6, 1925, SSM.

35 **"What are the rules of the table?":** Mahmood Khan, interview with author, Oct. 13, 2017.

36 **". . . behave in courteous fashion":** "The Children Asking," Noorunnissa Khan, undated, DH.

36 **"Fairies of an enchanting sphere":** "Sweet Peas," Noorunissa Khan, undated, DH.

36 **"Take me gently":** "The Night Fairies," Noorunissa Khan, undated, DH.

36 **"it believes seriously":** HIK, *Education* (Claremont, CA: Hunter House, 1989), 32.

37 **"motor car":** HIK letter to NIK, undated, SSM.

37 **"Peace . . . is harmony":** Noor, untitled, undated essay, DH.

37 **"little ones are sheltered":** Inayat Khan, *Biography of Pir-o-Murshid Inayat Khan* (London: East-West Publications, 1979), unpaginated.

37 **birthday cakes . . . "dear past":** Overton Fuller, 42–43.

38 **Good Comrade prize:** Overton Fuller, 41.

38 **one Christmas:** "Under the Kerosene Oil Lamps," Khair-un-nisa Ray Inayat Khan (Claire Ray Khan), 2004, unpublished, SSM.

38 **pulmonary difficulties:** Hendrik J. Horn, "Introduction to Theo von Hoorn as a Sufi Memoirist," in *Recollections of Inayat Khan and Western Sufism,* ed. Theo von Hoorn (Leiden, Holland: Foleor Publishers, 2010), 130.

38 **Messenger of God:** Horn, 533.

38 **"My ancestors were Muslims":** "Indian Mystic Offers One Religion for All," *New York Times*, Dec. 7, 1926, 11.

39 **"I have no religion":** "Indian Mystic," 11.

39 **"I'm often homesick":** HIK, *The Mysticism of Sound and Music: The Sufi Teaching of Hazrat Inayat Khan* (Boston: Shambhala Publications, 1996), 182.

39 **"What is wrong with you?":** Malcolm Cameron Lyons and D. E. P. Jackson, *Saladin: The Politics of the Holy War* (Cambridge: Cambridge University Press, 1982), 357.

40 **formal caste:** Habeeb Salloum, *Muru'ah and the Code of Chivalry* (Washington, DC: Al-Hewar Center for Arab Culture and Dialogue, 2005), unpaginated.

40 **Inayat's rules:** PZIK, ed., *Caravan of Souls* (New Lebanon, NY: Suluk Press, 2013), 139–41. Inayat only had time to plant the seeds for Sufi chivalry before he died in 1927. In 2010 his nephew Mahmood Youskine Khan expanded on how to incorporate chivalry into daily life. To qualify as knights, Sufis had to recite a knightly rule for forty mornings, then apply it in their behavior on each of those days. Since there were forty rules, completing the entire roster took 1,600 days—four years plus 140 days.

40 **"cause our own troubles":** Noor, ms. on world religions, untitled, unpaginated, undated. Probably written in mid- or late 1930s, DH.

40 **"There is always a price":** Noor, ms. on world religions.

40 **planned to return home:** "Founder of Sufi Movement," *Madras Mail*, Dec. 18, 1926, page unknown.

40 **change his way:** Claire-un-nisa Khan, "Urs Commemoration," https://wahiduddin .net/mv2/bio/Claire_un_Nisa.htm.

40 **rented a house:** Title of article, name of newspaper in Delhi, and page number unknown, Nov. 16, 1926.

41 **"To serve God":** HIK, *Mysticism of Sound,* prologue, unpaginated.

42 **"architecture is music":** HIK, *Mysticism of Sound,* 3, 5.

42 **Inayat contracted pneumonia:** "The Death of Sufi Inayat Khan, the Great Preacher," *The Daily Haqiqat*, city unknown, India, Feb. 11, 1927, page unknown.

42 **"Abba's love":** HIK to NIK, telegram, Jan. 1, 1927. The family called Inayat "Abba," the term for "father" in many Muslim families.

42 **buckets of coal:** Zamir Rohrs, interview with author, Jan. 16, 2017.

42 **"*Hazrati zindagi*":** Mahmood Khan, interview with author, Oct. 13, 2017.

42 **"Little Mother":** Harper and Harper, 82.

42 **"Lazy girl, who slumbers still":** Harper and Harper, 114.

42 **Ora refused to eat:** Harper and Harper, 98.

42 **"Forgive us, dear Amma":** Noor-un-nisa Inayat Khan, "To our Amma," in Harper and Harper, 117.

42 **"little rays":** Noor, untitled poem to Ora, DH.

43 **"Father's pride":** Ora Baker Khan, "Graduation Day," in Hidayat Inayat-Khan, *Once Upon a Time* (Groningen, The Netherlands: Sufi Brotherhood Centre, 1998), 58.

43 **"sent it from above":** Ora Khan, "Graduation Day."

43 **"mystery of the night":** Noor, "Nocturnal," written in 1927, DH.

43 **"come to seek rest":** Noor Inayat Khan, "Song to the Madzub," probably written in the late 1920s, NF.

43 **"What must have been":** Mahmood Khan, interview with author, Oct. 9, 2017.

43 **"leave this world":** Noor Inayat Khan, "Life in the Solitude," undated, DH.

Chapter 3: "This Is Not Good for Your Health"

45 **Alladad's father proposed:** Mahmood Khan, interview with author, Oct. 13, 2017. Inayat's brothers liked Alladad, but his drinking concerned them. Sufis were encouraged to be abstinent. They also didn't believe Ora's claim that Inayat's uncle intended to marry her. In their culture, an uncle marrying a nephew's widow was considered close to incest.

46 **"gratitude in the smallest little way":** NIK, "The Four Little Children of Murshid," undated essay, DH.

46 **"Although life gives us":** Noor-un-nisa Inayat Khan, "To Our Beloved Amma," undated, DH.

46 **"It is wrong":** Noor, untitled, undated essay, DH.

46 **"Moïse" by the poet Alfred de Vigny:** Letter from a student in NIK's classes to David Harper, Apr. 7, 2013, DH.

47 **". . . will it never end?":** "Alfred de Vigny's 'Moïse,'" trans. Jeanne Curran, http://www5.csudh.edu/dearhabermas/moise01.htm.

47 **"Share only your happiness":** Letter from student to Harper, DH.

47 **Noor gave books . . . bonbons:** Letter from student to Harper.

48 **"a very gentle girl":** Jean Overton Fuller, *Noor-un-nisa Inayat Khan* (The Hague: East-West Publications, 1988), 51. On screen, Harpo was chaotic. Off screen, he was disciplined, especially about his music: he practiced his harp three hours a day when home in California.

48 **"It is necessary":** Odette de Montesquiou, *The Legend of Henriette Renié,* trans. Robert Kilpatrick (Bloomington, IN: Author House, 2006), 58.

48 **Two dogs were carved:** Claire Ray Harper and David Ray Harper, *We Rubies Four* (New Lebanon, NY: Omega Publications, 2011), 107.

48 **One of the more expensive harps:** Howard Bryan, emails to author, Jan. 9 and 11, 2018.

48 **tapered soundboard:** Nancy Hurrell, email to author, Dec. 28, 2017.

48 **Ora's wish:** Mahmood Khan, email to author, Feb. 18, 2018.

48 **Elie Goldenberg:** Previous writing about NIK refer to Goldenberg as "Elie Goldberg," "Eli Goldberg," or simply "Goldberg." In Noor's address book, compiled in the 1930s, she wrote "M. Elie Goldenberg, 11 bis Rue Diderot, Suresnes."

50 **Elie moved from Paris:** NIK's personal address book, DH.

50 **world's center for cosmetics:** Vincent Cronin, *Paris: City of Light, 1919–1939* (New York: HarperCollins, 1994), 47.

51 **They were too angry:** Mahmood Khan, interview, Oct. 9, 2017.

51   **Azeem as a stray . . . a mésalliance:** Khan interview, Oct. 9, 2017.

51   **"Who has heard my painful cry":** Noor-un-nisa Inayat Khan, "The Song of the Night," undated, DH.

52   **Pablo Casals:** PVIK, "Memories of Noor," undated, unpublished essay, DH.

52   **"I detest living":** Pablo Casals, quoted in Albert E. Kahn, *Joys and Sorrows: Reflections by Pablo Casals* (New York: Simon & Schuster, 1970), 49.

52   **"the perfectability of man" . . . "the good in you":** Kahn, 49.

52   **"An affront to humanity":** Kahn, 99.

52   **Noor and Vilayat went to Milan:** Overton Fuller, 63.

53   **Champéry:** PVIK, "Memories of Noor."

53   **bicycles they had brought:** PVIK, "Memories of Noor," 64.

53   **humor and jests:** Mahmood Khan, interview with author, Oct. 13, 2017.

53   **wrote to Azeem:** Noor, letters to Azeem, 1934–1938, DH. Unfortunately, Azeem's letters to Noor have disappeared.

54   **"My dear Azeem":** Noor, letter to Azeem from The Hague, dated only "1938," DH.

54   **"We will see the years pass":** Noor, untitled poem to Azeem written on her birthday, Jan. 1, 1935. DH.

54   **she was the only student:** Program from Mar. 31, 1935, recital at salon of Henriette Renié, DH. Other students played work by French and German composers—Francis Thome, Charles Oberthur, Alphonse Hasselmans, Marcel Tournier. The program listed NIK as "Mlle. Inayat." Her first and last names were omitted. Other students were listed by their full names.

Chapter 4: The Road Is Weeping

55   **meeting with Hitler:** William L. Shirer, *The Collapse of the Third Republic* (New York: Simon & Schuster, 1969), 403.

55   **"peace for our time:** David Drake, *Paris at War* (Cambridge, MA: Belknap Press, 2015), 7–8.

55   **"Our enemies are worms":** Jeffrey Record, *Making War, Thinking History* (Annapolis, MD: Naval Institute Press, 2014), 15.

55   **"the profound conviction" . . . "the imbeciles":** Drake, 8.

56   **"We menace no one":** Joachim C. Fest, *Hitler* (New York: Harcourt Brace, 1974), 607–8.

56   **350,000 French reservists . . . 31,000 children . . . Ritz Hotel . . . the *Mona Lisa* . . . Astrologers . . . the chief rabbi . . . Jean Verdier:** Drake, 13–15.

56   **"no other war":** "Crusade," *Time* magazine, Feb. 19, 1940.

57   **Trains were free:** Drake, 19.

57   **Blackouts were enforced:** Drake, 28.

57   **a new law extended:** Drake, 23.

57   **waiters asked customers:** Drake, 27.

57   **as a nurse on the front:** Jean Overton Fuller, *Noor-un-nisa Inayat Khan* (The

Hague: East-West Publications, 1988), 84–85. NIK's course list from her Red Cross training, courtesy, DH. On May 8, 1940, the French Red Cross issued Card #40693 to NIK as a nurse's aide.

57 **Maginot Line:** The seven-mile-wide Maginot Line stretched 230 miles along the Franco-German border—12 million cubic feet of earthworks, 150,000 tons of steel, fifty-eight underground fortresses, barbed wire, pill boxes, land mines, thousands of antitank spikes set in concrete and hospitals, barracks, tunnels, and cinemas sixty feet below ground. Throughout were fixed machine guns and artillery unable to follow the movement of any invader. The Line was pure folly. Vincent Cronin, *Paris: City of Light, 1919–1939* (New York: HarperCollins, 1994), 188.

57 **Suresnes's railroad station and its airplane factories:** Michel Hébert and Guy Noël, *Memoire en Images: Suresnes Tome II* (Joue-les-Tours, France: Alan Sutton, 1996), 17, 115.

57 **air-raid shelter:** "Germans Bomb Paris," Pittsburgh (Pa.) Press, June 3, 1940, 1.

57 **twenty-eight bombs . . . Plumes of black smoke:** Edouard Duval, "Journal de Guerre, 1939–1942," unpaginated, MUS.

58 **Half of Europe:** Helen Mackay, *With Love for France* (New York: Charles Scribner's Sons, 1942), 94.

58 **"desolate and dreadful":** Quoted in Jonathan Fenby, *The Sinking of the Lancastria* (New York: Simon & Schuster, 2005), 17.

58 **"Somewhere in northern France":** Antoine de Saint-Exupéry, *Airman's Odyssey* (New York: Mariner Books, 1984), 350.

58 **"all religions, all races":** PVIK, "Memories of Noor," unpublished essay, DH.

59 **"impervious":** Arthur Herman, *Gandhi & Churchill* (New York: Bantam Books, 2008), 447.

59 **Czechoslovakia to respond passively:** Judith M. Brown, *Gandhi: Prisoner of Hope* (New Haven, CT: Yale University Press, 1989), 320.

59 **"massacre":** Robert Payne, *The Life and Death of Mahatma Gandhi* (New York: E. P. Dutton, 1960), 485.

59 **"German Jews will score":** M. K. Gandhi, "Zionism and Anti-Semitism," in *The Gandhi Reader*, ed. Homer A. Jack (Bloomington, IN: 1956), 320–21. "Even after the war," wrote a Gandhi biographer, "when the full extent of the Holocaust became known, Gandhi still felt that 'the Jews should have offered themselves to the butcher's knife. . . . It would have aroused the world and the people of Germany. . . . They succumbed anyway in their millions." Herman, 445.

59 **"take your beautiful island":** M. K. Gandhi, "To Every Briton," in *Gandhi Reader*, 345.

59 **"We are engaged in a struggle":** Payne, 489.

59 **"Do you know":** Martin Buber, "A Letter to Gandhi," Feb. 24, 1939, in Buber, *A Land of Two Peoples*, ed. Paul Mendes-Flohr (Chicago: University of Chicago Press, 2005), 115. By contrast with Gandhi, other Indian leaders recognized early the peril facing European Jews. The Indian spiritual teacher Aurobindo advocated suspending the independence movement until Hitler—"the greatest menace the world had

ever faced"—was defeated. Nirodbaran, *12 Years with Aurobindo* (Pondicherry, India: Sri Aurobindo Publications Dept., 1988), 128, 152–53. And in December 1938, Gandhi's close associate, Jawaharlal Nehru, urged the head of an Indian province to provide government positions to skilled Jewish refugees—"things are moving so fast that . . . these unfortunate persons may simply be crushed out of existence." Yasmin Khan, *The Raj at War* (London: Vintage Press, 2018), 9.

60 **"Right at our door":** PVIK, "Memories of Noor."

60 **"millions of Jews":** PVIK, "An Recognizable Face from Suresnes: Who Was Noor Inayat Khan?," unpublished essay, DH.

60 **"if revolvers or swords":** PVIK, *Creating the Person* (New Lebanon, N.Y.: Omega Publications, 1995), 32–33. The price of refusing to fight for our country, Inayat said, was leaving it and "stay[ing] in solitude under the shade of a tree"—with no homeland, no refuge, and few friends. HIK, *Education* (Claremont, CA: Hunter House, 1989), 38–39.

61 **"kill with the sword of wisdom":** *Bhagavad Gita*, ed. Juan Mascaro (Baltimore: Penguin, 1971), 65.

61 **"the ruler of his soul":** *Bhagavad Gita*, 67.

61 **"in the heart of all":** *Bhagavad Gita*, 71. In an aside to Gandhi in his 1939 letter to the Indian leader, Martin Buber's comments on war as a spiritual calling closely mirrored what the *Gita* said: "We should be able even to fight for justice—but to fight lovingly." Buber, "A Letter to Gandhi," in Buber, *A Land of Two Peoples*, 125.

61 **"The essence of spirituality":** HIK, "Nirtan: Dance," TTHIK.

61 **"awaken man":** HIK, letter to Ada Martin, an undated Wednesday in 1917.

61 **"drunkenness":** HIK, "Social Gothekas: The Intoxication of Life," TTHIK.

62 **Vilayat's MG:** Claire Ray Harper and David Ray Harper, *We Rubies Four* (New Lebanon, NY: Omega Publications, 2011), 124. The MG must have been an 18/80. Claire Khan wrote in *We Rubies Four*, and Mahmood Khan, NIK's cousin, told me over dinner in Suresnes in 2019, that Vilayat's MG had a jump seat. Of the prewar MGs with jump seats, the 18/80 was produced from 1929 to 1933, the closest to 1940, the year the Khans left Paris. Older MGs with jump seats were the 14/28 (manufactured 1925–1927) and the 14/40 (manufactured 1927–1929). The 18/80s had a 40 hp motor with a top speed of 55 mph. John Day, president of MG Car Club, Ltd, email to author, Mar. 13, 2018.

63 **body of a grandmother:** Drake, *Paris at War*, 54.

63 **"One would think":** Léon Werth, *33 Days* (Brooklyn: Melville House, 2015), 9.

63 **"bright green lawns":** Mark Twain, *The Innocents Abroad* (New York: Modern Library, 2003), 71–73.

63 **"black congestion":** Jean-Paul Sartre, *Troubled Sleep* (New York: Alfred A. Knopf, 1951), 14.

63 **"the scraping of boots . . . hot, stale stench":** Sartre, *Troubled Sleep*, 21.

63 **population of Chartres . . . Bordeaux:** Julian Jackson, *France: The Dark Years* (New York: Oxford University Press, 2001), 120.

65 **"frantic young mothers":** Noor-un-Nisa Inayat Khan, "Escape from St. Nazaire (1940)," unpublished, unpaginated, DH.

65 **"If someone said to me":** Werth, 48.

66 **insisted on tagging along:** DH, interview with author, Oct. 17, 2017.

66 **9,000 passengers . . . Stanley Rimmer:** Fenby, 3–5, 9–10, 14–15, 97, 104, 155.

66 **"noises ceased":** Khan, "Escape from St. Nazaire."

66 **"being guarded by":** Khan, "Escape from St. Nazaire."

67 **"We just walked and walked":** Harper and Harper, 127.

67 **Vilayat was furious:** Harper and Harper, 128.

68 **the first German bombers:** Juliet Gardiner, *The Blitz* (London: Harper Press, 2010), 4.

68 **"beautiful and summery":** Daphne Wall, *The World I Lost: A Memoir of Peace and War* (Brighton, England: Sorties Ltd, 2014), ebook.

68 **Four days later:** Number of days determined by the stamp on page 9 of NIK's passport: "Immigration Officer, 22 Jun 1940, Falmouth." This was four days after Noor boarded the *Kosongo* in France.

69 **Oxford, three hours away:** Harper and Harper, 130. The *Kasongo* was sunk by a German submarine, Feb. 26, 1941, eight months after it took NIK to England.

69 **black convertibles prowled:** Ronald C. Rosbottom, *When Paris Went Dark: The City of Light under German Occupation, 1940–1944* (New York: Back Bay Books, 2014), 72–82. As Hitler was touring Paris, Oscar Hammerstein remembered visiting the city, smitten with its beauty and gaiety. Certain that Paris would never be the same, Hammerstein wrote the saddest song ever written about that city: "The last time I saw Paris / Her heart was warm and gay." Hammerstein's lyrics had to satisfy him until Paris was liberated. Otherwise, he possessed only a dread that the Nazis would destroy the city's spirit and dampen its soul. Hugh Fordin, *Getting to Know Him* (New York: Da Capo Press, 1995), 172–73.

70 **Crossing the Seine:** Rosbottom, 83–91.

70 **"It was the dream":** Alex Kershaw, *Avenue of Spies* (New York: Crown, 2015), 31.

70 **"not covet foolish things":** Noor Inayat Khan, "The Children Asking," unpublished, undated poem, DH.

Chapter 5: The Bloody World's on Fire

73 **did "not obtrude":** Jean Overton Fuller, *Noor-un-nisa Inayat Khan* (The Hague: East-West Publications, 1988, 91.

73 **some sort of liaison . . . "becomes a fighter pilot":** Overton Fuller, 92.

74 **"use without limit":** David Drake, *Paris at War* (Cambridge, MA: Belknap Press, 2015), 69.

74 **247 one night:** Philip Ziegler, *London at War, 1939–1945* (London: Sinclair-Stevenson, 1995), 114–15.

74 **400 another:** William Sansom, *The Blitz: Westminster at War* (Oxford: Oxford University Press, 1990), 60.

74 **civilians were killed:** Juliet Gardiner, *The Blitz: The British Under Attack* (New York: HarperCollins, 2011), 33, 70.

74 **"The whole bloody world's on fire":** Gardiner, 113.

74 **St. Thomas's Hospital:** Gardiner, 38–39.

74 **House of Commons:** Sansom, 92.

74 **a colossal cave:** Sansom, 71.

75 **Café de Paris:** Gardiner, 324.

75 **"The people are marvelous":** Sansom, 59.

75 **"a queer sensation":** Sansom, 97.

75 **only fifty tanks:** Sansom, 59.

75 **looters slid rings:** Gardiner, 324.

75 **In Cardiff:** Gardiner, 329.

75 **claimed that Jews . . . "Because two days ago":** Ziegler, 175.

75 **"heart sank":** Claire Ray Harper and David Ray Harper, *We Rubies Four* (New Lebanon, NY: Omega Publications, 2011), 133.

75 **Fulmer Chase Maternity Home:** Overton Fuller, 93–94.

76 **#754197 . . . "N. Inayat-Khan":** NIK's WAAF identity card, DH.

76 **"Nora":** Overton Fuller, 95.

76 **straw mattresses . . . wore shoes . . . pay was two-thirds:** Beryl E. Escott, *The WAAF* (Buckinghamshire, England: Shire Publications, 2003), 8, 10, 11, 21.

76 **"lumps of grisly meat":** Juliet Gardiner, *Wartime: Britain, 1939–1945* (London: Headline Book, 2005), 511.

76 **Women's uniforms:** "WAAF Service Dress Uniform Buyer's Guide," http://www.wadhamsfamilyhistory.co.uk/FortiesWAAFuniform, html.

77 **three weeks of basic training:** Escott, 7.

77 **"The constant marching":** Gardiner, *Wartime*, 511.

77 **"Would you like":** Gardiner, *Wartime*, 316.

77 **2,298 Scots:** Les Taylor, *Luftwaffe Over Scotland: A History of German Air Attacks on Scotland 1939–1945* (Caithness, Scotland: Whittles Publishing, 2010), xi.

77 **more than two feet of snow fell:** "February 1941—Rather cold; considerable snow," Monthly Report of the Meteorological Office, Air Ministry, vol. 58, no. 2, Mar. 26, 1941.

77 **chilblains:** Overton Fuller, 96.

77 **in a basement . . . cannon . . . Edinburgh Castle:** Dorothy Barnes, "A Chelsea Girl," WW2 People's War: An Archive of World War Two Memories, BBC History. www.bbc.co.uk/history/ww2peopleswar/stories/63/a2026065.shtml.

78 **"in tune with the universe":** HIK, "The Power of the Word," TTHIK.

78 **"Our cheers are going":** Noor, poem to Ora, untitled, undated other than "May 1941"— probably on or near May 8, Ora's birthday, DH.

78 **sent a telegram:** Harper and Harper, 132. The family did not hear from Hidayat until September 1945, when a telegram came from Dieulefit, France. The Germans had prohibited communicating with England during the war. In those years, Hidayat hid in the mountains with his wife and children. Harper and Harper, 150.

79 **tossing a bun:** Abingdon-on-Thames municipal website, "Bun Throwing: a

400-Year-Old Moment of Mayhem," www.abingdon.gov.uk/witness-living-tradition/bun-throwing.

79 **decorated their room . . . they started mumbling Morse:** Overton Fuller, 95–96.

79 **"Heidenroslein":** A more risqué interpretation of the song focuses on a young man seeing a beautiful woman ("young and lovely as the morning"), confessing his desire ("I will pick you, my red rose!"), and forcing himself on her ("I will prick you") as she tries to fend him off.

80 **Two Whitleys crashed:** "RAF Abingdon 10 OTU," www.rafabingdon10otu.co.uk.

80 **"mouse-brown hair":** Overton Fuller, 115. Noor's nickname, "Bang away, Lulu," was adapted from a folk song of that same title. Sung to the tune of "Good Night, Ladies," each version was bawdy and funny. A relatively tame version goes: "My Lulu gal's a daisy / She wears a big white hat / I bet your life when I'm in town / The dudes all hit the flat."

80 **her Raleigh bicycle:** NIK's bicycle permission pass, RAF Compton Bassett. Issued July 4, 1942, DH.

80 **train to London:** John "Blossom" Bloom's memories of RAF Compton Bassett, www.newtonmyers.com/The%20Fifties20-%20Part%20one.html.

80 **"generous, but reckless character":** Overton Fuller, 137.

80 **"there is such peace":** Overton Fuller, 115.

80 **finished Milton's *Paradise Lost*:** Overton Fuller, 118.

80 **modern German novel:** Overton Fuller, 124.

81 **Poor night vision:** Harper and Harper, 133.

81 **not have to kill anyone:** Harper and Harper, 139.

81 ***Fantasia*:** Overton Fuller, 100–101.

81 **Beethoven's Sixth was "exciting":** William Glock, "Music," *London Observer*, Aug. 10, 1941, 7.

81 **"Noor is a deer":** Overton Fuller, 101.

81 **"live in this world . . . I do all things for you":** HIK, "The Inner Life," TTHIK.

81 **"A lady-like hair style":** Overton Fuller, 102.

82 **seventy-four thousand fatalities:** Yasmin Khan, *The Raj at War: A People's History of India's Second World War* (London: Vintage, 2016), 20.

82 **India's "natural friends":** Khan, *Raj at War*, 113.

82 **"Hundreds, if not thousands perished":** Khan, *Raj at War*, 107. A few months before Noor went before the commission board, England sent Sir Stafford Cripps to Delhi to negotiate greater cooperation between India and Britain. The major stumbling block was a 1939 law that let British governors control food distribution, suspend newspapers, seize property, and detain indefinitely anyone suspected of jeopardizing the war effort. Cripps offered to loosen some of these measures if Britain controlled every military matter related to India. Neither pacifists nor

independence leaders approved, and Cripps's mission was a failure. Khan, *Raj at War,* 12.

83 **"At present":** Overton Fuller, 104.

83 **draw an equivalence:** Overton Fuller. Though an Indian Home Guard was never formed, two million Indians served, 1939–1945, in the Indian Army in Ethiopia, Egypt, Libya, Tunisia, Algeria, Burma, and Malaya. Elsewhere, forty-three thousand pro-Japanese Indians fought in the Indian National Army for independence from Britain. Khan, *Raj at War,* 18, 118, 310.

83 **If India's situation:** Overton Fuller, 105.

83 **"I should like to have appeared":** Overton Fuller, 105.

84 **"completely lit by electricity":** Ad for Hotel Victoria, date undetermined, http://www.historyworld.co.uk/content/hotelvictoria.jpg.

84 **"linguistic qualifications":** NIK file, NA HS9/836/5.

Chapter 6: A Thing No Human Could Face with Anything but Terror

86 **"Where are the enemy?":** David Stafford, *Churchill and Secret Service* (New York: Overlook Press, 1998), 12.

86 **"rightly esteemed":** Churchill, quoted in "The Greatest Deed I Ever Saw," Ronald I. Cohen, "Finest Hour," 1st quarter 2019, 36 (National Churchill Library and Center, George Washington University, and the National Churchill Museum, Westminster College).

86 **Churchill didn't want spies:** Noor's family has been adamant since the war that she was an "agent," not a "spy." On Feb. 14, 2014, Hidayat, Noor's brother, told a Sufi living in California, "My sister was not a spy! She was a resistant officer fighting against criminal dictatorship." Hidayat Khan, email to Jeanne Kassof, Nov. 30, 2018.

87 **"the outfit," "the firm," or "the racket":** Patrick Yarnold, *Wanborough Manor: School for Secret Agents* (Guildford: Hopfield, 2009), 18.

87 **"smash things up" . . . "set Europe ablaze":** Hugh Dalton, *The Fateful Years* (London: Frederick Muller Ltd, 1957), 366.

87 **Fifty-four agents:** Albert E. Riffice, "Intelligence and Overt Action," in *Studies in Intelligence,* Winter 1962, vol. 6, no. 1: 76.

87 **destroyed 350 kilograms:** Patrick Howarth, *Undercover* (London, Phoenix Press, 2000), 214. After the war, it was discovered that the Germans were actually proceeding down the wrong theoretical road toward a bomb.

87 **twelve thousand German soldiers:** Howarth, 214.

87 **Forty-eight trains:** Giles Milton, *Churchill's Ministry of Ungentlemanly Warfare* (New York: Picador, 2017), 194.

87 **two thousand trainloads:** Milton, 209.

88 **"better than men":** Selwyn Jepson oral history, IWM.

88 **"to give worth and meaning" . . . "truants," "human decency":** E. H. Cookridge, *Inside SOE* (London: Arthur Barker, 1966), 63–64.

88 **too impulsive:** M. R. D. Foot, *SOE: The Special Operations Executive, 1940–1946* (London: Pimlico, 1984), 59.

88 **"an intuitive sense":** Jepson oral history, IWM.

89 **"I realized it would be safe":** Jepson oral history, IWM.

89 **"I have to decide":** Foot, *SOE: Special Operations Executive*, 73.

89 **"My object was always":** Foot, *SOE in France*, 59.

89 **"a thing no human could face":** Jean Overton Fuller, *Noor-un-nisa Inayat Khan*, 110.

89 **One line of thinking:** Foot, *SOE: Special Operations Executive*, 60.

89 **There was little doubt:** Jepson oral history, IWM.

90 **Noor had assumed:** Mahmood Khan, interview with author, Oct. 9, 2017.

90 **"I wish you would decide":** Ora letter to NIK, undated, DH.

90 **"gratefully accepting":** NIK letter to Selwyn Jepson, Nov. 11, 1942, DH.

Chapter 7: "I Am a Busy Little Girl Now"

91 **MI5 . . . checked:** Selwyn Jepson, oral history, IWM.

91 **"If I begin":** Jean Overton Fuller, *Noor-un-nisa Inayat Khan* (The Hague: East-West Publications, 1988), 120.

91 **Official Secrets Act:** Form signed by Noor, Feb. 15, 1943, DH.

91 **"I am a busy little girl":** Noor letter to Vilayat, in Overton Fuller, 121. Overton Fuller says the letter "must have been" sent shortly after NIK began her SOE training.

92 **not telling . . . venereal disease . . . kill a sentry with a knife:** Anonymous, *SOE Syllabus,* introduction by Denis Rigden (Richmond, Surrey, England: The National Archives, 2004), 19, 39, 132, 260, 366–67.

92 **"then kick him . . .":** Gary Kamiya, *Shadow Knights: The Secret War Against Hitler* (New York: Simon & Schuister, 2010), 48.

92 **do "not turn your back":** HIK, "Social Gathekas: What Is Wanted in Life?," TTHIK.

92 **training was hand-tailored:** M. R. D. Foot, *SOE: The Special Operations Executive, 1940–46* (London: British Broadcasting Corporation, 1984), 64–65.

92 **one-man submarine:** Anonymous, *The British Spy Manual,* introduction by Sinclair McKay (London: IWM, 2014), 90, 186–87.

92 **basic training at Wanborough Manor:** Patrick Yarnold, *Wanborough Manor: School for Secret Agents* (Guildford: Hopfield, 2009), 21.

93 **"first-class shooting" . . . 280 acres:** 1912 ad for sale of Wanborough Manor Estate. Courtesy, Patrick Yarnold.

93 **neighbors ignored:** Yarnold, email to author, May 5, 2018.

93 **"Bravery was what they had":** Atkins, quoted in Sarah Helm, *A Life in Secrets* (New York: Anchor Books, 2007), xxi.

93 **Noor's group:** Yarnold, 97–100.

94 **"fit for no more":** Yarnold, 99.

94 **Jaap Bateman:** Beryl E. Escott, *The Heroines of SOE: Britain's Secret Women in France F Section* (Stroud, England: History Press, 2010), 121.

94 **Cecily Margot Lefort:** Escott, 103–4.

94 **over 102 aviators:** Michael Tillotson, ed., *SOE and the Resistance: As Told in the Times Obituaries* (New York: Continuum, 2011), 89–90.

94 **Yvonne Cormeau:** Escott, 115–16.

94 **6:30 in the morning:** Yarnold, 37.

94 **"sheer perfection":** *Jane Austen's Letters,* edited by Deirdre Le Faye (New York: Oxford University Press, 2011), 216–19.

94 **"only French was spoken . . . French chef . . . students shot pistols:** Yarnold, 38–39.

94 **At night:** Yarnold, 38.

95 **"The act of shooting":** Noor-un-nissa Khan, "Symbologies," unpublished essay almost certainly written in 1943.

95 **"A person for whom":** Cpl. Gordon (first name not given), Report on Noor for the SOE, Mar. 11, 1943.

95 **"slow to get the hang" . . . "no aptitude" . . . called her clumsy:** Major R. C. V. de Wesselow, Preliminary Report on Nora Inayat-Khan, Mar. 10, 1943.

96 **"From a shaky start":** de Wesselow.

96 **Agents disguised antennas:** *British Spy Manual,* 219.

96 **with a gun ready:** *SOE Syllabus,* 125.

96 **"unless absolutely unavoidable":** *SOE Syllabus,* 218.

97 **their "fist":** Leo Marks, *Between Silk and Cyanide: A Codemaker's War, 1941–1945* (New York: Free Press, 1998), 601.

97 **up to twenty percent:** Marks, 9.

97 **"That is very possible":** Thomas Wemyss Reid, *Memoirs and Correspondence of Lyon Playfair* (New York: Harper & Brothers, 1899), 158–59.

98 **Lawrence of Arabia . . . John F. Kennedy's PT 109:** David Kahn, *The Code-breakers* (New York: Macmillan, 1967), 312, 592.

98 **Germans had trucks . . . fat men in raincoats:** Foot, *SOE: Special Operations,* 106–7, 111.

99 **"any romantic ideas":** NIK file, NA HS9/836S.

99 **"always tells the truth":** HIK, "Chalas: An Illuminated Word," TTHIK.

99 **"the light in which the true nature":** "Chalas."

100 **"Glad to know" . . . "I hope you retire":** Ora, letter to Noor, 16th of an unidentified month, late spring 1943, DH.

100 **"short meals and short drinks":** *SOE Syllabus,* 68.

100 **take a taxi:** *SOE Syllabus,* 69.

100 **Noor became skilled:** *SOE Syllabus,* 55–56.

100 **a Parisienne:** *SOE Syllabus,* 82.

101 **"some small idea":** Maurice Buckmaster, *They Fought Alone* (London: Odhams Press, 1958), 46–49.

101 **"seemed absolutely terrified"**: Overton Fuller, 127.

101 **"This . . . is the life"**: *SOE Syllabus,* 48-49.

102 **to research children's impressions**: Noor's notes from her May 19–23, 1943, "scheme" in Bristol, NA.

102 **"responsible, understanding"**: Noor's notes.

102 **uncertain, wary**: SOE report on NIK's "scheme," NA.

102 **For a dead-letter box**: Noor's notes.

103 **"kindly" . . . "very deaf"**: Noor's notes.

103 **"stupid" mistakes**: SOE report on NIK's "scheme," undated, NA.

103 **"I'm training to be"**: Marks, 311.

103 **"a little nervous"**: SOE report on Noor, May 24, 1943, NA.

104 **"Highly temperamental"**: Monthly Progress Report for Inayat-Khan, Signal Training. For Major R. Signals, Commanding STS 52, May 31, 1943, NA.

104 **"Not over-burdened"**: Col. Frank Spooner report to SOE at conclusion of NIK's "finishing school" training, May 21, 1943, NA.

104 **"We don't want them overburdened"**: Buckmaster's scribbling on Spooner's report, undated, NA.

105 **Hindu *Vedas***: Overton Fuller, 129.

105 **"so many things"**: Overton Fuller, 130.

105 **"Do you remember"**: Noor, untitled poem, May 1943, DH.

105 **"mind quite at ease"**: Ora, letter to Noor, 16th of an unidentified month, late spring 1943.

105 **wanted to marry her**: Overton Fuller, 114.

106 **she was engaged**: Overton Fuller, 132.

107 **"She spends so much of her time"**: Overton Fuller, 126.

Chapter 8: "I Have Gained My Subjects' Freedom"

108 **going at first was slow**: M. R. D. Foot, *SOE in France* (HMSO, 1966), 84.

108 **impeccable bearing**: E. H. Cookridge, *Inside SOE* (London: Arthur Barker, 1966), 199.

108 **chef in Paris**: Cookridge, 196.

108 **smuggled spies**: Cookridge, 256.

108 **German mine sweeper**: Cookridge, 235.

108 **twenty trains**: Cookridge, 237.

108 **twenty-two transformers**: Cookridge, 238.

109 **locks on canals**: Cookridge, 222.

109 **Hitler was furious**: Foot, 169.

109 **"All traitors"**: John Vader, *The Prosper Double-Cross* (Mullumbimby, Australia: Sunrise Press, 1977), 28. Regarding "All male relatives of these traitors between 1 and 65 will be shot," the Nazis actually planned to execute one-year-olds. That is not a typo.

109 **ultimate responsibility . . . flush with cash . . . more effective**: E. H. Cookridge, *Set Europe Ablaze* (New York: Thomas Y. Crowell, 1967), 132.

109 **sixty cells:** Cookridge, *Set Europe Ablaze*, 202.

110 **"lack of ruse":** Sarah Helm, *A Life in Secrets* (New York: Anchor Books, 2007), 13. Several accounts claim Noor—needed in France sooner than expected—was flown to the Continent the night of May 21/22, then returned to England because her pilot didn't see landing signals near Compiègne. No archival records confirm this. Confusion arose because the name of that flight was "Madeleine"—the same as Noor's code name. Records state that two Lysanders flew to France on May 21/22. One dropped agents near Issoudun. The other returned to England when the pilot saw no landing signal, probably because Germans had jammed radio broadcasts for the reception committee to meet the flight. Hugh Verity, *We Landed by Moonlight* (Manchester, England: Crecy Publishing, 2005), 197.

110 **"most powerful personality":** Helm, xv.

110 **"childlike":** Helm, 13.

111 **"There is only one crime":** Helm, 17.

112 **bend one of your rules:** Helm, 18.

112 **"There were questions":** Helm, xxii.

112 **"hadn't had to teach her":** Marks, 308.

112 **"damn busybody"** . . . **"mystical upbringing'** . . . **"Indian prince"** . . . **only one available:** Marks, 308–10.

113 **"Any longer than that":** Marks, 310.

113 **"potty princess":** Marks, 311.

114 **sometimes riding:** Jean Overton Fuller, *Noor-un-nisa Inayat Khan* (The Hague: East-West Publications, 1988), 58.

114 **"It's beautiful":** Letter, Noor to Azeem, date unknown, probably mid-1930s, DH.

114 **Le Mair was an ideal partner:** Le Mair's paintings were so comforting that, in the early 1920s, Colgate, the American beauty-goods manufacturer, asked her to illustrate twelve advertisements for Fab, a new soap being marketed for sensitive skin. Henriette delivered what Fab needed: a soft touch for soft skin. Brochure for "A Gallery of Children," a show devoted to Le Mair's art, Bethnal Green Museum, October-November 1975.

115 **rose at six:** Overton Fuller, 72. A cousin of Noor's was bothered by the Buddha's death in her jatakas. Said Mahmood Khan, "At least the good characters in Grimm stories always live long and happily. What vexed me was that, once the Buddha sacrificed himself, Noor made the lucky survivors live long and happily ever after. This was callous. How could they?" Mahmood Khan, email to author, Apr. 6, 2018. Noor had another literary breakthrough in 1939: on Aug. 13, the children's section of the Paris newspaper *Le Figaro* published her adaptation of the Greek myth of Echo.

115 **"Oh Noor, what the hell":** Marks, 315.

115 **"slender figure":** Marks, 315.

115 **"suspected she'd written":** Marks, 316.

116 **"Returning suddenly":** Marks, 316.

116 **"I have gained my subjects' freedom":** NIK, *Twenty Jataka Tales*, 21.

116 **"Coded messages":** Marks, 317.

116 **"You've told me a lie":** Marks, 318.

117 **Checks could take many forms:** David Kahn, *The Codebreakers* (New York: Macmillan Co., 1967), 534.

117 **"If you tell them":** Marks, 320.

118 **"My little sister" . . . "Please don't worry" . . . "We will meet someday":** Claire Ray Harper and David Ray Harper, *We Rubies Four* (New Lebanon, NY: Omega Publications, 2011), 138–39.

Chapter 9: The Business Is Underway

121 **green oilskin coat:** Hugh Verity, *We Landed by Moonlight* (Manchester, England: Crecy Publishing, 2005), 94.

121 **Rymills was twenty-three:** Verity, 15.

122 **Rymills's cocker spaniel:** Verity, 15.

122 **specially treated cotton:** Larry Doyle, email to author, Nov. 25, 2015.

122 **"a wonderful sense of humor":** Bernard O'Conner, *RAF Tempsford* (Stroud, England: Amberley Publishing, 2010), 127.

123 **"proof in ourselves":** John Vader, *The Prosper Double-Cross* (Mullumbimby, Australia) Sunrise Press, 1977), 60.

124 **Jeanne Marie's cover story:** SOE's story for Noor, issued May 1943, DH.

124 **"Never . . . come out of character":** Anonymous, *SOE Syllabus,* introduction by Denis Rigden (Richmond, Surrey, England: The National Archives, 2004), 55.

124 **"Cinema" . . . transmit messages:** "Nurse Plan," SOE document, undated, 1. NA.

124 **3 p.m. daily:** NIK file, NA HS9/836S.

124 **sever contact:** "Operation: NURSE," SOE document, June 6, 1943, 1, NA.

125 **Passwords were crucial . . . "be extremely careful":** "Operation: NURSE," 1–2.

125 **numerous possibilities:** "Operation: NURSE," 2.

125 **It was rife . . . "with denunciations":** Maurice Buckmaster, *Specially Employed* (London: Batchworth Press, 1952), 185.

125 **Posters appealed:** David Drake, *Paris at War 1939–1944* (Cambridge, MA: Belknap Press, 2015), 328, 331.

126 **Tobacco rations . . . taxes on bikes . . . food rations . . . Métro stations:** Drake, 332–33, 335–36.

126 **"the joy of an exchange":** Jean Guehenno, *Diary of the Dark Years, 1940–1944,* trans. David Ball (New York: Oxford University Press, 2014), 195–96.

126 **"now resembled Shanghai":** Marie-Madeleine Fourcade, *Noah's Ark* (New York: E. P. Dutton, 1974), 310.

127 **"I was so disappointed" . . . "you will be in your uniform":** Jean Overton Fuller, *Noor-un-nisa Khan* (The Hague: East-West Publications, 1988), 175.

127 **"*Elle avait très peur*":** Jean Overton Fuller, *The German Penetration of SOE, France 1941–1944* (Maidstone, England: George Mann Books, 1996), 64.

128 **André Marsac . . . Odette Sansom:** E. H. Cookridge, *Inside SOE* (London: Arthur Barker, 1966), 209.

128 **acted like she was twenty:** Overton Fuller, *Noor-un-nisa Khan*, 143–45.

128 **seven hundred acres:** Herbert J. Little, "Report on Agricultural Education—A Summary," *Journal of the Royal Agricultural Society of England*, vol. 21, 1885 (London: John Murray), 147.

129 **"would have coincided":** Prosper Report, June 19, 1943, NA/HS9/91/1.

129 **her first message to England:** "Plaque in Tribute to the Agents in the Prosper Network of Grignon, Historical Context," http://museedelaresistanceceenligne .org, accessed May 21, 2018.

129 **Noor's suitcase:** Overton Fuller, *Noor-un-nisa Khan*, 149.

129 **Mrs. Balachowsky immediately telephoned . . . buried Gilbert Norman's radio . . . leave immediately:** "Plaque in Tribute," http://museedela resistanceceenligne.org.

130 **1 Square Malherbe:** Report to SOE recommending Noor for a George Medal, undated, 6, NA.

130 **"I picked this up":** Overton Fuller, *Noor-un-nisa Inayat Khan*, 146.

130 **putting milk in her teacup:** Overton-Fuller, *Noor-un-nisa Inayat Khan, 146.*

131 **"It isn't written on them":** Overton-Fuller, *Noor-un-nisa Inayat Khan*, 150.

131 **security is "a frame of mind":** British SOE, *How to Become a Spy: The World War II SOE Training Manual* (New York: Skyhorse, 2015), 7–8.

131 **"That does not mean everything is all right":** Overton-Fuller, *Noor-un-nisa Inayat Khan*, 152.

132 **"Always assume":** British SOE, *How to Become a Spy*, 96.

132 **she sensed something was wrong:** "Plaque in Tribute," http://musee delaresistanceceenligne.org. Some accounts of NIK at the college that day claim she had a shootout with the Germans. There is no evidence of this, or that she carried her pistol with her while in France.

132 **groups of ten:** Renaud General Report [to SOE], July 1943. "Renaud" was another name for France Antelme.

132 **"Long live France":** "Plaque in Tribute," http://museedelaresistanceceenligne.org.

133 **Balachowsky was arrested . . . Vandervynck was arrested:** http://musee delaresistanceceenligne.org. Balachowsky was deported to Buchenwald and survived the war. Vandervynckt died in Dachau, May 1, 1945, two days after the camp was liberated.

133 **"the most dangerous place:** Maurice Buckmaster, *They Fought Alone* (London: Odhams Press, 1958), 208.

133 **"Laying low":** Leo Marks, *Between Silk and Cyanide: A Codemaker's War, 1941–1945* (New York: Free Press, 1998), 364.

133 **at least a month:** Colin Gubbins, Noor's recommendation for the George Award, Feb. 24, 1944. NA JH9/91/1.

133 **"the principal and most dangerous":** Overton Fuller, *German Penetration*, 87.

Chapter 10: The Joy of Sacrifice

134 **"the greatest joy":** Noor, ms. on world religions, undated, unpaginated, DH. Probably written mid- or late 1930s.

134 **"expressed in sacrifice":** Noor, ms. on world religions.

135 **"the light of the soul":** HIK, "The Magnetism of the Soul," TTHIK.

135 **"as soon as one touches the barrier":** HIK, "The Healing Papers: Likes and Dislikes," TTHIK.

135 **"not afraid of keeping the enemy":** HIK, "Magnetism of the Soul."

135 **"raises you higher":** HIK, "Social Gathekas: Sufi Mysticism, Human Actions Become Divine," TTHIK.

135 **"awakened souls":** HIK, "Nirtan: Dance: Aphorisms," TTHIK.

135 **"not advisable"** . . . **"as many as ten times":** Renaud General Report, July 1943.

136 **"What have you got in that case":** Jean Overton Fuller, *Noor-un-nisa Inayat Khan* (The Hague: East-West Publications, 1988), 156.

136 **a German soldier standing next to Eliane Plewman:** Beryl E. Escott, *The Heroines of SOE: F Section: Britain's Secret Women in France* (Stroud, England: History Press, 2012), 113.

136 **As she walked toward the box office:** Jerrard Tickell, *Odette* (London: Headline Review, 2007), 159.

137 **"The great thing":** Overton Fuller, 172.

137 **"I have come to Paris"** . . . **"But you run the risk":** Overton Fuller, 156.

138 **Madame Salmon:** Overton Fuller, 157.

138 **"It seemed so natural":** Overton Fuller, 157.

138 **light summer frock:** Overton Fuller, 157.

138 **To make their hair lighter:** British SOE, *How to Become a Spy,* 55.

138 **café near the Champs-Elysées:** Overton Fuller, 157.

139 **parked next to a field:** Overton Fuller, 158. When transmitting from a car parked along a country road, power for NIK's radio came from the car's battery or from the battery in the radio's "suitcase." Either way, Noor had to wait almost a minute for the radio's vacuum tubes to warm up. In those sixty seconds, the Germans couldn't find her: her radio was only detectable while transmitting and it couldn't transmit until its tubes were hot. But sitting in a dark car alongside a dark road for a minute longer than necessary must have frayed the nerves of everyone in it.

139 **"A little dark girl":** Overton Fuller, 157.

140 **a small rosebush:** Overton Fuller, 159.

140 **always have someone:** British SOE, *SOE Syllabus,* 125.

140 **"a chain is as strong":** British SOE, *SOE Syllabus,* 97.

140 **"My only good moments"** . . . **"these little things":** Overton Fuller, 161.

141 **SABlons 80.04:** Overton Fuller, 160.

141 **Aisner's boyfriend visited:** Report from SOE recommending NIK for the George Medal, undated though probably submitted Feb. 1944, 8. NA HS/9/91/1.

141 **new neighbors were Nazis:** Report from SOE, undated, unpaginated, NA.

141 **"Mademoiselle" . . . "he would never think":** Overton Fuller, 171.

142 **"These people are working":** Overton Fuller, 161.

142 **To acquire those funds:** SOE's "Second Interrogation of Bricklayer" aka France Antelme, July 23, 1943, NA.

143 **a flight that Noor arranged:** Jean Overton Fuller, *The German Penetration of SOE, 1941–1944* (Maidstone, England: George Mann Books, 1996), 97.

143 **"The entire Prosper organization":** Nicolas Bodington file, NA HS9/171.

143 **his first choice. His second choice:** M. R. D. Foot, *SOE in France* (HMSO, 1966), 287.

143 **Noor introduced Bodington:** Foot, 287.

143 **Robert Gieules:** Francis J. Suttill, *Shadows in the Fog* (Stroud, Gloucestershire: 2014), 182.

144 **With five exits . . . Bodington was strict . . . established their bona fides:** V. M. Atkins file, IWM 8/3/1-44 & 8/4/1-7.

145 **known each other since childhood:** Foot, 280.

145 **75 Boulevard Lannes:** "Physician Prosper Circuit, Major Francis Alfred Suttill's Organization," NA.

145 **the night of August 16/17:** Hugh Verity, *We Landed by Moonlight* (Manchester, England: Crecy Publishing, 2005), 199.

145 **one on the floor:** John Vader, *The Prosper Double-Cross* (Mullumbimby, Australia: Sunrise Press, 1977), 41.

145 **Three nights after:** Verity, 199.

146 **"is really wonderful":** Overton Fuller, 163.

146 **Noor arranged for all the flights:** NIK file, NA HS9/836S.

Chapter 11: "I Need Trees"

147 **Gestapo arrested his wife:** M. R. D. Foot, *SOE in France* (HMSO, 1966), 288.

147 **with twenty agents hidden:** Jacques Delarue, *The History of the Gestapo* (New York: Skyhorse Publishing, 2008), 200.

148 **"lives, but his soul":** HIK, "Religious Gathekas: #18-19 The Coming World Religions," TTHIK.

148 **"crocodile tears":** Delarue, 72.

148 **"Harm no one":** PZIK (ed.), *Caravan of Souls* (New Lebanon, NY: Suluk Press, 2013), 139–40.

148 **"My honor is my loyalty":** Delarue, 74.

149 **"I no longer recognize":** Charles-Ferdinand Ramuz, quoted in Philippe Burrin, *France Under the Germans* (New York: The New Press, 1996), 31.

149 **Soldiers patrolled:** Anonymous, "Diary of the Second World War by a Young Girl Living in Suresnes," MUS.

149 **Under a bridge:** "Diary of the Second World War."

149 **a twenty-year-old:** Anne Sebba, *Les Parisiennes* (New York: St. Martin's Press, 2016), 175.

149 **high-school girl:** Jacqueline Fleury, interview with author, Jan. 16, 2017.

149 **hid downed Allied pilots:** Sebba, 165.

149 **occupying 180 homes and apartments:** M. Wilpert, "Guerre 1939–1945—Note [sur] l'occupation de Suresnes par l'armée Allemande," Societé d'Historie de Suresnes, 4–8.

150 **thirteen hostages were killed . . . forty-four prisoners . . . given sauerkraut:** David Drake, *Paris at War 1939–1944* (Cambridge, MA: Belknap Press, 2015).

150 **forty-six Frenchmen were executed:** Delarue, 266.

150 **killed one soldier and injured thirty others:** "116 Die for Paris Bomb Incident," *Melbourne (Australia) Argus*, Sept. 21, 1942, 1. The 116 were executed for bombing the cinema. Everyone killed was innocent. Those responsible were arrested a few days after the executions.

150 **all eighteen years old:** Agnes Humbert, *Resistance* (New York: Bloomsbury, 2008), 109, 350.

150 **Joseph Axelrod . . . and others:** Memorial for slain Resistance fighters, Mont Valérien.

150 **twenty-eight officers:** Census of occupied homes in Suresnes, Societé d'Histoire de Suresnes.

151 **Noor was disguised:** Overton Fuller, 164.

152 **so inconspicuously:** Overton Fuller, 164.

152 **hidden by a curtain . . . she would never tell her mother:** Overton Fuller, 165.

152 **made Noor uneasy . . . "I need trees":** Overton Fuller, 165.

152 **how foolish Noor had been . . . weren't hostile:** Overton Fuller, 165.

153 **Geneviève Vanlaere:** Overton Fuller, 166.

153 **a gauntlet of homes:** Wilpert, 8.

153 **she would like to use their home:** Overton Fuller, 166.

153 **"Oh, Raymonde":** Overton Fuller, 41.

153 **some clothespins:** Overton Fuller, 166.

153 **opening and closing the curtains . . . heard the racket:** Overton Fuller, 167.

154 **"Mother dearest":** Claire Ray Harper and David Ray Harper, *We Rubies Four* (New Lebanon, NY: Omega Publications, 2011), 140.

Chapter 12: A Date at Le Colisée

155 **several hundred secret radios:** Stephen Tyas, *SS-Major Horst Kopkow: From the Gestapo to British Intelligence* (Stroud, England: Fonthill, 2017), 102.

155 **Noor explained her code:** Overton Fuller, *Noor-un-nisa Inayat Khan* (The Hague: East-West Publications, 1988), 168.

156 **the Germans would torture her:** Overton Fuller, 168–69.

156 **tricks the SOE had taught:** Anonymous, *SOE Syllabus,* introduction by Denis Rigden (Richmond, Surrey, England: The National Archives, 2004), 69–70.

156 **she had a sixth sense:** *SOE Syllabus*, 169–70.

157 **"I am very well":** *SOE Syllabus*, 176.

157 **healthy meals . . . two fresh eggs:** Overton Fuller, 167.

157 **waterproof cape . . . navy-blue scarf:** Overton Fuller, 172.

158 **"brought me luck":** Sarah Helm, *A Life in Secrets* (New York: Anchor Books, 2007), 46.

158 **"Please arrange everyday scheds":** NIK file, NA HS9/836S.

159 **Madame Peineau scolded her . . . "I didn't think" . . . "*Petite*, there are some things":** Overton Fuller, 178–79.

160 **"two American airmen":** NIK file, NA HS9/836S.

160 **sixteen representatives . . . Jean Moulin:** Julian Jackson, *France: The Dark Years, 1939–1944* (Oxford: Oxford University Press, 2003), 456.

160 **Noor sat in the kitchen:** Overton Fuller, 181.

160 **Bidault had been elected . . . De Gaulle was pleased:** Jackson, 465.

161 **"take Message No. 6":** NIK file, NA HS9/836S.

161 **Frank Pickersgill:** Pickersgill file, NA HS 9/1406/8.

161 **"the most depressing":** Roy Maclaren, *Canadians Behind Enemy Lines* (Vancouver: UBC Press, 2004), 45.

161 **talking in his sleep:** Pickersgill file, NA HS 9/1186/2.

161 **Macalister . . . had studied at Oxford:** Maclaren, 51.

162 **"loyal, truthful, honest":** Macalister file, NA HS 9/954/2.

162 **Macalister's French:** Jonathan F. Vance, *Unlikely Soldiers* (Toronto: HarperCollins, 2008), 200.

162 **Pickersgill scribbled . . . Macalister . . . jotted down:** M. R. D. Foot, *SOE in France* (HMSO, 1966), 189.

162 **In the trunk of the Citroen:** Foot, 279–80.

163 **eighty miles an hour . . . Bullets ripped:** E. H. Cookridge, *Inside SOE* (London: Arthur Barker, 1966), 234.

163 **Culioli wrote down the names:** Vance, 212.

163 **eighty-four containers:** The Organization of the SUTTILL Prosper Circuit on 1 June, NA.

163 **Josef Goetz:** Foot, 270.

163 **the Gestapo's *Funkspiel*:** Foot, 242.

164 **seventeen agents:** Foot, 244–45.

164 **"reception committees":** Foot, 293.

164 **Karl Horst Holdorf . . . Josef Placke:** Vance, 226.

165 **ask the coatroom attendant:** Overton Fuller, *The German Penetration of SOE, 1941–1944* (Maidstone, England: George Mann Books, 1996), 106.

166 **No one followed Noor:** Patrick Yarnold, email to author, Aug. 9, 2018.

166 **the "Canadians" met Noor:** Statement by Placke to the DST, the French domestic intelligence agency, quoted in Jean Overton Fuller, *Double Agent?* (London: Pan Books, 1961), 69.

166 **6 Rue Cambacérès:** Overton Fuller, *Double Agent*, 69.

166 **six SOE agents . . . two million francs . . . over three hundred contain-ers:** Tyas, 244.

166 **kept sending messages:** Jonathan Vance, email to author, Aug. 14, 2018.

167 **list of factories:** NIK file, NA HS 9/836/5.

167 **secret SOE report:** Vera Atkins file, NA HS 6/4-6.

167 **"she realized now and then":** Noor, letter to Vilayat, Sept. 15, 1943, DH.

167 **"the leave I was hoping for":** Noor, letter to Ora, Sept. 15, 1943, DH.

168 **"do be good":** Noor, letter to Ora.

168 **Noor memorized . . . tin of sardines:** Overton Fuller, *Noor-un-nisa Inayat Khan,* 179.

168 **exposés about the mistreatment of children:** Jacques Bourquin, "Pascale Quincy-Lefebvre, "Children's Fighting Path of an Opinion Maker: Alexis Danan," *Review of the History of Irregular Childhood,* 17/23015, posted Oct. 30, 2015, http://journals.openedition.org/rhei/3742.

168 **Noor's "being and her substance":** Alexis Danan, "Serenade to Madeleine," *Franc-tireur,* Feb. 17, 1957.

169 **"defend life against all":** Bourquin.

169 *Beautiful Age:* Danan, "Serenade to Madeleine."

169 **grandson of a rabbi:** Bourquin.

169 **"wonderful astonished eyes" . . . Twice, she came closer:** Danan.

169 **"the little black suitcase" . . . "most detached" . . . "softest" person:** Danan.

170 **Allied air raids were routine:** Ronald Rosbottom, *When Paris Went Dark: The City of Light under German Occupation* (New York: Back Bay, 2014), 292. One warehouse was near Gare d'Austerlitz, another in a mansion on Rue Bassano, the third in a fur-niture store formerly owned by Jews.

170 **sometimes twice a day:** Jean Guehenno, *Diary of the Dark Years, 1940–1944: Col-laboration, Resistance, and Daily Life in Occupied Paris,* trans. David Ball (New York: Oxford University Press, 2014), 217.

170 **three hundred civilians . . . seven people at Longchamps:** David Drake, *Paris at War* (Cambridge, MA: Belknap Press, 2015), 336.

170 **In September, bombs fell:** Drake, 339–40.

171 **One *résistant* was stopped:** Verity, 141.

171 **an unflattering yellow . . . looked "hunted":** Overton Fuller, *Noor-un-nisa Inayat Khan,* 196.

171 **"dead tired":** Pierre Viennot, "SFR, a French Company Under the German Boot," account of the war years Viennot wrote for his family around 1985, unpaginated.

172 **sabotaged the products . . . eighteen-month-old-son:** Viennot.

172 **"Louis Deux" . . . blueprints . . . two hand grenades:** Viennot.

173 **Viennot became her guardian:** Viennot.

173 **they sometimes used his flat:** Emmanuel de Chambost, "History of the CSF

Under Occupation: Instruction Against Girardeau and Brenot," http://siteedc
.Edechambost.net/CSF/Resistance_Viennot.html.

173 **Au Roi de la Bière:** Viennot. Au Roi de la Bière is now a McDonald's.

173 **Viennot saw his uncle:** Overton Fuller, *Noor-un-nisa Inayat Khan*, 186.

174 **Noor hadn't heard from Gieules:** de Chambost.

174 **He drove slowly:** Viennot.

174 **five minutes too late:** Overton Fuller, *Noor-un-nisa Inayat Khan*, 188.

174 **"I can't believe":** Overton Fuller, *Noor-un-nisa Inayat Khan*, 189.

174 **Viennot told Noor:** Viennot.

174 **phone number . . . get her address:** Overton Fuller, *Noor-un-nisa Inayat Khan*,
189.

174 **"I have to leave that place":** Overton Fuller, *Noor-un-nisa Inayat Khan*, 189.

175 **a friend of Viennot's:** Viennot.

175 **"My hair has been":** Overton Fuller, *Noor-un-nisa Inayat Khan*, 191.

175 **A pleated skirt . . . everything she wore:** Viennot.

175 **"Madame . . . I won't see you again":** Overton Fuller, *Noor-un-nisa Inayat
Khan*, 193.

175 **"No . . . this place isn't safe":** Overton Fuller, *Noor-un-nisa Inayat Khan*, 193.

176 **"I gave it to you":** Overton Fuller, *Noor-un-nisa Inayat Khan*, 195.

176 **"shameful," "revolting":** Overton Fuller, *Noor-un-nisa Inayat Khan*, 195.

176 **"No! We must not say that:** Overton Fuller, *Noor-un-nisa Inayat Khan*, 195.

176 **"We cannot judge":** HIK, "In an Eastern Rose Garden: Mind, Human and
Divine," TTHIK.

176 **"strife may be his blessing":** Noor, ms. on world religions, undated, unpaginated, DH.

Chapter 13: "When I See You Again, It Will Be after the War"

177 **"I wish I were":** Jean Overton Fuller, *Noor-un-nisa Inayat Khan* (The Hague: East-
West Publications, 1988), 195.

177 **"I know I can rely":** Overton Fuller, 195.

177 **"I didn't think":** Overton Fuller, 197.

178 **"You must go":** Overton Fuller, 197.

178 **Gare Saint-Lazare:** Emmanuel de Chambost, "The Resistance of Pierre Viennot,"
http://siteedc.Edechambost.net/CSF/Resistance_Viennot.html.

178 **a café near Porte Maillot:** Overton Fuller, 198.

178 **"I am going to England":** Overton Fuller, 198.

179 **Pont de Levaillois-Bécon Métro station:** Pierre Viennot, "SFR, a French
Company Under the German Boot," unpaginated.

179 **did not appear at Madame Peineau's:** Overton Fuller, 202.

179 **"if I have not been arrested by then":** Overton Fuller, 202.

179 **Simone Truffit:** "Biographie de Simone Truffit (alias André, Paco)," cnd-castille.fr
› index.php › annuaire › download.

179 **a shed full of Metoxes:** de Chambost. German subs had been outfitted with Metox radar detectors since August 1942. Invented and manufactured by a small French company, they could detect airborne radar up to fifteen miles away—enough time for a sub to crash-dive to safety.

179 **The other nine flights:** Hugh Verity, *We Landed by Moonlight* (Manchester, England: Crecy Publishing, 2005), 201–2. Several accounts about NIK claim she was slated to fly to England on Oct. 14. That would have been ironic, as it was the day before she was arrested. Contrary to these accounts, however, there were *no* flights to England on Oct. 14.

180 **for one hundred thousand francs:** M. R. D. Foot, *SOE in France* (HMSO, 1966), 299.

180 **half payable:** Jean Overton Fuller, *Double Agent?* (London: Pan Books, 1961), 13.

180 **description of Madeleine:** Statement by Josef Goetz, Nov. 20, 1946, NIK file, NA HS 9/836/5.

180 **About thirty years old:** Werner Reuhl, statement to British, November 1946, NA HS 9/836/5.

180 **The address Renée gave . . . Removing the key:** Overton Fuller, *Noor-un-nisa Inayat Khan*, 207.

180 **Renée and André entered:** Overton Fuller, *Double Agent?*, 13–14.

181 **matched the description the agents had been given:** Reuhl statement.

181 **He betrayed a photographer:** Jean Overton Fuller, *The German Penetration of SOE, France 1941–1944* (Maidstone, England: George Mann Books, 1996), 24. Cartaud worked for the Gestapo until D-Day, often going under the name of Albert von Kapri, a Prussian twist on "Capri."

181 **"victims of the treachery":** Rémy, *Ten Steps to Hope* (London: Arthur Barker, 1959), 137.

182 **his service with the Gestapo:** Overton Fuller, *German Penetration*, 24.

182 **Cartaud's father:** Rémy, *Memoirs of a Secret Agent of Free France* (New York: Whittlesey House, 1948), vol. 1, 187.

182 **"Wouldn't it be best":** Rémy, 187.

182 **"I have every confidence":** Rémy, 187.

182 **pulling Cartaud's hair:** Overton Fuller *Noor-un-nisa Inayat Khan*, 225.

183 **drawing more blood:** Overton Fuller, *Noor-un-nisa Inayat Khan*, 225.

183 **"This would happen":** Overton Fuller, 208.

183 **Each left-hand page:** M. R. D. Foot, *SOE: The Special Operations Executive, 1940–46* (London: British Broadcasting Corporation, 1984), 139.

183 **the Gestapo's knowledge:** Buckmaster, in NIK file, NA HS 9/836/5.

184 **she needed money:** Overton Fuller, 206.

184 **Renée had a crush:** Foot, *SOE: Special Operations*, 139.

184 **"if absolutely necessary":** Anonymous, *SOE Syllabus*, 125.

184 **Odette Sansom:** Jerrard Tickell, *Odette* (London: Headline Review, 2007), 159–60.

184 **agent Hans Zomer . . . Herbert Lauwers:** Foot, *SOE: Special Operations*, 131.

185 **"prerequisite":** Foot, *SOE in France*, 59.

185 **"She was of the greatest interest":** "Translation of the Voluntary Statement Made by the Commandant of the Paris Gestapo, Hans Kieffer." NA, HS 9/836/5.

Chapter 14: "Madeleine, Don't Be Silly. You Will Kill Yourself"

189 **one of several buildings:** The Germans confiscated 82, 84, and 86 Avenue Foch. All were sacked. The worst thefts were at 86, the home of Hélène de Zuylen, who escaped to Portugal in 1940. Germans stole her rare silver, twenty-six cases of wine from the Rothschild vineyards, and five tapestries by the finest weaver in France. Zuylen, The American Commission for the Protection and Salvage of Artistic and Historic Monuments in War Areas, www.fold3.com/image/269988830.

189 **Gestapo started torturing prisoners:** Atkins file, IWM 8/3/1-44 & 8/4/1-7; Stephen Tyas, *SS-Major Horst Kopkow: From the Gestapo to British Intelligence* (Stroud, England: Fonthill, 2017), 117. Sometimes a driver for the Gestapo was told to run water in the tub on the second floor for a prisoner who allegedly wanted a bath. If the prisoner didn't answer questions satisfactorily, Gestapo agents held his head under water for what the driver told Allied investigators was "a few seconds," adding "The whole thing lasted about ten minutes," as if that made the torture more humane.

189 **map of France:** Sarah Helm, *A Life in Secrets* (New York: Anchor Books, 2007), 73.

190 **green blanket . . . detective novels:** Jean Overton Fuller, *Noor-un-nisa Inayat Khan* (The Hague: East-West Publications, 1988), 226.

190 **Eighty-four Avenue Foch was the Ritz:** Paul Leverkuehn, *German Military Intelligence* (London: Weidenfeld and Nicholson, 1954), 115.

190 **chocolates, pastries, and cigarettes:** Testimony in Overton Fuller, *Noor-un-nisa Inayat Khan,* 224, and "Rough Report by Capt. J. A. R. Starr dictated to C. S. M. Goddard at Stn. XXVIII commencing 9 May 1945," NA, KV 6/29.

190 **tall, thin, brown-haired . . . Vogt could swim across:** Jean Overton Fuller, *Conversations with a Captor* (London: Fuller d'Arch Smith, 1973), 3, 51–52.

190 **color-blind and nearsighted:** Jean Overton Fuller, *The German Penetration of SOE, France 1941–1944* (Maidstone, England: George Mann Books, 1996), 74.

191 **given a pistol:** Overton Fuller, *Conversations,* 3, 51–52.

191 **"Here, things are different":** Thomas Childers, *In the Shadows of War* (New York: Henry Holt, 2003), 289–90.

191 **"Will you take tea with me?":** Overton Fuller, *Conversations,* 25.

191 **an enemy "of his country":** Jean Overton Fuller, *Double Agent?* (London: Pan Books, 1961), 15.

192 **"You know who I am":** Overton Fuller, *Noor-un-nisa Inayat Khan,* 208.

192 **Assuring Noor:** Overton Fuller, *Noor-un-nisa Inayat Khan,* 208.

192 **"Madeleine, don't be silly":** Overton Fuller, *Noor-un-nisa Inayat Khan,* 209.

192 **"When I looked out":** Overton Fuller, *Noor-un-nisa Inayat Khan,* 209.

193 **Jean-Paul Archambault:** Overton Fuller, *Noor-un-nisa Inayat Khan,* 210.

193 **dinner for two:** Overton Fuller, *Noor-un-nisa Inayat Khan*, 210.

194 **"You know everything":** Overton Fuller, *Noor-un-nisa Inayat Khan*, 211.

194 **He admired her . . . her fists clenched:** Overton Fuller, *Conversations*, 4.

195 **names that appeared:** Overton Fuller, *Noor-un-nisa Inayat Khan*, 211.

195 **more frustrating than helpful:** Overton Fuller, *Noor-un-nisa Inayat Khan*, 212.

195 **"She's impossible":** Overton Fuller, *Noor-un-nisa Inayat Khan*, 212.

195 **"How far did you get?":** Overton Fuller, *Noor-un-nisa Inayat Khan*, 212.

195 **"square-headed, not tall":** "Report by S/LDR M. Southgate," HS 9/1395/5, NA.

195 **"To you, I will tell":** Overton Fuller, *Noor-un-nisa Inayat Khan*, 212.

195 **"Why don't you give":** Overton Fuller, *Noor-un-nisa Inayat Khan*, 212.

196 **"Madeleine, you should not be rough":** Overton Fuller, *Conversations*, 12.

196 **"It's all one to me":** Overton Fuller, *Noor-un-nisa Inayat Khan*, 212. The phrase, meaning "It doesn't matter to me," echoes Shakespeare's *Troilus and Cressida*: "she [Cressida] would be as / fair on Friday as Helen is on Sunday. But what care I? / I care not an she were a black-a-moor; 'tis all one to me."

196 **most on her mind:** Overton Fuller, *Noor-un-nisa Inayat Khan*, 213.

196 **on the third floor:** Jerrard Tickell, *Odette* (London: Headline Review, 2007), 270.

196 **toenails were pried out . . . "born to endure":** Odette Sansom oral history, IWM, https://www.iwm.org.uk/collections/item/object/80009265.

196 **"like they were your servants":** Sansom oral history.

196 **"Make the snake your friend":** HIK, "Boulas: A Kindled Word," TTHIK.

197 **requesting fresh clothing:** Overton Fuller, *Noor-un-nisa Inayat Khan*, 214.

197 **writing poems and stories:** Overton Fuller, *Noor-un-nisa Inayat Khan*, 226.

197 **"I don't like people to read my stories":** Overton Fuller, *Noor-un-nisa Inayat Khan*, 214.

197 **"understood that I was her friend" . . . "No. It's not you":** Overton Fuller, *Conversations*, 13.

197 **"Don't forget":** Overton Fuller, *Conversations*, 13.

197 **would not have pleased Hans Kieffer:** Overton Fuller, *Conversations*, 13.

197 **"Nora Baker":** Overton Fuller, *Noor-un-nisa Inayat Khan*, 212.

198 **"What are you trying to know":** Overton Fuller, *Conversations*, 212.

198 **"Don't you feel it's a pity":** Overton Fuller, *Conversations*, 212.

198 **"It doesn't matter":** Overton Fuller, *Conversations*, 216.

199 **"MY CACHETTE UNSAFE":** Atkins file, NA HS 6/4-6.

200 **Funkspiel on radios:** data calculated from Tyas, 242–50.

201 **"His whole manner":** Marie-Madeleine Fourcade, *Noah's Ark* (New York: E. P. Dutton, 1974), 32.

201 **"like so many other young men":** Lynne Olson, *Madame Fourcade's Secret War* (New York: Random House, 2019), 133.

201 **"completely fearless":** Fourcade, 31.

201 **"Since 1917":** Olson, 101. Alliance's specialty was providing intelligence to the British. Without Alliance, the British would have been poorly informed about troop

movements, or which German units were camouflaged and where, and which French industrialists were getting rich manufacturing war equipment for Hitler.

201 **Faye returned to France:** Hugh Verity, *We Landed by Moonlight* (Manchester, England: Crecy Publishing, 2005), 192, 194–95, 197, 199–200.

201 **The Resistance smuggled a rope:** Fourcade, 233–34.

202 **three arrests, two escapes:** Fourcade, 339.

202 **"Never, do you understand":** Fourcade, 339.

202 **"the Nazi vise is getting tighter":** Fourcade, 339.

202 **Nazis knew he was coming . . . :** Abwehr report, in Fourcade, 340.

202 **Aulnay-sous-Bois . . . no time to pull out his revolver:** Fourcade, 348.

202 **he was questioned:** Fourcade, 348.

202 **preferred "living in Avenue Foch" . . . "Don't lead them":** Nigel Perrin, *Spirit of Resistance* (Barnsley, England: Pen & Sword Military, 2008), 134.

203 **he purchased large amounts . . . leaped onto the footboard:** Starr file, NA HS 9/140/8.

203 **thirty-five thousand francs:** Jean Overton Fuller, *The Starr Affair* (London: Victor Gollancz, 1954), 39.

203 **passed through the gates:** Starr file, NA KV 6/29.

204 **"it was a huge mass of pus":** Starr file.

204 **pushed a steel rod:** Overton Fuller, *Starr Affair*, 46.

204 **light-brown hair, navy-blue slacks:** Starr, in Overton Fuller, *Noor-un-nisa Inayat Khan*, 225.

204 **"Cheer up":** Overton Fuller, *Noor-un-nisa Inayat Khan*, 227.

204 **Using a bottle:** Account by a French prisoner, in Roy MacLaren, *Canadians Behind Enemy Lines, 1939–1945* (Vancouver: UBC Press, 2004), 62–63. This prisoner, whom MacLaren does not name, said Pickersgill "came within an inch of freeing the whole prison"—surely, an exaggeration. After recovering from his wounds in a hospital, Pickersgill was returned to 84 Avenue Foch. In August, a boxcar took him to Buchenwald. In September, he was strung up with piano wire. His body was thrown into a crematorium.

205 **Almost every bone:** Overton Fuller, *Starr Affair*, 97.

205 **down the stairs:** Starr, letter to Overton Fuller, May 26, 1953, in Atkins file, IMW Box 8, File 2.

205 **After a prisoner escaped . . . Germans had installed bars:** Fourcade, 368.

205 **she kept badgering:** Fourcade, 368.

Chapter 15: Sacred Honor

206 **delay the escape until Christmas:** Atkins file, IWM 14/1-13.

206 **he had a screwdriver:** "Rough Report by Capt. J. A. R. Starr dictated to C. S. M. Goddard at Stn. XXVIII commencing 9 May 1945," NA KV 6/29; and Jean Overton Fuller, *No. 13, Bob* (Boston: Little, Brown, 1954), 72–73.

207 **she concocted a compound:** Atkins file, IWM 14/1-13.

207 **tickets for the Paris Métro:** Charles Glass, *They Fought Alone* (New York: Penguin Press, 2018), 126.

207 **attempted to hang herself:** Glass, 125.

207 **never told the Germans . . . word of honor:** Overton Fuller, *No. 13, Bob,* 76–78.

208 **planned to send it to his wife:** Hans Kieffer, "A Report About John Starr," HS 9/1096/8, NA.

209 **he'd learned what they knew:** "Rough Report by Capt. J. A. R. Starr." After the war, several prisoners who had been at no. 84 claimed Starr was a collaborator. He successfully explained that he had gotten close to the Germans to learn as much as he could about them. If he escaped to England, that information could benefit the Allies.

209 **"As you will have realized":** Jean Overton Fuller, *The Starr Affair* (London: Victor Gollancz, 1954), 76.

209 **Kissing Noor:** Overton Fuller, *Starr Affair,* 77.

209 **"We've done it!":** Faye in Overton Fuller, *Noor-un-nisa Inayat Khan,* 234. The early morning of Nov. 25—when the escapees were on the roof of 84 Avenue Foch—was Thanksgiving in the United States, a day when Americans pause to appreciate what they have. If Noor's escape had been successful, she would have given thanks for her newfound freedom.

209 **Suddenly, air-raid sirens:** "Rough Report by Capt. J.A.R. Starr."

210 **one rope . . . didn't have the flashlight . . . smashed the glass:** Overton Fuller, *Noor-un-nisa Inayat Khan,* 235.

210 **"What do we do now?":** "Report by Starr," NA KV 6/29.

211 **German troopers barged in:** "Report by Starr."

211 **photo of Kieffer:** Overton Fuller, *Starr Affair,* 80.

211 **gave his word of honor:** Excerpt from deposition on oath of Hans Kieffer, sworn before War Crimes Investigation Unit, Jan. 19, 1947, HS 9/835/5 NA.

211 **Twelve SOE agents . . . the escape had been Noor's idea:** "A Report about Captain John Starr," Kieffer HS 9/1096/8, NA.

211 **he vowed not to escape:** Overton-Fuller, *No. 13, Bob,* 88-89.

212 **Both refused:** Overton Fuller, *No. 13, Bob,* 89.

212 **"Break not your word of honor":** PZIK (ed.), *Caravan of Souls* (New Lebanon, NY: Suluk Press, 2013), 141.

212 **"on what shall we build":** HIK, "Boulas: A Kindled Word," TTHIK.

212 **Gare de l'Est:** Jerrard Tickell, *Odette* (London: Headline Review, 2007), 322, 324–25.

212 **three months before Faye flew:** Lynne Olson, *Madame Fourcade's Secret* War (New York: Random House, 2019), 220.

212 **told only one *résistant*:** Olson, 260.

212 **remained at Bruchsal for eight months . . . military court . . . Angelo Chiappe . . . SS guards killed him**: Marie-Madeleine Fourcade, *Noah's Ark* (New York: E. P. Dutton, 1974), 373. Several accounts of NIK's second escape from

84 Avenue Foch say Starr plotted the escape. Most likely, Faye initiated the escape with NIK's assistance, then with Starr's, since Starr knew the layout of no. 84. Faye probably would have succeeded if he had escaped by himself: he had to wait on the roof while NIK loosened the bars in her cell, and Starr failed to bring equipment he'd promised and lost his courage mid-escape. The confusion about Faye's and Starr's roles possibly originated with Jean Overton Fuller's *The Starr Affair*. She believed everything Starr told her and compromised her journalistic integrity by letting him read her book before publication. For the escape, I rely on both *The Starr Affair* and Fourcade's *Noah's Ark*. Fourcade relied on Faye's handwritten account, which he hid in a German prison. Both women had a bias: Fourcade and Faye had been lovers: possibly she was seeking to burnish his legacy. And Overton Fuller was convinced Starr was a maligned servant of England, not the collaborator many claimed. The one account of the escape that is missing is Noor's.

212 **"Ein wichtiger Terrorist":** Fourcade, 373.

213 **"absolute uncertainty" . . . "When everything and everyone":** Floris B. Bakels, *Nacht und Nebel,* trans. Herman Friedhoff (Cambridge: Lutterworth Press, 1993), 25.

213 **"a strange phenomenon":** Bakels, 36.

213 **to end "all chivalry":** Walter Gorlitz, "Keitel, Jodi, and Warlimont," in Corelli Barnet (ed.), *Hitler's Generals* (New York: Grove Press, 2003), 152.

213 **"Efficient and enduring intimidation":** Nurnberger Dokumente, PS-1733, NOKW-2579., NG-226, in Karl Dietrich Bracher, *The German Dictatorship* (New York: Praeger Publishers, 1970), 418.

213 **"vernebelt":** William Manchester, *The Arms of Krupp* (New York: Back Bay Books, 2003), 519.

Chapter 16: The Realm of Ghosts

214 **"plump and richly dressed":** Jerrard Tickell, *Odette* (London: Headline Review, 2007), 326.

214 **In Karlsruhe, Noor was placed:** Jean Overton Fuller, *Conversations with a Captor* (London: Fuller d'Arch Smith, 1973), 45–46.

215 *Angaben zur Person . . . Nummer des Gefangenbuches:* From prisoners' registration book, Pforzheim prison, DH.

215 **an ordinary prison:** Dr. Martin Stingl, Karlsruhe archivist, email to author, Nov. 27, 2018.

215 **political prisoners, *résistants*, and SOE agents:** Brigitte and Gerhard Bernhard, email to author, Nov. 21, 2018.

215 **eleven were women:** Report on Pforzheim prison by a Mr. Backfisch (first name unknown), senior official in public prosecutor's office, to Gestapo HQ in Karlsruhe, Feb. 14, 1944, 63, NA.

215 **uniform worn by all *Nacht und Nebel* prisoners:** Bernhard email, 141.

215 **leg irons that were chained to the handcuffs:** Report by George Bucher, chief guard at Pforzheim prison, to Gestapo in Karlsruhe, in Christian Haller, *Der "Ausländereinsatz" in Pforzheim* (Heidelberg: Ubstadt-Weiher, 2004), 29.

215 **"Bracelets of steel":** Hugh Oloff de Wet, *The Valley of the Shadow* (London: Panther Books, 1956), 133.

215 **Noor's cell:** Guy Caraes, email to author, Dec. 26, 2018.

216 **"Here are three French women":** Deposition of Yolande Lagrave, to War Crimes Investigation Unit, Jan. 26, 1947, WO 309/1022, NA.

216 **"To a prisoner":** Overton Fuller, *Conversations*, 47.

216 **"She could subvert":** *Conversations*, 48.

216 **"unhappy, very unhappy"... "I cannot give it"... "Think of me":** Lagrave deposition.

217 **"Here's to the Fourth"... "Long live free France":** Lagrave deposition.

217 **"Give me some news":** Lagrave deposition.

217 **they sang loudly in French:** Caraes, email to author, Dec. 26, 2018.

218 **"basket of cherries":** Hugh Verity, *We Landed by Moonlight* (Manchester, England: Crecy Publishing, 2005), 97.

218 **cells on either side of Noor's:** Overton Fuller, *Conversations*, 46–47.

218 **they talked about music:** Overton Fuller, *Noor-un-nisa Inayat Khan*, 244.

218 **"I felt sorry":** Deposition of Wilhelm Krauss to War Crimes Investigation Unit, Oct. 6, 1946, DH.

218 **"weird sensation to be able to move":** de Wet, 153.

219 **"a little indication of chivalry":** de Wet, 67.

219 **only three times:** Lagrave deposition.

219 **"expect a violent escape attempt":** Report on Pforzheim prison, Backfisch to Gestapo, Feb. 14, 1944.

219 **"The warden of the prison":** HIK, "Talas: The Rhythmic Expression of an Idea," TTHIK.

219 **the women in one cell:** Lagrave deposition.

219 **her "state of mind":** Report by Bucher, in Haller, *Der "Ausländereinsatz" in Pforzheim*, 29.

220 **"the beauty of simple things":** de Wet, 144–47.

220 **her "true self"... "before realization shall come":** Noor, ms. on world religions.

220 **one air raid ... thirty-five air raids:** Tony Redding, *Bombing Germany: The Final Phase: The Destruction of Pforzheim and the Closing Months of Bomber Command's War* (Pen and Sword Aviation, 2015), 1.

220 **in December, police warned:** Redding, 2.

220 **ninety-eight American bombers:** Redding, 38.

221 **In early October ... "had serious accident":** NIK file, NA HS 9/836S.

221 **prayed "that Noor was not having":** Leo Marks, *Between Silk and Cyanide: A Codemaker's War, 1941–1945* (New York: Free Press, 1998), 399.

221 **Gerry Morel:** Sarah Helm, *A Life in Secrets* (New York: Anchor Books, 2007), 52.

221 **aide he sent to Pforzheim:** Kieffer file, NA HS 9/836/5.

221 **fifteen percent of transmissions . . . "Identity Check Omitted":** David Kahn, *The Codebreakers* (New York: Macmillan, 1969), 534.

222 **first at 84 Avenue Foch . . . more notorious cellars:** E. H. Cookridge, *Inside SOE* (London: Arthur Barker, 1966), 303.

222 **Buckmaster was recommending Noor:** Maurice Buckmaster, "Recommendation for the Award of the George Medal," Feb. 24, 1944, in NIK file, NA HS 9/836/5.

222 **fist on her radio had changed:** Marks, 411.

222 **Marks looked away:** Marks, 411.

222 **"Please God":** Marks, 416.

223 **"We have just received":** Capt. E. G. Bisset, letter to Mrs. Baker-Inayat, Jan. 5, 1944. DH.

223 **"news of your daughter":** Major Jack Mackenzie, letter to Mrs. Baker-Inayat, May 29, 1944. DH.

223 **"dearest little daughter":** Ora, letters to NIK over several months, 1944, DH. Ora often failed to date her letters.

Chapter 17: Gethsemane and Golgotha

224 **"Stalingrad means a turning point":** Joachim Fest, *Hitler (New York: Harcourt, Brace, 1974)*, 666.

224 **over one million British:** Fest, 706.

224 **almost five thousand were killed:** 4,980 to be exact. William Shirer, *The Rise and Fall of the Third Reich* (New York: Touchstone, 1988), 1072.

225 **"all terror and sabotage troops":** M. R. D. Foot, *SOE in France* (HMSO, 1966), 169.

225 **"large deliveries of arms":** Atkins file, IWM 14/1-13.

225 **from Nancy in France, then in Germany:** Jean Overton Fuller, *The German Penetration of SOE, France 1941–1944* (Maidstone, England: George Mann Books, 1996), 154–55.

225 **136 SOE agents:** Stephen Tyas, *SS-Major Horst Kopkow: From the Gestapo to British Intelligence* (Stroud, England: Fonthill, 2017), 173. The Nazis never intended to treat SOE agents decently. SS chief Heinrich Himmler said Germany's enemies should die after "torture, indignity and interrogation had drained from them the last shred . . . of evidence which should lead to the arrest of others. Only then should the blessed release of death be granted them." Foot, 373.

225 **agents . . . at Gross Rosen, Mauthausen, and Buchenwald:** Overton Fuller, *The German Penetration of SOE*, 172–74; Tyas, 172–74.

225 **"I am going" . . . "She was no longer":** Deposition of Yolande Lagrave to War Crimes Investigation Unit, Jan. 26, 1947, WO 309/1022, NA.

226 **"small, shrunken and gray-looking":** Sarah Helm, *A Life in Secrets* (New York: Anchor Books, 2007), 275.

226 **"would make an excellent wife":** Patrick Yarnold, *Wanborough Mano: School for Secret Agents* (Guildford: Hopfield, 2009), 99.

226 **twenty large deliveries . . . more than a hundred miles of tracks:** Beryl E. Escott, *The Heroines of SOE: F Section: Britain's Secret Women in France* (Stroud, England: History Press, 2012), 123.

226 **They tortured her:** Escott, 123–24.

226 **paint imaginary feasts:** Helm, 228–29.

226 **seventy-five Allied aviators . . . Noor's radio:** Escott, 140–41.

227 **"Because I hate them":** "8 Rue Merentie, a narrative by Jean Contrucci, with the collaboration of Jacques Virbel," https://www.alliancefrancaise.london/8-rue -Merentie-ENG-AFL.pdf.

227 **240,000 Germans . . . tortured with electric shock:** Escott, 112–14.

227 **Cell no. 16:** Helm, 225.

227 **"the usual manner" . . . drove the women to Bruchsal . . . train for Stuttgart:** Deposition of Christian Ott to British investigators, Oct. 23, 1946. Atkins file, IWM 8/3/1 & 8/4/1-7.

227 **In Stuttgart, the group waited:** Ott deposition.

227 **twenty-six bombing raids . . . firestorm:** Jorg Friedrich, *The Fire* (New York: Columbia University Press, 2003), 293.

228 **"We thought the end had come":** Friedrich, 291. The air raid occurred between 11 and 11:30 p.m., Sept. 12, 1944. The women were at the train station around 4 a.m., just short of 24 hours before the attack.

228 **"The four prisoners will be transferred" . . . "If I had known":** Ott deposition.

228 **they had no idea:** British War Office, letter to J. Beekman, July 10, 1946. Archive of KZ-Gedenkstatte-Dachau, D.A. 20965.

228 **they would farm:** Ott deposition.

228 **munitions factory . . . clinic:** Harold Marcuse, *Legacies of Dachau* (Cambridge: Cambridge University Press, 2001), 18–19.

228 **The first prisoners:** Marcuse, 9.

229 **thirty thousand prisoners:** Andre Scharf, historian at Dachau Concentration Camp Memorial Site, interview with author, Oct. 19, 2017.

229 **death rate:** Marcuse, 49.

229 **"*Eine Welt*":** Marcuse, 18–19.

229 **Around 10 or 11 p.m:** Ott deposition.

229 **the women would be executed . . . Wassmer read the death sentence . . . Beckman asked:** Ott deposition.

230 **"upon arriving":** J. Beekman letter to a Mrs. Dystel, Nov. 25, 1985. Archive of KZ-Gedenkstatte-Dachau, D.A. 20965.

230 **four prisoners loaded the bodies:** Beekman letter.

230 **tall hedge:** Lt. Col. Fellenz, 42nd Rainbow Division, report to his commanding officer, May 6, 1945, https://www.scrapbookpages.com//DachauScrapbook/ KZDachau/CrematoriaArea/New Crematorium.

231 **In Wassmer's telling:** Jean Overton Fuller, *Noon-un-nisa Inayat Khan*, 249.

231 **a "receipt" for their bodies . . . explicitly denied:** Atkins file, NA WO 309/1022.

231 **"they were in rags" . . . "almost naked" . . . "who was fond of this type of sport" . . . "the bunker":** H. J. Wickey, letter to Pan Books, Ltd., Apr. 23, 1958. David Harper.

231 **136 cells:** Official website of Dachau Concentration Camp Memorial Site.

232 **"dead or half-dead":** Wickey letter.

232 **According to Peters:** Letter signed "A.F." from Dirk Peters to Jean Overton Fuller, Dec. 5, 1958, DH.

234 **like a blacksmith:** www.scrapbookpages.com/DachauScrapbook/DachauTrials/WilhelmRuppert.html.

235 **"What makes sense?":** Angelika Eisenmann, interview with author, Oct. 20, 2017.

235 **"We are so happy to know":** Ora, letter to Noor, Sept. 21, 1944 letter, DH.

235 **"Dear Mrs. Baker Inayat":** NIK file, NA HS 9/836S.

236 **"fulfilled the purpose":** HIK, *The Sufi Message of Hazrat Inayat Khan*, 165.

236 **"the attributes of the past souls":** HIK, "The Phenomenon of the Soul: Man, the Seed of God," TTHIK.

236 **"highest and most inconceivable" . . . "the experience of non-existence":** Noor, ms. on world religions.

237 **"Through love":** Rumi in John Baldock, *The Essence of Rumi* (London: Arcturus Publishing, 2016), 181.

Afterword: "I Pray *with* Noor"

239 **he fell into the water:** Claire Ray Harper and David Ray Harper, *We Rubies Four* (New Lebanon, NY: Omega Publications, 2011), 144.

239 **Between June 6 and 19:** Harper and Harper, 144.

239 **"Crowds gathered":** Ora, letter to Noor, Sept. 21, 1944, DH.

239 **"Camp after camp":** Harper and Harper, 145.

240 **"terribly worrying":** Harper and Harper, 146.

240 **"be so kind":** PVIK, letter to War Office, Feb. 12, 1947 letter, NA HS9/836/9.

240 **Vilayat dreamed:** Jean Overton Fuller, *Noor-un-nisa Inayat Khan*, 253.

240 **"I hope," the War Office wrote:** Harper and Harper, 152.

240 **British newspapers would soon publish:** Harper and Harper, 188.

241 **"attempting . . . to fill the void" . . . "Where is mother?" . . . "She is no longer here":** Harper and Harper, 189.

241 **"the Nazis used psychopaths":** PVIK, *Awakening* (New York: Jeremy P. Tarcher/Putnam, 2000), 149.

242 **"requires much of us":** PVIK, *Awakening*, 150. In 1975, Vilayat's Sufi order established its American headquarters in New Lebanon, New York. Now known as the Inayati Order and headed by Vilayat's son, Pir Zia Inayat Khan, it is currently based in Richmond, Virginia.

242 **"otherworldly":** Sarah Helm, *A Life in Secrets* (New York: Anchor Books, 2007), 15.

242 **"all the radio plays":** Helm, 353.

242 **"dangerous":** Helm, 355.

243 **worked in the prison before the war:** Jean Overton Fuller, *The German Penetration of SOE, France 1941–1944* (Maidstone, England: George Mann Books, 1996), 144.

243 **"overfull":** Helm, 355.

243 **"It was nice for you":** Overton Fuller, 144.

243 **"Kieffer," Atkins chided:** Overton Fuller, 144.

243 **"Snow Drop," a story:** Sandra Lillydahl, editor's notes in Noor Inayat Khan, *King Akbar's Daughter* (New Lebanon, NY: Suluk Press, 2012), xvii.

243 **"bouncing out from every hole":** *King Akbar's Daughter*, 215.

243 **"If you wish":** *King Akbar's Daughter*, 217.

243 **"Are you there, Little Daughter?" . . . "If you don't return":** *King Akbar's Daughter*, 219.

244 **"a flower as tiny as a drop":** *King Akbar's Daughter*, 219.

244 **"as never before":** *King Akbar's Daughter*, 221.

244 **"more phlegmatic kind of courage":** Jean Overton Fuller, *Noor-un-nisa Inayat Khan*, 128.

245 **57 Grande Rue Saint-Maurice . . . "arrested in Paris" . . . *"Umgekommen":*** Index card from International Tracing Service, #1245867.

245 ***Recherches d'équilibre:*** Album cover, "Les Formes de la Dance Contemporaine," Niles Editions Touristiques et Artistiques, Paris, 1971.

245 **family motto:** "Tuyll" entry, Wikipedia.

245 **hid for a year:** Jean Overton Fuller, *Conversations with a Captor* (London: Fuller d'Arch Smith, 1973), 16.

245 **"If I had known":** Vogt, quoted in Overton Fuller, *Conversations*, 16.

246 **"a town out of fairyland":** Overton Fuller, *Conversations*, 35.

246 **"What do you want?":** Overton Fuller, *Conversations*, 26–27.

246 **"There was nothing Kieffer could do":** Overton Fuller, *Conversations*, 12.

246 **"I should have liked . . . I cannot believe":** Overton Fuller, *Conversations*, 5, 49.

247 **"Truth . . . is the most powerful":** Overton Fuller, *Conversations*, 57.

247 **"Monstrous and intolerable accusations" . . . helped "shorten the war":** "Statement by Buckmaster," in E. H. Cookridge, *Inside SOE: The Story of Special Operations in Western Europe 1940–1945* (London: Arthur Barker, 1966), 603–5.

248 **470 agents:** Cookridge, 604.

248 **Fewer than forty:** M. R. D. Foot, *SOE in France* (HMSO, 1966), xxv.

248 **"Nothing, neither her nationality":** Geneviève de Gaulle-Anthonioz, in Private Papers of Noor Inayat Khan, IWM 12248.

248 **"very brave, very bold":** Jacqueline Fleury, interview with author, Jan. 16, 2017.

248 **Atkins convinced them:** Sarah Helm, *A Life in Secrets* (New York: Anchor Books, 2007), 367.

248 **"How they exchanged mugs":** Helm, 367.

249 **St. James's Palace announced:** Supplement to the *London Gazette*, Apr. 1, 1949, 1.

249 **accepted the medal:** Photo in *The* [Melbourne, Australia] *Age*, Aug. 8, 1949, 1.

249 **"To Vera Atkins. With gratitude":** Helm, xxvii.

250 **"G/C For Braver Than They Thought Girl":** Headline, *Continental Daily Mail*, Paris edition, Apr. 6, 1949. Page uncertain.

250 **"Betrayed, Chained":** Jerrard Tickell, "Betrayed, Chained, She Did Not Flinch," *Times Colonist*, Victoria, BC, Sept. 3, 1949, 26.

250 **"Secret agent 'Madeleine'":** Jill James, "For Four Months, She Bluffed the Gestapo," [London] *Junior Express Weekly*, July 16, 1955, 12.

250 **"heard champagne corks":** Tickell.

250 **"tenderest of voices":** Overton Fuller, *Noor-un-nisa Inayat Khan,* 124.

250 **"inner poise":** Overton Fuller, 114.

250 **"not a doubt":** Overton Fuller, 245.

250 **"extraordinary achievements" . . . "one of the silent heroes":** Royal Mail Mint Stamps, "Remarkable Lives," issued Mar. 25, 2014.

252 **Was it a contradiction:** PVIK, "An Unrecognizable Face from Suresnes," DH.

252 **"Noor-un-Nisa Inayat Khan was":** Jusy Joseph, "India Pays Homage to World War II Spy," DNA India, Sept. 5, 2006, https://www.dnaindia.com/india/report -india-pays-homage-to-wwii-spy-1051414/.

253 **"This is a beautiful place":** Maev Kennedy, "Statue Honours Indian Secret Agent Killed at Concentration Camp," *Guardian*, Nov. 8, 2012, https://www.theguard ian.com/world/2012/nov/08/statue-indian-secret-agent-killed.

253 **"think about the fantastic work":** Helena Horton, "Ministers Back Campaign to Put Noor Inayat Khan on 50 Pound Note," [London] *Telegraph*, Oct. 17, 2018, https:// www.telegraph.co.uk/news/2018/10/17/ministers-back-campaign-putnoor-inayat -khan-50-note/.

255 **"I do not pray":** Sister Irmengard, interview with author, Oct. 19, 2017.

255 **"I don't understand":** Sister Irmengard interview.

255 **"One more thing":** Year 6 students, Chorlton C of E Primary School, *Liberté: The Life of Noor Inayat Khan,* 2.

256 **"Yet . . . for all the tears":** Mary Inayat Khan, interview with author, Jan. 19, 2017.

256 **"Noor always believed":** Mary Inayat Khan interview.

ILLUSTRATION CREDITS

INDEX

Page numbers in *italics* refer to illustrations. Page numbers
beginning with 267 refer to endnotes.